Edith A. Sisson has been a
popular and enthusiastic teacher
at the Massachusetts Audubon
Society for many years. She has
led many natural history
explorations with children and
has published articles on nature-
related topics.

And hark! how blithe the throstle sings!
He, too, is no mean preacher:
Come forth into the light of things,
Let Nature be your Teacher.

From the poem
"The Tables Turned"
by William Wordsworth

nature
with children
of all ages

activities &
adventures
for exploring,
learning, &
enjoying the world
around us

edith a. sisson

The Massachusetts Audubon Society

PRENTICE
HALL
PRESS

New York   London   Toronto   Sydney   Tokyo   Singapore

PRENTICE HALL PRESS
15 Columbus Circle
New York, NY 10023

Originally published by Prentice-Hall, Inc.

PRENTICE HALL PRESS and colophons are registered trademarks
of Simon & Schuster, Inc.

Library of Congress Cataloging-in-Publication Data

Sisson, Edith A.
   Nature with children of all ages.

   Includes bibliographies and index.
   1. Nature study.   2. Natural history—Study and
teaching.   3. Outdoor education.   I. Title.
QH51.S527   372.3′57   81-23371
                    AACR2

ISBN 0-13-611542-X

Interior design by Maria Carella
Page layout by Diane Heckler-Koromhas

Manufactured in the United States of America

20 19 18 17 16 15 14 13 12

contents

preface

In order to live *with* the environment, modern society should have appreciation, care, and concern for natural forces and beings. There is no better way to foster these attitudes than with our children, who have innate senses of curiosity and wonder. They are natural naturalists, and we adults have only to encourage this talent. Hold a small hand while quietly watching clouds tinged like flames of orange and red in an evening sky, and feelings of awe will be shared. Pick up litter in a neighborhood park with a group of small helpers, and feelings of responsibility will grow. Take care that feet, both small and large, carefully step around a colony of ants, and attitudes of reverence for all life will be nourished.

Sharing nature with children can be easy, especially when we have enthusiasm ourselves for learning about the natural environment. The purpose of this book is to help readers to realize how easy this sharing can be and to feel confident about teaching outdoors. The natural history information and activities in this book will also serve as samplers of informative materials (both theoretical and practical) that will act as catalysts, encouraging readers to develop their own outdoor teaching methods and styles. If you achieve these goals, pass this book along to someone else or keep it on a shelf as a handy reference work that suggests specific natural history learning activities.

acknowledgments

Much of the information in this book represents a synthesis of teaching ideas and experiences shared by fellow workers at Massachusetts Audubon Society, especially the Drumlin Farm tour staff. I am indebted to many, especially to Anne S. Cheatham, who started me on my way at Audubon, and to Leona G. Champeny, who generously shared her expertise, which is particularly manifest in the pond chapter. Elizabeth S. Paynter and Frances D. Francis have also been special sharers. Charles E. Roth, Chief Educator/Naturalist of the Massachusetts Audubon Society's education department, is responsible for the night mammal-watching plan in Chapter 8, as well as for numerous other natural-history facts and teaching insights. He and the education department also have given me invaluable support in my teaching endeavors. Mary S. Shakespeare's drawings and Jane H. Caulfield's photographs greatly enhance the text, and I appreciate their assistance, which went far beyond the production of illustrations. I also thank the Massachusetts Audubon Society for the use of some of its illustrative teaching materials, and Mary E. Kennan of Prentice-Hall, whose support carried me through preparation of the book. Then there are the thousands of children, adults, and senior citizens who come to Audubon's Drumlin Farm, and the fifth-graders in the Sharon Intermediate School, all of whom have taught me much while I have been teaching them.

My greatest acknowledgment goes to my family. Long ago my husband, Tom, with his vegetable garden and honey bees, established a family emphasis on living with the natural world, an emphasis that has enriched us all. Jinny, Kathy, Edie, and Polly, each in her own way, have shared with us their own senses of curiosity and wonder about the natural world. Bonnie and Gay and their varied winged and four-footed followers have shared much, too, in their special ways. All this has contributed to my own caring and concern for the natural world, which have been the foundation of this book.

introduction

Nature always offers discoveries. The more we learn about the natural world, the more we realize how much more there is to learn, and how much there is that no one knows. For instance, information is too scanty for a conclusive answer to the simple question "Where are the tiny frogs called spring peepers during the wintertime?" We know where these frogs are in early spring by their bell-like choruses from neighborhood ponds. In summer, bright-eyed children easily spot these Lilliputians of the frog family in the woods. We assume that during the winter they hibernate, but where? Perhaps a child whose curiosity you foster on outdoor trips will someday discover the answer.

Field guides and other natural history books are helpful, but to know and understand the outdoor world we must experience it by seeing, touching, hearing, smelling, and sometimes even tasting. Allowing all our senses to respond increases our sensitivity to nature and our feelings of being a part of the environment. We can add the benefits of sharing different individuals' observations and knowledge when we go out with a group. It is often surprising how the youngest child or the least-informed adult in a group may ask the most right-to-the-point question, and how working out the answer becomes interesting to the whole group.

Some answers to simple questions are given in the natural-history sections of the chapters in this book. Much of this information is based on my own observations and is designed to provide foundations for the related learning activities. Although both the information and the activities are intended to be comprehensive, they necessarily reflect my own tastes, biases, and experiences, and the choice of material is somewhat arbitrary and purposely personal. I have included many of my own first-hand experiences in order to point out how activities may be particularly effective and where pitfalls may exist.

Age groups for each activity are not given since an activity's suitability depends on many factors, especially the participants' previous experiences. In some cases activities are described as particularly suited for younger, or older, children; and sometimes suggestions are given for adapting an activity for a different age group. You are the best judge of the needs of the children with you, and you can make your own adaptations of activities when needed. Many of the activities are also suitable for adults.

The activities offer a diversity of helpful learning ideas for a variety of interests for people of all ages and degrees of experience. The activities relate directly to natural-history studies, as well as to other disciplines, since the natural environment is by no means limited to one subject. Quite the contrary, it is all-embracing, as described by the ecological maxim: "Everything is hitched to everything else." Estimating the weight of the leaves on a tree becomes a math problem. Researching how the Indians used cattails for weaving is a social studies project. Studying erosion touches on geology, and studying pollution is an environmental-education topic. Reports, poems, art projects, and music are also included in the activities, along with numerous botanical and zoological activities, such as experiments with growing seeds or learning how fish are adapted for life in water. Most of the activities are designed to be as experiential as possible, in line with the old proverb "I hear, and I forget; I see, and I remember; I do, and I understand."

Although diverse, all the activities have been limited to those that call for simple, inexpensive, easy-to-obtain items. The intention is to offer experiences that are not difficult to do; those requiring technical equipment or experiments in a well-equipped laboratory are not included. Consult technical references for such activities.

The bibliography at the end of each chapter includes books that are generally informative about the chapter's subject matter, as well as examples of the different types of books available. Children's natural history books are often excellent sources of information for adults, too. For this reason the bibliography includes books for "Children and Adults" as well as books for "Adults." The latter, however, include books that can be used by older children, and many of these books have illustrations that appeal to people of all ages. There is a blank page following the index for you to write down activities to try, techniques to remember, what did not work well, and so on. I invite you to add your own thoughts and comments to this book.

credits

Photographs on pp. 5, 9, 13 (top), 18, 20, 28, 45, 49, 76, 85, 86, 89, 94, 149, 153, 154, 161, 172, and 181 by Jane H. Caulfield.

The photograph on p. 90 and the line drawings on pp. 6, 13, 16, 17, 22, 30, 31, 38, 41, 44, 46, 47, 48, 50, 51, 54, 55, 56, 57, 58, 59, 60, 67, 68, 70, 75, 76, 78, 79, 81, 82, 95, 111, 116, 118 (left), 120, 123, 130, 131, 132, 134, 151, 152, 153, 154, 155, 163, and 185 are by Mary S. Shakespeare.

The poem "The Little Turtle" is reprinted with permission of Macmillan Publishing Co., Inc., from *Collected Poems* by Vachel Lindsay. Copyright 1920 by Macmillan Publishing Co., Inc., renewed 1948 by Elizabeth C. Lindsay.

Excerpt from Henry David Thoreau, *Walden* (New York: Thomas Y. Crowell Co., 1961), pp. 234-235.

The poem "Stopping by Woods on a Snowy Evening" from *The Poetry of Robert Frost*, edited by Edward Connery Lathem. Copyright 1923, © 1969 by Holt, Rinehart and Winston. Copyright 1951 by Robert Frost. Reprinted by permission of Holt, Rinehart and Winston Publishers and Jonathan Cape Ltd., and the Estate of Robert Frost.

Photographs on pp. 2 and 124 are used by permission of the Ministry of the Environment, Government of British Columbia.

Photograph on p. 83 by Hugh R. Smith and photographs on pp. 3, 4, and 171 are used by permission of the American Nature Study Society.

Photographs on pp. 7, 13 (bottom), 21, 39, 40, 62, 105, 108, 112, 115, 119, 128, 135, 164, and 180 by E.A.S.

The photograph on p. 9 and the drawings on pp. 81 and 163 are used by permission of the Massachusetts Audubon Society.

Photographs on pp. 15, 67, and 145 by Cecil W. Stroughton are used by permission of the United States Department of the Interior, National Park Service.

Photograph on p. 21 used by permission of Katherine S. Kingsford.

Illustration on p. 23 from *The Life of the Forest*, Copyright 1969, St. Regis Paper Company, 150 East 42nd St., N.Y., N.Y. 10017. All rights reserved. Some captions have been paraphrased.

Photographs on pp. 28, 34, 57, and 71 by R.L. Coffin are used by permission of S.T. Coffin.

"Manypeeplia Upsidownia" on p. 32 is from *The Complete Nonsense Book* by Edward Lear, published by Dodd, Mead, & Co. and Faber and Faber, Ltd.

Photographs on pp. 33 and 43 are from *Art Forms from Plant Life* by William M. Harlow, published by Dover, 1976, used by permission of the author.

Photograph on p. 65 used by permission of the Tennessee Department of Conservation.

Photograph on p. 72 used by permission of the U.S. Fish and Wildlife Service, Okefenokee Wildlife Refuge, Georgia.

Photograph on p. 80 used by permission of the Florida Department of Commerce, Division of Tourism.

Photographs on pp. 90 and 166 are used by permission of the Arizona Office of Tourism.

Photograph on p. 92 is used by permission of the Wyoming Game and Fish Department.

The following are used through the Courtesy of the Museum of Fine Arts, Boston: *The Cow*, Alexander Calder, 60.240, Decorative Arts Special Fund; *The Great Wave*, Hokusai Katsushika, 21.6765, Spaulding Collection; and *Coffin of Djehuty-Nekht*, Dynasty XII, ca. 1860 B.C. 20.1822, Harvard Boston Expedition.

Photograph on p. 110 used by permission of Margaret W. Arnold

Photographs on pp. 113 and 118 are used by permission of Sarah Fraser Robbins.

Photographs on pp. 124 and 147 used by permission of the Maine Department of Inland Fisheries and Wildlife.

Photograph on p. 138 by Jack Swedberg used by permission of the Massachusetts Division of Fisheries and Wildlife.

Photograph on p. 139 used by permission of the Florida News Bureau, Dept. of Commerce.

Photograph on p. 148 used through

Courtesy of Dover Publications, Inc.

Photographs on pp. 158 and 175 (bottom) used by permission of the Montana Travel Promotion Unit.

Photograph on p. 175 (top) used by permission of the Wyoming Travel Commission and Grand Teton Lodge Co.

Photograph on p. 177 by Marianne Pernold and photograph on p. 186 by George Robinson used by permission of the USDA.

Photograph on p. 179 by Richard Frear is used by permission of the United States Department of the Interior.

The Victorian wreath algae print on p. 112 is used by permission of the Peabody Museum of Salem, Salem, Mass.

1

tips & techniques for teaching out-of-doors

Anyone who has an open mind and a little curiosity can teach, and learn, outdoors. Children, and others with inquisitive minds, are ideal for sharing learning experiénces. Many parents learn about natural history right along with their kids, as I know, having done so with my own. Teachers and other youth group leaders, as well, can, and do, learn with their children. Whether you are a parent, a classroom teacher, a group leader, or in some other situation, do not hesitate to participate in outdoor experiences with children.

basics of outdoor teaching

attitudes, not facts

The good news for beginning or hesitant outdoor teachers is that facts can be low-priority items. What benefit is it if children can memorize that an insect has six legs, three main body parts, and two antennae, or even that it has eleven abdominal segments, but fail to learn that there are helpful as well as harmful insects, all of which deserve recognition and respect for their roles in any natural system? Children acquire some facts; but unless they gain even a simple appreciation of the role of insects, they may grow up with dreams only of bigger and better insecticides. The teacher must teach attitudes first; facts come later. Watch a honeybee on an apple blossom and contemplate the healthful apple that may result from the visit. Is it not something to marvel at? Here is an attitude

that can spark the sense of wonder that children naturally possess.

There are wonders everywhere in the natural world, and it is not difficult to find them with a group of children. Admire the delicate structure of a dandelion seed head. Blow it and wonder how nature contrived the design of such effective parachutes to carry seeds away with the wind. Plant one of the seeds and you and the children become responsible for a birth—if only of a common weed, it's a small miracle nevertheless.

A teacher who enjoys a dandelion in this way with a group of children is helping those children to develop an awareness and appreciation of the natural world. Yet at the same time, foundations are being laid for facts about how plants reproduce. The dandelion parachutes are a means of seed dispersal, and the new plant is the result of seed germination. Both seed dispersal and germination are important factors in plant reproduction. After this experience, the teacher and the children can look up materials in books about seed dispersal and germination or try other experiences and experiments for further learning. If you

have curiosity to match that of the children, you will be able to do this.

Do remember, however, that it is your attitude that comes across. There is no point in trying to teach a group of children to appreciate snakes if, while you are explaining some of the wonders of snake construction, you are at the same time holding the snake at arm's length and your nervous apprehension shows in your eyes. Teach about beautiful wild flowers instead, for if you are not comfortable with the subject, your body language will betray your feelings. Choose subjects that you like, and then your own enthusiasm will come across.

explore together

Suppose that you decide to concentrate on wild flowers found out-of-doors. A child asks for the name of a specific flower, and you do not know it. Should you panic? No. Herein lies an opportunity for productive teaching. Readily admit that you don't know, and suggest that you and the child look it up together when you have finished the walk. This will mean that you will both have to make careful observations of the flower, maybe even make notes or sketches in order to look it up later. It also gives the child a feeling of shared exploration. If you suggest that the child find the answer later and tell you what was discovered, you generate further incentive to learn. Never be afraid to say that you don't know an answer, for it can be an effective way of raising curiosity.

Often, when you do know the answers, it works well to let the children discover the answers themselves. Ask them leading questions. Socrates used this method, and it is helpful in the outdoor classroom where there are often clues that lead to the answers. "Who made these tracks?" asks Mark, looking down at some hopping tracks in the snow. "I wonder," you respond, "where do the tracks come from?" Mark looks along the tracks in one direction. "That way. They seem to come from that tree," he says. Looking the other way he exclaims, "And that way they come from that other tree!" "An animal from the trees?" you ask. Mark looks puzzled; then suddenly the smile appears. "I know," he bursts out. "It's a squirrel! It just has to be because only a squirrel would be going up into trees like that." So Mark has answered his own question, and maybe later on, perhaps by watching how a squirrel hops, he will be able to answer the question, "In which direction was the squirrel going?"

use the senses

Look, feel, listen, smell and, with discretion, sometimes taste. By using their senses, children become truly involved, magnifying

Look, feel, listen, and smell.

the learning experience. "Seeing is believing," goes the old expression, and we might add that feeling, listening, smelling, and tasting also are believing, or, at least, leading to understanding. Concentration on feeling objects outdoors leads to appreciation of textures. Take leaves as an example. It is surprising how many different textures they have: smooth, rough, scratchy, hairy, silky, fuzzy. Try feeling some, and surely you will add to the list. Stopping to listen outdoors adds a new dimension to the experience, especially if you are with a large group. Ask everyone to be quiet for one minute, and listen. What do you hear? We are so accustomed to background music in the supermarket and the sound of the TV in the living room that it is a pleasant change to stop and try to hear noises rather than having them constantly crowding in on you. As with feeling, listening increases awareness.

Smelling, which also adds to awareness, deserves more use than we tend to give it, for no other sense evokes memories so strongly. Do you remember the smell of mud on a first warm spring day

when you were a child? My own picture is quite complete, including the backyard and the patch of melting snow. Try smelling leaves. Bruise them a little and notice the subtle differences that they have in odor. Some, of course, have decidedly distinctive smells: sassafras, yarrow, bayberry, black walnut, pine, to name a few. The sense of taste, which relates to that of smell, is the only sense that should be downplayed outdoors. Although there are many tasty items out there, there are many that are toxic as well. Use great caution; and, even when you come upon a field brimming with ripe wild strawberries, stop first to be certain about identification before enjoying the feast.

flexibility

Maintain a sense of humor and you will be able to incorporate flexibility into your outdoor teaching, for you will certainly need it. Unlike an indoor classroom where the conditions are familiar and subject to little change, the outdoors can produce sudden surprises. Accept these surprises as challenges, rather than aggravations, so that you can be ready to take advantage of them. You may be leading the children to the final understanding of whatever was the object of your outdoor expedition, but let a mother duck and her babies appear, and you have instantly lost the attention of your group. Nothing you can say will take attention off the duck family. Thus, the first thing to do is simple: Enjoy the ducks. Encourage observation. It is a special sight to see how the little ducklings walk neatly in a line behind their mother. While watching with the group, contrive how you might be able to link the subject of ducks or motherhood back to whatever it was that you were about to conclude; then, when the ducks have gone their way, you can smoothly turn attention back to where it was before the interruption. It's never quite that easy; but the fact remains, flexibility is essential. Perhaps it will suddenly start to rain the moment the ducks are out of sight, presenting you with a new challenge. Afterward, however, it might just turn out that the children remember "the time when we saw the baby ducks and got soaking wet" as an exciting adventure, perhaps even including an understanding of the material that the trip was designed to teach.

planning outdoor experiences

Outdoor visits with children benefit from forethought, whether the visit is a brief venture out into the school yard to gather a few autumn leaves, or an all-day outing to study woodland ecology in a national forest.

trip objectives

Decide first on the objective of the trip. Why are the students going out in the school yard to gather fallen leaves? If they are going to make colorful leaf mosaics, the objective would be to find leaves of different bright colors. However, if the class has been studying insects and plants, the objective of leaf collecting might be to find leaves that show holes and other signs of insect damage. Decide what activities will carry out your objective.

where to go?

The choice of the place to go depends on both objective and activities. It would be difficult to study woodland ecology in an asphalt urban school yard, but rural school grounds might include an appropriate wooded area. A national forest would be ideal but out of the question if it is not within reasonable distance of the school. If buses or other transportation are not available, obviously your choice has to be an area within walking distance.

Any outside area may be used for natural-history studies: national and state parks, forests and wildlife preserves; local parks and conservation areas; privately owned areas whose owners allow visiting groups; school yards and grounds; backyards or the vacant lot down the street; and even the sidewalks along streets. A city sidewalk, for instance, may offer an

Any outside area may be used for natural history studies, the shore of a pond . . .

... or the vacant lot down the street.

astonishing amount of natural-history discoveries—anything from a patch of moss growing in a crack in the pavement to birds high up in a tree.

If possible, visit the site of the outside visit before taking the children there. This will enable you to plan how best to use the area for the objective and activities you have in mind. Check the route you will take to know where you are going and to enable you to judge the timing of the visit. Also, check the site for possible hazards. One time I did not check a route; and, inadvertently, I led a group of four-year-olds right into the middle of a bramble patch, where suddenly the menacing thorns at every move became overwhelming. Fright and scratches led to tears. It was a mistake that should have been avoided, although for an older group it might have been a challenging adventure.

Remember that flexibility is a maxim for outdoor teaching; and however well you may have planned the trip, there may be surprising diversions. Planning at least will give you a schedule to

vary from, and it nearly always makes the learning experience go more smoothly.

field trip mechanics

There are a myriad of small details that may, or may not, be involved with the outdoor visit you are planning. Will you need buses or other transportation? Arrangements should include date, time and place of pickup, destination, and route, as well as plans for the return trip. What, if any, clearances are necessary with school officials; are permissions needed from school, parents, or the place you will visit? Will snacks or lunches be needed? If so, you must make arrangements for them. If trash cans will not be available at the site, you will probably have to bring your trash back with you; you can point out to the children how this demonstrates the ecological maxim that "everything has to go somewhere." Should you take a first-aid kit? Do any of the children have allergies that may

require special attention? Will bathrooms be available?

How many children will be going on the trip? If it is a large number, try to subdivide it into smaller groups, with an adult leader for each group. Will you need additional adults to assist with supervision? Parents and student teachers are helpful field trip assistants. If possible, keep the groups small, and, generally speaking, the younger the children, the smaller the groups should be. For instance, eight is a good number for a group of preschoolers, whereas twelve is a reasonable number for groups of junior high or high schoolers.

Naturally, the larger the group, the less individual attention per student and the more a student's attention can wander; but many times small groups are not feasible. Groups of fifteen can be manageable; even groups as large as twenty-five to thirty are possible to manage, although it can be difficult to project a voice outdoors to so many and to be certain that everyone has opportunities to observe or participate in the activities. Structured planning and limiting the duration of the outside visit can help toward success with a large group. However, these guidelines for group size are only general, and many factors can cause variations. At times I have led groups of seventy-five children on hill-climbing excursions. My insistence that no one go ahead of the leader (myself) and the use of a large cowbell (a whistle would probably serve as well) as a signal to return to the group after a period of dispersal at the top of the hill helped to keep the trips manageable and, thus, enjoyable for all.

The length of an outdoor visit will depend on the trip objective and activities, the weather, and the ages of the children. Preschoolers can pay good attention to a specific outdoor program for about three-quarters of an hour to an hour; first- and second-graders for about an hour and a half; and older children and adults for about two hours. These times, like group size guidelines, are general; with any age group, variations in the program, chances to sit down and relax, snacks or lunch, and other breaks make longer outdoor sessions possible. Flexibility is also important because of weather. People who are uncomfortably hot, cold, or wet are not going to learn well. Cut the trip short or transfer some activities to more comfortable inside quarters if possible.

On outdoor trips, take little equipment beyond what is necessary for the activities planned. Carrying items not only may be tiring, but may limit activity as well. Sometimes the use of the item becomes an end in itself, and may serve as a subtle barrier to the child's ability to relate directly to the natural world. I have seen this happen with insect nets and four- and five-year-olds. We were sharing nets in the group and, even though it was

awkward and difficult for these young children to carry and use the nets, the children began to compete for turns with the nets. The goal of finding and observing insects soon took second place to the net competition. And I also felt, by intuition, that perhaps the message coming across to the children was that an insect net was necessary to observe and enjoy watching insects. The learning experiences improved greatly when we left the nets behind.

Sometimes, however, extra equipment is helpful. Useful items will vary with the objective and activities of the trip, as well as with the ages and stages of the children. Hand lenses with strings attached so that they can be worn around the neck are a generally useful item for children old enough to use them effectively. Binoculars, which also can be worn around the neck, are especially helpful for bird watching. Small notebooks that can fit into a pocket are useful for recording observations. Clipboards are helpful for holding sheets of paper and recording. Simple clipboards for every student can be made easily: cut pieces of cardboard to a size slightly larger than the paper to be used and secure each paper on a cardboard piece with two elastic bands. In winter when mittens or gloves are worn, index cards and crayons work well for brief note-taking. Over-the-shoulder bags are handy when everyone has to carry a number of items, and they are particularly useful for the group leader. The leader can take objects for the whole group, such as identification guides, plastic bags for collecting, clippers for plant samples, small plastic boxes for holding and observing insects and other small creatures, writing materials, pocketknife, ruler, string, and so on. Sometimes with younger children it's a good idea to carry a book for story-reading

during the trip, and almost always, with any age, a snack is appreciated.

Before taking children outside, try to make sure that they are prepared. Without a doubt, the most important preparation is that they dress for the weather. I cringe when I see sneakers and street shoes worn on a field trip when snow is on the ground; the wearers are going to be uncomfortable in a very short time, a state of affairs not conducive to learning. Give the children a brief outline of what will be done outdoors, including explanations of how to use any new equipment. It may be necessary to explain whether they must stay with the group, walk in a line, have partners, or follow other rules. Sometimes it helps to have the children learn vocabulary terms that may be new to them and that are applicable to the subject of the trip.

Dress for the weather.

Depending on any previous outdoor experiences of the children and on what section of the country you are in, it may be necessary to warn about certain potentially harmful animals and plants. Ask a group of children, "What should you do if a bee comes near you?" If the replies suggest swatting it or running away, help the children to understand that such motion could disturb the bee enough so that it might sting. Staying as still as possible is the correct answer, even though it may take courage to do so. Incidentally, if a member of the group is stung by a bee or other insect, try to identify the kind (yellow jacket, hornet, honey bee); this information is helpful in case of an allergic reaction. Other harmful animals include ticks, chiggers, and some kinds of snakes and spiders. Familiarize yourself with any that may be in your area, and learn how to deal with them by consulting field guides for your locality and individuals experienced in the outdoors and knowledgeable about the area's harmful animals and plants. Certain government agencies may also have helpful information. Plants that are harmful to touch include poison ivy, poison sumac, poison oak, poison wood, and nettles; some plants, such as jimsonweed, can cause dermatitis, or skin inflammation, with some people. Be certain that the children can identify any of the potentially harmful plants that grow in the area so that they will take care to avoid contact with them. If you suspect that biting insects, such as mosquitoes, are going to cause discomfort, you may want to take along an insect repellent. A better solution would be to plan your trip at a time of day or season when biting insects are not out or to choose an area

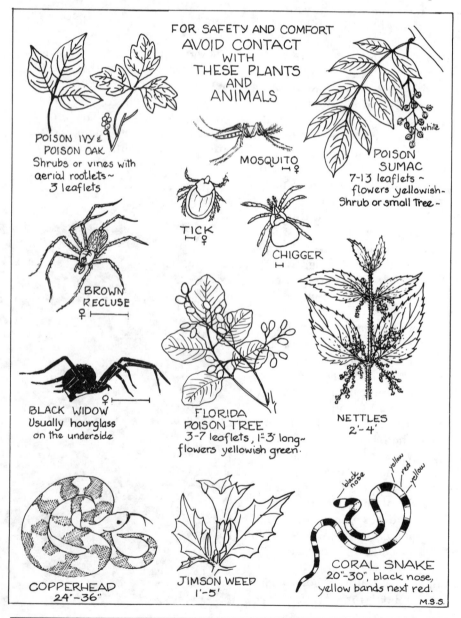

FOR SAFETY AND COMFORT
AVOID CONTACT WITH THESE PLANTS AND ANIMALS

POISON IVY & POISON OAK
Shrubs or vines with aerial rootlets ~ 3 leaflets

MOSQUITO

POISON SUMAC
7-13 leaflets ~ flowers yellowish-
Shrub or small Tree ~

TICK

CHIGGER

BROWN RECLUSE

BLACK WIDOW
Usually hourglass on the underside

FLORIDA POISON TREE
3-7 leaflets, 1-3' long~ flowers yellowish green.

NETTLES
2'-4'

COPPERHEAD
24"-36"

JIMSON WEED
1'-5'

CORAL SNAKE
20"-30", black nose, yellow bands next red.

M.S.S.

Warning!
Some plants and animals can be harmful.

where they are not likely to be found.

If collecting items is a planned part of the trip, help the children to follow conservation ethics. Do not pick flowers or remove plants from roadsides or along pathways; leave them for others to enjoy also. Never pick rare or endangered species of plants. Take samples of other plants or items sparingly and only as needed, and always be certain to have landowners' permissions for collecting. In areas of fragile ecology, such as sand dunes, stay on designated trails. Point out to the children that if every visitor took just one short walk off the designated trails, erosion could follow and drastically change the habitat. Also, explain that if each visitor took just one sample of a rare plant, it would quickly disappear. Such attitudes will help young people to develop a feeling of responsibility for the environment.

Collecting is fun!

outdoor teaching tips

helpful hints

Here are a few simple suggestions for aiding group learning outdoors. The sun can get into people's eyes. When you stop to address a group in an open area, take note of where the sun is. Position yourself so that you are looking toward the sun while you speak. This means that only one person may be squinting (you), not the whole group. When leading a group down a trail, walk until about half of the members have gone by an object you wish to point out; stop and step back to the middle so you can discuss the object where both ends of the group can see it and hear you. Always try to project your voice to everyone. Remember that those on the outside fringes of a group are particularly susceptible to being distracted by other noises in the area.

If your group has broken up into small working parties for activities, give these groups a feeling of your support by paying frequent visits to each one. Sometimes the children that stay nearest to you on a trip may be the most interested and have the most questions. They deserve your attention, but do not forget others in the group. Try to see them as individuals rather than as a mass, even if these are children you do not know. Try to address and hear from each individual. Asking questions of the group encourages members to participate. A little humor in your own style often helps to make a group feel comfortable with you.

grabbers

Grabbers are various devices for "grabbing" the attention of a group. A physical grabber is an object that is startlingly unusual and unexpected. If, when you are talking to a group about animal bones, for instance, you reach quietly into your bag and suddenly pull out an enormous bone, you will galvanize attention. (Beef thigh bones are well suited for this; they are huge and can be obtained from a butcher or supermarket meat department. However, they are heavy and thus not easily portable during a field trip.)

Other grabbers are more subtle. To focus group attention on an object, try looking at it yourself, intently. Invariably other eyes in the group will follow yours. Let group members help out as much as possible by carrying items and assisting with other tasks. If there is something you do not want to forget to show the group later on, ask the children to remind you about it. They will; and even such simple participation helps to keep their attention on what the group is doing.

There are moments on outdoor trips when lowering your voice can be a grabber. You spot a bird in a nearby tree; stop, point to it, and look at the group. Then, in a whisper ask the children if they can see it. What is it doing? Does anyone know what kind of bird it is? Probably every child in the group will be trying to catch each word as you whisper it, and you will indeed have their attention.

Sitting down with the group is a useful technique (weather and ground conditions permitting). No shuffling feet, no wandering off; you have them right with you, and while everyone relaxes it is an opportunity for you to explain something, show an object, or ask questions to encourage the children to express their thoughts about the trip. Individual tasks are useful grabbers, too. Ask the children to take notes during the trip. Have them collect specific items, look for things on a list, or sketch certain objects. Give them sample paint chips and let them find items with colors that match the samples.

group control

Controlling a group outdoors is quite different from doing so inside. A group of active children can explode in all directions like so much popcorn. Be warned, but not dismayed, for in a real sense you have the world to make up for the slight inconvenience of maintaining control safeguards. Both the helpful hints discussed earlier and grabbers aid in controlling groups. Following are a few techniques that work well for me. Consider them, and add some of your own to suit your own teaching manner.

At the start of the trip, especially, be firm about whatever rules you may have set. It is easier to relax rules as time goes on, rather than the other way around. In any case, hurting or frightening animals, needless plant destruction, or littering should never be tolerated. If you sense that the group has pent-up energy about to erupt, find an area where the children can safely run. Point out a route (for instance, around a big pine tree and back), and enjoy the sight of the exhilarated takeoff as abundant energy is channeled into good spirits and a run. If space is limited, try somersaults, cartwheels, or finding out which students can stand on their heads. If the children stray during such an exercise time, or if they have dispersed for doing activities, use a prearranged signal, like the old-fashioned dinner bell, to call everyone back. The signal may be "time's up," a whistle, hand clapping, even a cow bell (effective with very large groups), or it may be a hand signal—a technique with a built-in control. It keeps the children in contact with you, for they must glance occasionally in your direction to see if the signal is being given.

Sometimes keeping the group

with you becomes a challenge. Instead of yearning for four containing walls, consider some of your other options. Try playing follow the leader. Everyone goes in single file, and while you lead the line in and out and around and about, the children's attention focuses on staying with the group, right where you want it to be. Young children enjoy playing baby ducks following their mother (you), and don't forget to flap your wings a bit as you go along. When snow is on the ground, you can all travel as wolves do, each person carefully walking in the tracks of the leader. At other times, skipping or hopping uses surplus energy and keeps the group with you. Do the children push to be at the head of the line? If so, here's a neat trick. Patiently wait for the pushing to subside. When everyone is lined up behind you, step firmly around to the end of the line, where you are likely to find the unaggressive children who need recognition. Ask everyone to turn around, and off you go with the reversed line behind you.

When your group is around you, desperately eager to reach a certain destination, and about to "take off," try an altered, simplified version of the game of Red Light. Explain only that no one is to go ahead of you. Walk along, wait until some eager ones are a few paces ahead, and then stop with some fanfare and a claim that you have "caught" those that are ahead. They must come back behind you. Then, go forward again. The children will be avidly watching your feet. Stop abruptly. Have you "caught" anyone this time? This is fun and also achieves your own aim of keeping everyone together. But do not overuse it so that boredom sets in.

Sometimes, when the children seem to want to rush ahead, turn around at the front of the group, walk backward, and find something to talk about that will hold their interest. The children will keep their distance to converse with you. Be cautious, however, and watch your backward stepping. One time I forgot and found myself in collision wth a street sign. (Outdoor teaching has its own particular challenges!)

Two or three excited kids, all trying to tell you something at the same time, is inevitable. Ask for raised hands and allow for fair turns to speak—techniques that work well indoors and out. A subtle and effective ploy to use with an outdoor group is, as you recognize and listen to one enthusiastic speaker, to put your hand calmly on the shoulder of the other eager-to-speak child. Your body language whispers reassuringly, "I know you are anxious. Your turn next."

There may come a rare time when you have exhausted all your helpful hints, grabbers, and

Put your hand on the shoulder of the eager-to-speak child.

group control techniques, and the group still tends toward out-of-bounds behavior. Accept defeat to a degree rather than keep up a pointless battle. Use flexibility, that password for the outdoor

teacher, and change your program to encompass places and activities that you feel your group will be able to handle. The children will be happy to achieve some success, and so will you.

ages, stages & special needs

There are no limits to who can appreciate and relate to the natural world. Its glories are there for everyone. A two-year-old can become very excited at discovering a tiny ant on its deliberate travels, and most senior citizens enjoy being close to animals. A blind person can learn far more about the texture of tree bark than others who have not had to develop such sensitivity of touch. It is the responsibility of the outdoor leader to understand the individuals in the group and to create experiences appropriate to them, whatever their age, stage, or special needs.

Children go through developmental phases, as we know, but coordinating these phases with learning experiences requires

Senior citizens enjoy being close to animals.

thought and perhaps some intuition. We can talk to children, but how do we know what they are hearing? I once showed a horse's bridle to a group of preschoolers, naturally calling it a "bridle." But I received a jolt when a little girl responded that she didn't know "horses got married." That jolt steered me into using objects and activity as much as possible with young children, keeping verbal teaching to a minimum.

Children's early years are largely devoted to the accumulation of experiences. A young child does not understand the water cycle, but, if he or she has watched clouds, felt rain, jumped in puddles, and noticed that puddles disappear, the basis of information about the water cycle is there, ready to be put together when the child reaches that stage of development. The child can then make deductions, understand cause and effect, and benefit from an increased knowledge of words. Explain evaporation, and the child will know that puddles disappear quickly when the sun shines. The ability for abstract thinking is on its way, but, by this time, adolescence is around the corner and the child may be preoccupied with ego development and how to relate with peers. The child can understand the water cycle in the abstract, but may direct his or her attention elsewhere.

Although learning by experience for any age is generally more pervasive than other methods, some youngsters with special needs do not benefit. Some children understand better when an explanation of the information is given first and the activity follows. Students with language barriers, however, need the opposite approach: minimal verbal explanation and emphasis on objects and activity. However, do not bypass the op-

portunity to teach some words of your language, or to learn a few words of theirs.

Many children with learning disabilities require special educational approaches, as do the emotionally disturbed. Teachers of these children with special needs can adapt their techniques to encompass natural-history education, generally with success, since these children, like most others, have an innate curiosity about the natural world. Sometimes in studying nature, the child who is having difficulties with other academic subjects can achieve, and at last gain a feeling of success. Mentally retarded children also respond positively to natural-history experiences, and there is no reason why many of the activities in this book cannot be tailored to suit their needs. Often these children have a particular interest in animals. This is an interest to build upon, but you must sometimes take extra care to make sure that a child does not inadvertently harm an animal or frighten it into harming anyone.

Some physically handicapped children at first may feel hesitant about participating in outdoor experiences. Those with walking disabilities or those dependent upon wheelchairs will have difficulties with rough terrain. Choose areas with easy access and smooth paths for these children. Inclement weather may seem especially threatening to children who may be unable to move quickly to shelter. Keep a special eye out for weather conditions and remember that in a pinch the large plastic bags used for trash can be made into raincoats by cutting holes at the bottom ends of the bags for heads to go through. Observation activities, such as birdwatching, are naturally easy for the physically handicapped. And tape recorders are useful tools for children who

cannot use their hands for writing. Pair these children with those with manual dexterity when doing activities requiring the use of hands. Also, pair children with speaking disabilities with those without; this kind of pairing allows the children to help each other by sharing their abilities. Try, as with able-bodied children, to make the outdoor activities as experiential as possible. Imagine how a child accustomed to seeing the ground from a wheelchair might feel to be allowed to sit on the ground and feel grass, smell the earth, and observe this new world closely.

Blind and deaf children, as well as those with multiple handicaps, require teaching that is suited to their individual needs, and many of the activities in this book can be adjusted for them as well as for the physically handicapped. Capitalize on the special sensitivities of these children. Blind children generally have acute hearing. Learning and identifying bird songs might be easier for them than for children with sight. Experiences involving touch and smell are also particularly appropriate for the blind. Deaf children have keen powers of observation that will assist them greatly in wildflower identification, as well as in many other observation exercises. Help handicapped children to share in childhood's natural love for things of the outdoor world. Also remember that natural history experiences will help these children to catch up with information that their nonhandicapped peers have more easily acquired.

Now we are ready to start with some outdoor experiences. The world is filled with eager children of all ages. Take some of them out with you and share their own sense of wonder as you rekindle your own. You certainly will enjoy it!

bibliography

natural history

Books
BROWN, VINSON, *The Amateur Naturalist's Handbook*. Englewood Cliffs, N.J.: Prentice-Hall, 1980.

BUCK, MARGARET WARING, *In Yards and Gardens*. New York: Abingdon, 1952 (and other titles by same author).

LAUN, H. CHARLES, *The Natural History Guide*, 4th ed. Alton, Ill.: Alsace Books, 1967.

PALMER, E. LAURENCE, and H. SEYMOUR FOWLER, *Fieldbook of Natural History*. New York: McGraw-Hill, 1975.

WORTHLEY, JEAN REESE, *The Complete Family Nature Guide*. New York: Avon, 1976.

Series
Doubleday Nature Guides. New York: Doubleday.

Golden Guides. Racine, Wis.: Western.

How to Know Series. Dubuque, Iowa: William C. Brown.

Life Nature Library. New York: Time-Life.

Our Living World of Nature. New York: McGraw-Hill.

Peterson Field Guides. Boston: Houghton Mifflin.

outdoor teaching

CARSON, RACHEL, *The Sense of Wonder*. New York: Harper, 1956.

CHINERY, MICHAEL, *Enjoying Nature with Your Family*. New York: Crown, 1977.

COMSTOCK, ANNA BOTSFORD, *Handbook of Nature Study*, 24th ed. Ithaca, N.Y.: Cornell University Press, 1967.

Examining Your Environment, series. New York: Holt, 1974.

GROSS, PHYLLIS, and ESTHER P. RAILTON, *Teaching Science in an Outdoor Environment*. Berkeley: University of California Press, 1972.

HAMMERMAN, DONALD R., and WILLIAM M. HAMMERMAN, *Teaching in the Outdoors*. Minneapolis: Burgess, 1973.

HILLCOURT, WILLIAM, *The New Field Book of Nature Activities and Hobbies*. New York: Putnam, 1970.

LAUN, H. CHARLES, *Natural History Field Notebook*, 3rd ed. Alton, Ill.: Alsace Books, 1979.

NICKELSBURG, JANET, *Nature Activities for Early Childhood*. Reading, Mass.: Addison-Wesley, 1976.

PECK, RUTH L., *Art Lessons That Teach Children about Their Natural Environment*. West Nyack, N.Y.: Parker, 1973.

PRINGLE, LAURENCE P., ed. *Discovering the Outdoors*. Garden City, N.Y.: Natural History Press, 1969.

RUSSELL, HELEN ROSS, *Ten-Minute Field Trips*. Chicago: Ferguson, 1973.

SCIENCE 5/13, *McDonald Educational Series*, School Council Publications. Milwaukee: McDonald Raintree, 1973.

SWAN, MALCOLM, *Tips & Tricks in Outdoor Education*, 2d ed. Danville, Ill.: Interstate, 1979.

VAN MATRE, STEVE, *Acclimatization*, American Camping Association. Martinsville, Ind.: Bradford Woods, 1972.

VINAL, WILLIAM GOULD, *Nature Recreation*. New York: Dover, 1963.

WENSBURG, KATHERINE, *Experiences with Living Things*. Boston: Beacon, 1966.

2 trees are almost everywhere

Let's start our exploration with a tree. Nearly everyone has access to a tree, from an urban park or city street to suburban yards and country areas. Even one backyard tree can offer natural-history experiences, studies, and take-off points for further investigation.

Imagine a visit with some young children to an oak tree. Here we go, through the field toward the tree. We see that the tree is tall, a lot taller than a nearby house. We notice its shape, and some of the children try to make their bodies into the same shape. Arms go out disjointedly, mimicking the branching, craggy oak style. Underneath the tree, where the grass is shorter, we feel the cool shade and hear the wind rustling the leaves. What do the leaves look like? We look closely at some, and the children think of many descriptive words: pointy, rough, lots of corners, long, jagged, even "funny." (These descriptive words would not suit the smooth-edged leaves of some oaks, such as willow, shingle, and live oaks.) We pull off a leaf. It feels tough and has some little holes in it. How large is the trunk? Can we reach our arms around it? Sarah tries, but it is too big. Joshua joins her, and together they can just reach around. We all feel the bark with our cheeks. How rough and bumpy it is! How does it smell? We lie down and gaze upward through the leaves. Look, high up by that big patch of blue sky, there's a nest. What bird family do you suppose grew up there? A squirrel scolds us while quietly we watch the fluttering leaves. Adam feels a lump under his back. Why, it's an acorn with a sprout coming out! What is it doing? Has anyone heard the expression "from little acorns mighty oak trees grow?"

Already this oak tree visit has touched on a wide variety of tree subjects. The observations of the overall tree shape and the way the leaves look are important facets of tree identification. The shorter grass under the tree shows that in the shade of the tree there is a different habitat from that of the open field. The size of the trunk gives a clue to how much lumber the tree could provide. Those tiny holes in the leaf attest to an insect's meal. The nest and the squirrel are signs that the tree offers shelter for wildlife. The sprouted acorn opens the subject of tree reproduction.

From this short visit there are many possible follow-up activities. Paint silhouettes of the tree. Make oak leaf prints. Find items made from oak wood in the classroom or at home. Hunt for different kinds of insects on the tree. Plant a sprouted acorn and watch the baby tree grow. Gather acorns and make them into cups and saucers. Learn to blow an acorn cap whistle. Estimate the height of the tree. Study how ancient peoples, such as Druids in Britain, venerated oaks. Use a field guide, and identify the different kinds of oaks commonly found in the community. (There are well over fifty species of oak in the United States.) Have an oak leaf contest. Sometimes oak leaves grow to be very large. Who can find the longest oak leaf?

The oak tree visit demonstrated several basic tenets of outdoor learning. We explored together and were flexible in our approach. We used our senses well: looking at the tree and the leaves; listening to the wind blowing the leaves and to the squirrel's scolding; feeling the texture of the leaves and the bark; smelling the bark. The oak tree has offered concrete experiences, as well as enticements for follow-up activities. Best of all, little or no prior knowledge was required. It was the tree itself that did much of the teaching.

Here we go toward the tree.

The oak leaf contest adds a decorative touch to the classroom window. (The leaf with the star is the winner.)

PIN OAK

SWAMP WHITE OAK

LIVE OAK

SHINGLE OAK

WHITE OAK

WILLOW OAK

trees are our friends

Trees are friends to people, especially because of their vital roles in ecology. Photosynthesis is the most important of these roles. Simply put, photosynthesis is the process by which leaves make food for the plant; leaves are "food factories" for trees. The green chlorophyll of leaves utilizes energy from the sun to convert carbon dioxide from the air and water from the roots into sugar, food for the tree. The waste product given off by these "factories" is oxygen, a basic requirement for all animal life. Without green plants and leaves, we could not exist.

Trees are also important as "nature's motels and restaurants." They provide shelter for countless animals, from squirrels and birds to hives of bees and tiny insect larvae. They are even used by other plants, such as wild grapes, the parasitic mistletoe, and many mosses and lichens. A tree "restaurant" attracts many clients, from beavers and bark beetles to numerous kinds of birds, as well as humans, who consume many fruits and seeds of trees. Sometimes we use trees for shelter, too, by standing under them in rainstorms (but never in electrical storms). For children, tree houses are distinctly special places.

Trees are also superb "recyclers." Every year deciduous (leaf bearing and shedding) trees contribute their leaves to nature's compost. At first these leaves act as mulch, preventing the underlying soil from drying out. Then, as the leaves decay, they return valuable nutrients to the soil. A wise gardener adds raked leaves to the compost pile for use on next year's garden. The

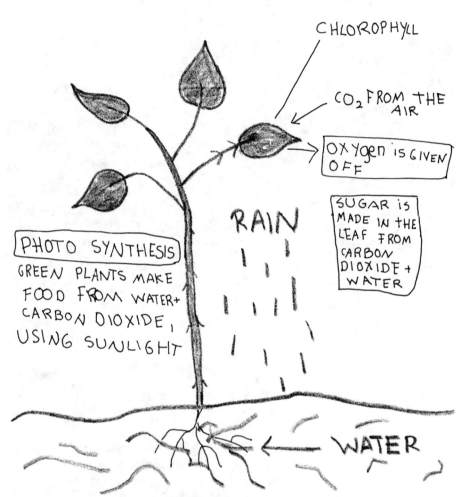

A fifth-grader's illustration of photosynthesis.

soft brown pine needles on the ground in a pine woods show that evergreens also recycle their leaves. The same principle of recycling takes place when a tree falls in the forest. Numerous agents, such as millipedes, sow bugs, mushrooms, and decay bacteria, break down the wood, returning it to the soil. Look under a log in the woods; children as young as three can be transfixed by discovering the many small creatures contributing to the recycling effort.

learning about trees

How can we learn about trees? By looking at them, listening to them, touching them, smelling, and sometimes even tasting them (with caution); by appreciating their roles in the natural world, as well as their importance to us; by being curious about them with enthusiasm for discoveries.

As a starter, here is a specific tree activity, one I have often used as an introduction to tree studies. It is designed for a class of twenty-four fifth-graders in a school that has a yard large enough to accommodate a fair number of trees, but it can be geared for older or younger children, for adults, or otherwise altered to suit particular situations. Its purpose is to sharpen observation skills, leading toward basic tree identification.

introductory tree activity

Materials: Leaves from four different kinds of common trees in the school yard (six leaves from each kind of tree, twenty-four in all), paper bag, four large index cards, four pencils.

Procedure:

1. Form four groups, each with six students, by leaf matching. Have each student take a leaf from the paper bag, find the other students with the same kinds of leaves, and group themselves accordingly.

By finding the matching leaves, the students on their own have already started leaf observation.

2. Each group makes leaf descriptions. Give each group a card and a pencil and have them list words that describe their leaves.

One way to learn about a tree is to sit beneath it and write down your observations and feelings about it.

Encourage the students to observe and list different kinds of descriptive words. What shape are the leaves? What color? How big? Would they like to invent a name for the tree that grew their leaves?

3. Groups exchange descriptions and leaves. Have them put the leaves back together in a pile. Give each group a leaf description card made by one of the other three groups, asking the students of each group to find the kind of leaves that their new card describes. Then have the groups read the descriptive words aloud, showing the matching leaves.

Since more observation techniques have been used, now is the time for discussing and sharing the results. Which descriptive words seem especially apt? Why? By now the students, through their own observations and thinking, have become familiar with four different kinds of leaves.

4. Go outside and identify trees by their leaves. Have the students identify and count the trees in the school yard that have the same kinds of leaves as those their group described on their first card.

Here, earlier observation work is given practical application.

5. Record the numbers of the trees found by the students and discuss the results.

The emphasis should be to stimulate the students to identify trees using their own observations, rather than to make a highly accurate survey. Do any students have wide disagreements about the number of one kind of tree? Ask them to go off together to resolve their differences. Perhaps a student included some trees that did not have leaves that truly matched, or maybe a student walked right under some of the trees without looking up and spotting them. Did any of the students notice identifying features of a tree other than its leaves? That can be a starting point for further studies of tree identification.

Until this point, we have not needed to know the names of the four trees. Now, have the students look up the trees in identification guides. Curiosity may be such that the students will want to know the scientific names as well as the common names.

There can be many variations of this activity. The numbers of trees, leaves, children, and groups can easily be changed. The groups can make more sophisticated descrip-

tions of their leaves, using technical leaf terms (simple, compound, toothed, lobed, elliptic, and so on). If it is not feasible for the class to go out to identify trees, omit steps 4 and 5. If the students already have had some experience with tree identification, stress accuracy in the outside tree survey. With very young children, try a simple matching leaves and trees walk. Give each child a leaf and go on a walking hunt to find trees with matching leaves. Four-year-olds feel excited and proud when they can identify "their" trees.

What other factors besides leaves are considered in tree identification? One of the most obvious is habitat. You will not see a palm tree growing naturally in Montana, or a ponderosa pine in Florida. Knowing the likely areas where different trees may be found, or not found, is helpful. A pine in Florida, for instance, will not be a ponderosa pine, which is a western tree; but it could be a longleaf or a slash pine, both of which are southern species. Trees are common to certain ranges and often have preferred environments within a range. The silver maple is found in the eastern half of the United States, while the Rocky Mountain maple grows where its name indicates. Within these ranges, the silver maple is often found in or near wetlands; the Rocky Mountain maple thrives at higher altitudes, especially in the southern part of its range.

Various tree features are helpful in identification. In addition to leaf shape, the overall tree shape is indicative. The typical cone shapes of many evergreens, for instance, are markedly different from the rounder shapes of deciduous trees. Branching patterns differ. The twigs of most trees grow at alternate intervals from the branch, but some have twigs that grow opposite each other. Tree barks vary.

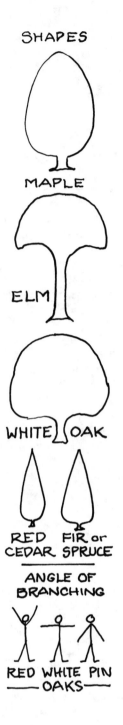

Almost anyone who sees a tree with white bark will think of birch. Trees with the rough brown variety of bark can seem confusing, but closer inspection will reveal differences. Tree flowers are another identifying clue. We can recognize the magnolia in spring by its showy flowers, but did you ever try to distinguish one species

MAGNOLIA

SUGAR

NORWAY

M95

METHOD OF
GROWTH
ON TWIG

Alternate

Opposite

of maple from another by the flowers? Maple flowers differ, even though they are inconspicuous, as are many tree flowers. Some tree fruits and seeds also are obscure, while others are obvious; but they all help with identification. Certainly anyone finding a tree in fall covered with delicious-looking red apples will be able to identify the tree!

Suppose you are outside with a group and someone asks, "What kind of tree is that?" If you don't know, never be afraid to say so; this can breed a genuine curiosity to find out. "Let's look it up" or "let's see how it differs from other trees" are natural responses that can lead not only to the name of the tree, but also to understanding and knowing the tree.

tree activities

Children see trees as friends—for climbing on, swinging from, or sitting under, and, most times, children enjoy activities with these friends. In the following pages are a wide variety of tree activities. Bear in mind that not all of these suggestions are suitable for all

ages, stages, or group sizes. Some are definitely for younger children, others for older children. Some are best suited for small groups, others for larger ones. Some may suit your own style and interests, others not. However, most of the activities can be geared up or down, or otherwise modified to suit your particular needs. Most important, the activities may suggest ideas of your own.

activities with leaves

For young children, one of the most pleasurable activities with leaves is simply jumping in them. Rake a large pile of autumn leaves and let the children enjoy jumping into it, absorbing the sounds, smell, and feel of the leaves as they do.

preserving leaves
with wax paper

Materials: Leaves, wax paper, scissors, old newspapers, electric iron.

Procedure: Cut pieces of wax paper. Arrange leaves between two pieces, and place these between several sheets of newspaper. Iron with a warm iron.

This is particularly effective with brightly colored autumn leaves, as the colors will last. Hang them up in a window for an attractive display. Try making place mats in this way. Wax paper sandwich bags may also be used. Simply place the leaves in the bags between newspaper sheets, and iron them.

preserving leaves
with clear self-adhesive
plastic

Materials: Leaves, heavy paper or cards, clear self-adhesive plastic, scissors.

Procedure: Arrange leaves on the paper or cards. Cut the plastic into pieces the size of the paper or cards. Peel the plastic and cover the arrangement with it, pressing it down carefully.

Very young children need help in peeling and applying the plastic. This activity is good for all ages, including the elderly, who often enjoy making decorative souvenirs on fall outings as a reminder of a pleasant trip. The colors last well. Make other leaf items with the plastic, such as postcards, bookmarks, or place mats. Put a leaf between two pieces of the plastic for a window decoration, or cut it into an oval shape, punch a hole at one end, and hang it as a pendant from a necklace made of string or yarn. Make leaf decorations to go around tin cans or other containers to be used as pencil and other kinds of holders. Holders can also be decorated with

other print-making methods—using paint, making spatter prints or leaf rubbings, or using blueprint paper.

leaf prints
using paint

Materials: Leaves, paint (water-based block-print ink, or oil-based for older children), plates, brayer (roller), old newspapers, paper, or other material to be printed.

Procedure: Put a leaf on the newspaper. Pour paint into the paint container, dip the brayer into the paint, and apply the paint to the leaf. Put the leaf, paint side down, on the article to be printed. Cover with a sheet of newspaper and press the leaf down gently. (It may help to use a rolling pin or to roll a straight-sided bottle over the leaf.) Remove the leaf to reveal its print.

Choice of paint colors and arrangements of leaves offer many creative alternatives. A variety of items can be decorated by this technique, from notepaper and place mats to wall hangings and curtains.

This leaf print curtain was made with fabric paints by the family together on a summer afternoon in the country. It reflects the plants that were at hand.

A leaf spatter print.

leaf spatter prints

Materials: Leaves, paper, paint (thinned poster paint, watercolors, or colored ink), old toothbrush, small piece of wire screening or a thin stick (about pencil length).

Procedure: Arrange leaves on the paper. Dip the toothbrush into the paint and let any drips fall back into the paint container. Hold the toothbrush several inches above the paper and rub the bristles against the screening or stick, spattering paint on the paper around the leaf.

Practice first, so that the spattering will land where you want it, not on yourself. You can also use a can of spray paint (without fluorocarbons, which scientists say are harmful to the environment). Either method produces pleasing leaf silhouettes.

leaf rubbings

Materials: Leaves, wax crayons, sheets of paper (not too heavy).

Procedure: Place leaf under a sheet of paper. Remove paper from a crayon and rub the crayon sidewise on the paper over the leaf. The leaf pattern will appear on the paper.

This technique is especially suitable for younger children. Even three-year-olds can do it with very little adult assistance, and they enjoy the magic-like appearance of the leaf pattern as they rub. For older children, leaf rubbings are an effective way to make a collection showing varieties of leaves.

matching leaves

Materials: Different kinds of leaves, several of each.

Procedure: Have each child take a leaf and then find the other children who have matching leaves.

This is a handy method for dividing a group arbitrarily into smaller groups (as in the introductory tree activity earlier in this chapter). Variations are possible. Use twigs from different kinds of evergreens. Cut a variety of leaves into halves; give a half to each child who then finds the child with the other half.

leaf sorting

Materials: Leaves.

Procedure: Sort the leaves into categories.

There are numerous possible categories: size—large to small, wide to narrow, long to short; texture—rough to smooth, thick to thin; insect damage—leaves with the most holes to those with the least, leaves with the most bumps or other kinds of damage; colors—reds, yellows, and other shades of autumn foliage, or variations of green; smell—leaves with a pleasant smell, with an unpleasant smell, with no smell. Most of these categories can be handled by young children. Older children can manage more exact or complicated versions, or they can sort leaves using technical leaf terminology, by shape (narrow,

oblong, elliptic, heartshaped, and others) or by appearance of edge (wavy, lobed, fine-toothed, and so on). Can anyone find two leaves that are exactly alike? Can anyone find leaves that show no sign of insect activity (a question for late summer or fall)?

leaf old maid

Materials: Twenty-one cards, clear self-adhesive plastic, two each of ten different kinds of leaves, one other kind of leaf, scissors.

Procedure: Put a leaf on each card and cover with the plastic. Play Old Maid using the cards; there will be ten matching pairs and one singleton, which is the "old maid."

Perhaps the children will change the name of the game, for instance, to Old Oak (if an oak is the singleton leaf). Other variations are possible. Make sets of four cards with the same kinds of leaves and the children can play Fish. Probably their ingenuity will lead them to create other variations.

how many leaves on a tree?

Materials: Tree, pencils, paper.

Procedure: Count the leaves on several of what seem to be typical branches, and figure the average number of leaves per branch. Count or estimate the total number of branches on the tree. Multiply the number of branches by the average number of leaves per branch to find the estimated number of leaves on the tree.

To find the number of leaves on the trees in a given yard, along a certain street, or in any particular area, first compute the estimated number of leaves on several representative trees in the area, and then figure the average number per tree. Next, either count or estimate the number of trees in the yard, street, or area. Multiply the average number of leaves by the number of trees, and there's the answer. This activity has potential for a number of math problems for older children. Also, it may lead to interesting discoveries about the numbers of leaves on different kinds of trees, as well as the variation in numbers on the same kinds of trees growing in different situations, such as sunny or shady places, or areas crowded with many trees.

To estimate the surface area of the leaves of a tree, use a ruler to make approximate measurements of each of several representative leaves. Then, compute the average surface area for a leaf. Estimate the total number of leaves on the tree, and multiply this number by the average surface area to find the estimated total leaf surface area of the tree. The leaf surface area of a tree is important because of photosynthesis. The more leaf surface area a tree has, the more food it may make for itself (and its boarders), and the more oxygen it will transpire.

how much do the leaves on a tree weigh?

Materials: Tree, scales (for delicate measurements), pencils, paper.

Procedure: Take enough leaves from the tree so that they will show a significant amount on the scales. Divide the weight shown on the scales by the number of leaves being weighed to find the weight of the average leaf.

Other math problems can follow. To find the estimated weight of all the leaves on a tree, figure the estimated number of leaves on the tree by the method described above. Multiply that number by the average weight per leaf for the total weight of the leaves on the tree. To figure out approximately

how many pounds of leaves must be raked to clear a given yard (assuming no wind, so that leaves are not blown in or out of the yard), take a number of leaves from representative trees in the yard and find the weight of the average leaf. Compute the estimated number of leaves on the trees in the yard as already described. Multiply that number by the weight of the average leaf. The results may show why raking leaves can be tiring! And a question about where to put so many pounds of leaves could lead to a discussion concerning the value of leaves for composting and how leaves are composted naturally in the woods.

autumn leaf mural

Materials: Leaves (colorful autumn leaves gathered by the children, if possible), glue, open containers for glue, applicators for glue (such as craft sticks), large mural-sized paper with several trees drawn in outline.

Procedure: Glue leaves on the trees in the drawing to produce an attractive "living" mural.

Three-year-olds enjoy making this mural of colorful autumn leaves. Gear this activity for slightly older children by drawing or gluing a different kind of leaf on each tree outlined on the mural. The children then glue the leaves they have collected to the appropriate trees on the mural. For still older children who have had some experience in tree identification, label the kinds of trees outlined on the mural and have the children glue their leaves accordingly.

activities with tree bark

making friends with a tree

Materials: One or more trees, preferably with trunks 2 feet (.6m) or more in diameter.

Procedure: Go up to a tree and "shake hands," using a branch if one is low enough, or otherwise using imagination. Then give the tree trunk a big hug.

Young children enjoy this activity. That "big hug" brings them into close contact with the bark of the tree. They are feeling it with hands and sides of faces, as well as with arms and bodies. They are smelling it; for instance, if the bark is moist, they may notice a wet, mossy smell. They are hearing the sounds made by their clothing rubbing against the texture of the bark. And they are having a truly

Give the tree a great big hug!

close-up view. Second-graders once became so enthusiastic about making "tree friends" on a walk that they ran to "try out" each tree we passed. We had already discussed how we could tell our own friends apart, and, during the walk, we found ways of telling our new tree friends apart, particularly by the differences in the bark. The children noted different bark colors and especially the variations in textures. Some barks were smooth, others rough. Some had fine ridges, others coarse. Some had deep furrows between the ridges, others shallow. We questioned what use the bark was to the tree and decided that it could certainly serve as a good protective covering. Older children can make these kinds of bark observations on their own, introducing themselves to tree identification by bark. They may be surprised to discover how varied tree barks are and also that the barks of young trees often are dissimilar from those of older trees of the same species.

Tree bark textures vary greatly.

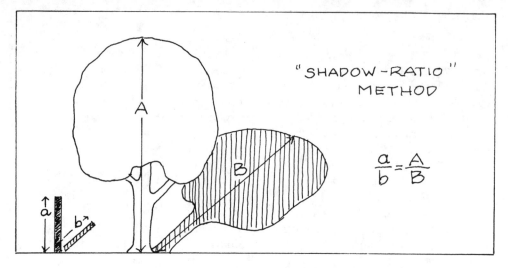

bark rubbings

Materials: Trees, paper (about typing paper weight), wax crayons.

Procedure: Peel the paper off the crayon. Hold a sheet of paper over the bark and rub with the side of the crayon over the paper, as in leaf rubbing. The pattern of the bark will appear on the paper.

Smooth barks tend to produce more effective rubbings than rough ones.

estimating tree height

shadow-ratio method

Materials: Yardstick, tree, pencil, paper.

Procedure: On a sunny day hold the yardstick perpendicular to the ground and measure the length of its shadow. Next, measure the length of the shadow of the tree. Then solve this ratio:

$$\frac{\text{Shadow of tree}}{\text{Height of tree}} = \frac{\text{Shadow of yardstick}}{\text{Height of yardstick}}$$
$$(36'' \text{ or } 90.2 \text{ c})$$

artist's method

Materials: Person (or a tall stick) of known height, pencil.

Procedure: Have the person stand next to the tree (or stand the stick next to the tree). Move away from the tree, holding the pencil vertically at arm's length. Sight over the top of the pencil to the top of the person (or stick); mark with thumb on pencil where the line of sight meets the feet of the person (or bottom of the stick). This length on the pencil represents the known height of the person (or stick). Determine how many of these lengths are in the height of the tree by moving the pencil upward, a length at a time. Multiply the number of lengths by the known height of the person (or stick) to find the approximate height of the tree.

finding the age of a tree

how old is a pine tree?

Materials: Pine trees (under 25 feet, or 7.5 m, tall).

Procedure: Count the number of circular growths of branches, or whorls, along the trunk of the tree and add five to find its approximate age.

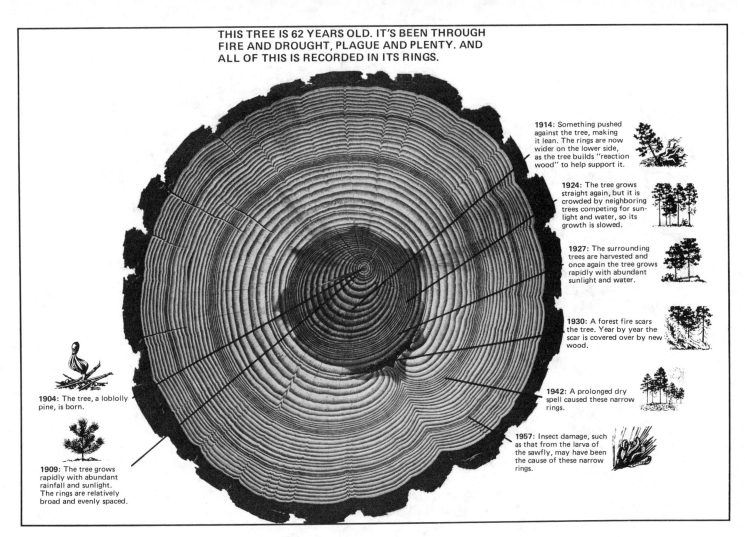

THIS TREE IS 62 YEARS OLD. IT'S BEEN THROUGH FIRE AND DROUGHT, PLAGUE AND PLENTY. AND ALL OF THIS IS RECORDED IN ITS RINGS.

1914: Something pushed against the tree, making it lean. The rings are now wider on the lower side, as the tree builds "reaction wood" to help support it.

1924: The tree grows straight again, but it is crowded by neighboring trees competing for sunlight and water, so its growth is slowed.

1927: The surrounding trees are harvested and once again the tree grows rapidly with abundant sunlight and water.

1930: A forest fire scars the tree. Year by year the scar is covered over by new wood.

1942: A prolonged dry spell caused these narrow rings.

1957: Insect damage, such as that from the larva of the sawfly, may have been the cause of these narrow rings.

1904: The tree, a loblolly pine, is born.

1909: The tree grows rapidly with abundant rainfall and sunlight. The rings are relatively broad and evenly spaced.

Read the rings.

The space on the trunk between two whorls represents a year's growth. It takes approximately five years from the sprouting of the seed for the tree to grow to the level of the first whorl; thus, counting the whorls and adding five gives the age. (This technique does not work with tall pines that have lost many lower branches, unless you can see where the branches had been on the trunk.) Have the children figure how high the tree was when it was their age, or when they were born.

count the rings on a stump

Materials: Tree stump.

Procedure: Count the rings on the stump. The number will be the age of the tree.

Each ring on the stump represents one year's growth. Rings that are far apart indicate years with favorable growth conditions, such as access to sunlight, ample nutrients, and water. Rings that are close together indicate unfavorable conditions, such as drought, crowding, or insect infestation. Stump rubbings can record these life histories. Use paper and the flat side of a wax crayon in the same manner as making leaf or bark rubbings.

role playing the lives of trees

Procedure: Tell the life story of a tree, from the sprouting seed and growth as a sapling, through winters, summers, storms, and fair weather spells, to the mature tree,

and perhaps even to the tree's being blown down in old age. Have the children be the tree, all curled up like a seed at first, then acting with their bodies to show sprouting and the tree's life story.

The students could also create a dance in which they portray the life of the tree.

tree pictures

drawings & paintings of trees

Materials: Paints, paintbrushes, crayons, pencils, paper, paper clips.

Procedure: Paint a picture of a tree using just twelve brush strokes. Draw silhouettes of trees to show the typical shapes of the different kinds. Paint a picture to illustrate

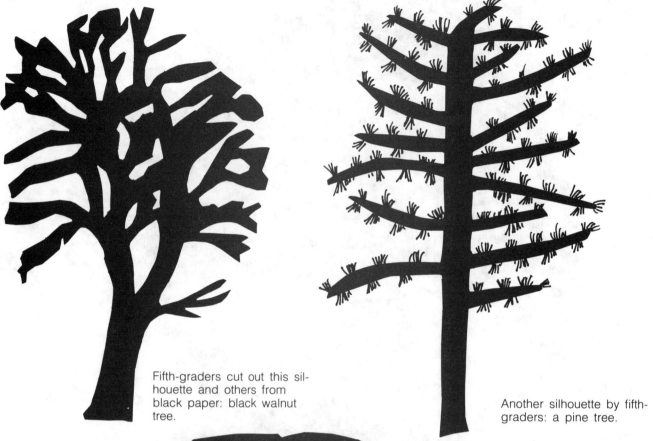

Fifth-graders cut out this silhouette and others from black paper: black walnut tree.

Another silhouette by fifth-graders: a pine tree.

Another silhouette by fifth-graders: weeping willow tree.

the concept that trees are nature's motels and restaurants. Cover a piece of heavy paper with black crayoning. Straighten out a paper clip and scratch away the black to make a scene showing trees. Draw or paint different kinds of leaves as accurately as possible; do the same with tree flowers, fruits, seeds, or nuts.

These are just a few suggestions. There are innumerable ways to sketch, draw, and paint trees. Remember that drawing an item necessitates close observation, which often reveals details that otherwise might be overlooked.

Visit an art museum to study different techniques of painting trees.

tree photography

Materials: Photographic equipment.

Procedure: Take photographic portraits of trees.

Make a tree photograph collection, labeling the species of each tree. Make close-up photographs of bark, buds, fruits, and so on. Make aesthetic pictures of trees and their shadows, or tree silhouettes. There are countless subjects and studies that can be done with a camera and trees.

properties of wood

density of wood

Materials: Equal-sized pieces of a variety of woods (oak, maple, pine, balsa, or others), a sink or other large container full of water.

Procedure: Float the different woods in the water and compare results.

Which wood floated high in the water? Which wood was heavier, thus floating lower? What does this tell about the density of these woods? Try using other kinds of wood and note the results. Weigh the woods on a small scale and compare results with the earlier observations.

hardness of wood

Materials: Pieces of oak and pine, hammer, nails.

Procedure: Hammer nails into the different woods.

Most children love to hammer. With this activity, they can have fun and learn about the properties of different woods at the same time. Nails that bend in the oak testify to its hardness; the ease of hammering into pine is obvious. This activity can lead to an understanding of the terms *hardwood* and *softwood*, and why certain woods are used for certain purposes. Why is a hardwood such as ash used for baseball bats? Why not use a softwood such as pine?

people's use of trees

historical uses of trees

Materials: Books and articles describing uses of trees historically and by different cultures, and/or an opportunity to visit a museum.

Procedure: Use reference materials and/or museum exhibits to learn about human uses of trees during a specific historical period or by a particular cultural group.

Trees have been used by humans for countless centuries, probably since a branch served as the first hunting spear or wood fueled the first cooking fire in a cave. People have always been dependent on trees. Many primitive societies worshipped trees, and in our modern society evergreen trees are brought into houses and decorated. Research into human uses of trees adds a new dimension to historical knowledge, as well as to an understanding of trees. Seeing a finely wrought wooden chair in a museum exhibit about ancient Egypt not only tells about life several thousand years ago, but also is mute testimony to the durability of some woods. A link between past and present can be made by studying how Indians of long ago used the kinds of native trees in your community, how they were later used by the white settlers, and how they are used today.

tree uses today

Procedure: Identify as many different uses of trees as possible in the classroom and in homes.

The lists will be long. They may include: wooden building materials, tools, furniture, boxes, musical instruments, toys; books, magazines, newspapers, cardboard cartons, and other paper pulp products; apples, bananas, tree fruits, and nuts of all kinds, including their products such as frozen orange juice or olive oil. Don't forget cocoa, cinnamon, nutmeg, and other common flavorings and spices; maple syrup, rubber pencil erasers, and turpentine, all of which are tree sap products; and firewood, now used in many households as an alternative to fossil fuels. Chemicals, resins, and other materials derived from trees are used in many items, such as chewing gum, perfumes, soaps, disinfectants, paints, shoe polish, crayons, cellophane, rayon, sausage cases, photographic films, sponges, and phonograph records. It might also be interesting to study the particular uses of different kinds of wood. For example, ax handles are commonly made of hickory; it is tough and hard, able to hold up under sudden shocks. Finally, trees are considered "America's renewable resource." Why?

recycling christmas trees

Materials: Old Christmas trees.

Procedure: Use the branches from several trees to make a winter shelter for small children to enjoy. Trim off the branches and secure the trunk in a stand to make a coat and mitten rack. Stand the tree up outside and use it to hold foods for the birds.

What other uses can you and the children devise?

writing about trees

diary of an "adopted" tree

Materials: One tree per child, paper, pencils; also, many of the materials listed in the preceding tree activities.

Procedure: Each child "adopts" a particular tree. The children study and observe their trees throughout the seasons, recording their observations and discoveries in a "tree diary."

An intensive knowledge of one tree can lead to a greater

understanding of them all. Following are suggestions for information and materials to include in a tree diary. Record the name of the tree and its location. Describe the tree, including its shape and an estimate of its height. Draw a picture of the tree. Describe its leaves, including size, shape, color, and texture, and record estimates of their number and their surface area. Include a leaf rubbing, a leaf preserved by clear self-adhesive plastic, a leaf print, or a drawing of a leaf. Describe the bark and include a bark rubbing. Do any roots show? With deciduous trees, record when the first leaves fall in autumn, the autumn color of the leaves, the date when all the leaves are gone, and draw a winter picture of the tree. Draw the buds and record when they open in spring. Do the same for the flowers and the seeds or fruit. Record animal activity in or under the tree during the seasons, including such signs as woodpecker holes, empty nests, or holes in leaves.

Tree diaries can be geared for younger children. For instance, in spring visit a tree weekly with a group of children. Write down some of their observations. Combine the observations into a text and make a copy for each child. Drawings, leaf prints or rubbings, bark rubbings, and other activities by the child can be included in each copy of the diary.

tree reports

Materials: Reference materials with information about trees, pencils, paper.

Procedure: Tell each child to choose a tree outdoors. Then, using reference materials, have each one research and write a report on the kind of tree chosen.

Tree reports can include a wide variety of information about a kind of tree, from its identification features and natural range to its historical uses by people and its present economic importance.

tree biographies

Materials: Trees, pencils, paper.

Procedure: Write a biography for a tree, describing events that may have happened around it from the tree's point of view.

The report can be factual or imaginative. Many communities contain old trees whose age is documented. Was the tree there when the community was settled? Before that, what Indians may have passed by the tree and what animals were common in the forest? What changes may have occurred in the tree's environment during the last fifty years?

tree poems

Procedure: Have the children look closely at trees and then ask them to write a tree poem. Here is one by a nine-year-old.

Branches hanging low and high
Look so nice against the sky.
Leaves so green, all shapes and sizes,
Trees have fruit, flowers and other
surprises
Big trunks, small trunks, white and brown,
I wonder how they grow out of the
ground.
Some will be used for houses and paper;
Logs will burn warmly in cold winter
weather.
All the birds making nests–
Boy do the trees need a rest!

bibliography

adults

BROCKMAN, C. FRANK, *Trees of North America.* New York: Golden Press, 1968.

BROWN, VINSON, *Reading the Woods.* New York: Macmillan, 1969.

EDLIN, HERBERT, and MAURICE NIMMO, *The Illustrated Encyclopedia of Trees.* New York: Crown, 1978.

HARLOW, WILLIAM, *Trees.* New York: Dover, 1957.

JACKSON, JAMES P., *The Biography of a Tree.* Middle Village, N.Y.: Jonathan David, 1979.

PARKER, SHELIA, and others, *Trees, Science 5/13.* London: MacDonald Educational, 1973.

PHILLIPS, ROGER, *Trees of North America and Europe.* New York: Random House, 1978.

SYMONDS, GEORGE W. D., *The Tree Identification Book.* New York: Morrow, 1958.

children & adults

ADLER, DAVID A., *Redwoods Are the Tallest Trees in the World.* New York: Crowell, 1978.

ANDERSON, MARGARET J., *Exploring City Trees.* New York: McGraw-Hill, 1976.

ATWOOD, ANN, *The Kingdom of the Forest.* New York: Scribner, 1972.

BUSCH, PHYLLIS S., *Once There Was a Tree.* Cleveland: World, 1968.

DONALDSON, FRANCIS, *Trees.* New York: Watts, 1976.

DOWDEN, ANN O., *The Blossom on the Bough, A Book of Trees.* New York: Crowell, 1975.

GUILCHER, J. M., and R. H. NOAILLES, *A Tree Is Born.* New York: Sterling, 1964.

HUTCHINS, ROSS E., *Lives of an Oak Tree.* Chicago: Rand McNally, 1962.

VESSEL, MATTHEW F., and HERBERT H. WONG, *Our Tree.* Reading, Mass.: Addison-Wesley, 1969.

ZIM, HERBERT S., and ALEXANDER C. MARTIN, *Trees.* New York: Golden Press, 1956.

3

have you thanked a green plant today?

Plants grow, breathe, reproduce, and use food, as do animals. However, most plants are green and can make their own food, unlike animals. The green chlorophyll of plants, from the tallest trees to the lowest mosses, uses energy from the sun to make food by the process of photosynthesis. Without this process there would be no food for animals, and we could not exist. Furthermore, photosynthesis removes carbon dioxide from the atmosphere and adds oxygen, a requirement for all animal life. Indeed, we should be extremely grateful for plants; we depend on them for our existence.

Trees are the largest of all plants; the largest of trees is in California, a giant sequoia, known as General Sherman. This tree measures 101.5 ft. (31 m) in circumference at the base and 242.7 ft. (83 m) in height. The smallest plants are microscopic. Unseen, they play vital ecological roles. For instance, the unicellular algae of the plankton community constitute primary food supplies in oceans and freshwater areas.

The simplest plants are nonflowering, reproducing by means other than seeds. Algae, fungi, lichens, and ferns traditionally have been considered as nonflowering members of the plant kingdom, but modern biologists may use different classifications. Of these plants, the algae have the simplest structure. They generally live in water or moist places and they usually possess chlorophyll. The green coatings sometimes apparent on the inside walls of aquariums or on moist tree barks are composed of millions of tiny alga plants. Seaweeds are algae, possessing chlorophyll, although in many seaweed varieties it is masked by red or brown pigments. In contrast to the algal plankton, some seaweeds grow to great lengths, one kind to as long as 200 feet (60 m).

Fungi do not have chlorophyll and, therefore, must obtain their food from other sources, generally dead plant or animal materials. A fungus plant sends out a network of white threadlike strands, called mycelia, through the material from which it is drawing its nourishment. At times these mycelia develop swellings filled with millions of spores. The swellings grow up through the surface, appearing as what we generally recognize as mushrooms. The mushroom is the fruiting body of the fungus plant in much the same way that an apple is a fruiting body of an apple tree. The mushrooms produce spores, which float away in the air to propagate new fungus plants. In the meantime, the feeding of the fungus plant plays a vital role in nature's natural recycling. For instance, if the fungus is feeding on the dead wood of a fallen tree, it contributes to the decay process by which the tree will eventually be returned to the soil where it once grew. Some fungi, however, are not so helpful from the human viewpoint—mold on bread or mildew on clothing, for example. Yet, penicillin comes from a mold, and yeast that makes bread rise is another helpful fungus.

Certain fungi and algae combine to form lichens, another group of nonflowering plants. To help children remember this partnership, tell them that "a fungus met an alga and they took a 'liken' for each other." Some lichens grow on tree barks, some grow on the ground, and a great many grow as encrustments on rocks. The fungus of the lichen holds the plant onto the rock and protects the alga from the cold, while the alga makes food for the lichen. Lichens are small, tough plants, and they do a gigantic task wedging themselves into cracks in the rocks upon which they live and also se-

creting acids; both these actions slowly cause rocks to crumble. This initiates one of the erosion processes by which rocks are eventually broken down to become part of soil.

Mosses are often the next soil builders after the lichens. They require only a little earth, and when a moss dies it adds to the organic content of its habitat. These low-growing plants have chlorophyll, and on the forest floor they look like soft, green blankets, inviting you to lie down on them. It is interesting how an entire moss plant can absorb water. Find a piece of dried-out moss, wet it, and you will see how the whole plant acts as a sponge.

Ferns are the most complex of the nonflowering plants. They are green with chlorophyll and are characterized by their graceful fronds. Geologic ages ago, ferns grew as tall as trees (today a few still persist in the tropics) and dominated the landscape. Coal is a product of these ancient plants, so we have ferns to thank for the energy that society derives from coal. Ferns reproduce by spores, and the location of the spore cases on the fern is often an identification aid.

It is easy to differentiate spore-bearing from seed-bearing plants, for the seed plants have flowers—and wouldn't the world be dull without them? We appreciate their beauty, as well as their function, which is to provide a means of reproduction by developing seeds. A typical flower has an ovary, which

Some people say that elves and fairies live under mushrooms.

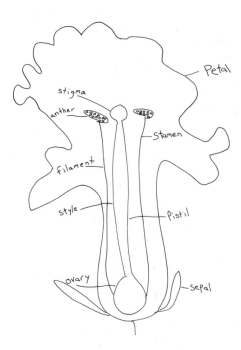

A fifth-grader's flower diagram.

has ovules inside, and pollen, which must unite with the ovules to fertilize them and start their growth into seeds. Pollination is the process by which pollen grains are spread from the stamens, where they grow, to the pistil, the flower part that contains the ovary in its base. The top of the pistil is the stigma, generally sticky in order to catch the pollen grains needed for fertilization.

Flowers have adapted in countless ways to achieve pollination and fertilization. Some depend on wind to spread pollen grains to the stigma. Others depend on insects or birds for pollination, and they have many lures, such as beautiful colors, attractive shapes, and delightful fragrances. A few flowers open at night and are pollinated by night-flying moths. Some plants have two kinds of flowers, those having pistils with ovaries and those having stamens with pollen.

Flowering plants are divided into three groups: annuals, biennials, and perennials. Annuals live for one growing season. Petunias, tomatoes, and milkweed are annuals; they must start anew from seed every year. Biennials, such as pansies and Queen Anne's lace, live for two years; their flowers and seeds are generally produced during the second year's growing season. Perennials live for many years. Some, such as chrysanthemums or dandelions, die down to the ground in winter, but they all produce flowers and seeds for many growing seasons.

Plants almost literally cover the earth. In many areas in the temperate zone, if you leave a garden untended just a little too long, weed plants will graphically demonstrate how quickly a plant covering can be made. Abandon the area to the weeds and they will thrive for a while, but eventually they will give way to woody plants, young bushes, and tree saplings. This is the process of plant succession, and, eventually, woods will cover the old garden area.

Plants have adapted to almost any habitat. Water hyacinths grow in warm climates, Canada mayflowers in cold ones. Cactuses thrive in desert conditions, cattails and most ferns need moist soils, and seaweeds and water lilies grow only in water. Mosses can grow in poor soils, and lichens may be the only plants on the rocky top of a high mountain. Some plants, like Spanish moss and orchids, grow in the air, although they are attached to trees. There are parasitic plants, such as mistletoe, a vine that saps energy from its host tree. There are carnivorous plants adapted for living in nutrient-deficient environments by supplementing their nitrogen intake with insects and other small creatures. Habitat is an important consideration in determining the identity of plants.

Size and manner of growth are also identification factors. Is the plant of medium height with

Cactuses thrive in deserts.

woody stems—a shrub perhaps? Is it long and trailing—a vine maybe? Does it look like green outdoor carpeting over a rock—most likely moss? Consider the leaves. Are they long and slender, as with cattails? Are they in three small leaflets, as with the clovers? Are they fronds, as with the ferns? Notice the shape, size, and placement of the leaves and also of the flowers. With wild flowers, color is often indicative, and many of these flowers are grouped in field guides according to the flower color. What are the fruits or seeds like, or are there spores? Does the plant have thorns? Are the stems round or square? Every feature of a particular plant may be helpful in identification.

Our direct and indirect uses of plants are countless. As an example, consider just one plant, the coconut palm. Some cultures have more than 200 uses for this one tree. We are all utterly dependent on plants. Perhaps it is in recognition of this dependency that so many people, no matter where they live, find pleasure in keeping plants indoors. African violets on the windowsill or ivy on the bookcase are not only decorative, but also seem to satisfy some basic yearnings of our inner selves.

Just as our uses of plants are innumerable, so are the possible activities that can be done with them at school, in the home, or outdoors. The activities described in the rest of this chapter are representative examples to do "as is," to adapt to particular situations, or to serve as catalysts for readers'

creativity in developing other useful projects. The subject of plants is so vast, however, that plant-related activities are also included in many other places in this book. (Chapters 2, 3, and 10 through 14 all include references to plants and plant activities.)

dandelions

As a starter, let's concentrate on just one plant, the common dandelion. A weed is a plant that grows where it is not wanted; and, although the dandelion has at times been cultivated as a vegetable, in most circumstances it eminently qualifies as a weed. As any careful lawnkeeper can testify, dandelions are well adapted for survival. Their leaves generally lie in flat rosettes, which defy the cutting blades of lawn mowers, while at the same time extinguishing growth of competing neighboring plants by covering them and blocking their access to sunlight. A long tap root stores an abundant food supply for the plant over the winter and makes it difficult for a gardener to eradicate the plant by pulling it up. As if these adaptations were not enough, the plant further ensures its success as a weed by the abundance of seeds that one plant can produce. Studying the adaptations of dandelions for survival can lead to studies of other plants and their particular adaptations for living in their own type of habitat.

The name dandelion comes from the French *dent de lion*—meaning tooth of the lion—probably a reference to the sharp, jagged edges of the leaves. Children are intrigued to learn this and enjoy learning about the traceable derivations of other flower names. The daylily, for instance, bears that name because its flowers bloom for one day only. A less common name for the dandelion is shepherd's clock, so called because the flower opens at the beginning of the day and closes at the end.

dandelion activities

watching the shepherd's clock

Materials: Pencil, paper.

Procedure: Find dandelion plants with flowers. Record the time that the dandelion blossoms start to open in the morning and the time that they finish opening. Record when they start to close in the evening and note how long the closing takes. Observe the flowers on cloudy and rainy days, and record what they do.

Some plants, such as clover, alfalfa, mimosa and locust have leaves that fold up in the evening; children often call them "sleepy head plants."

dandelion crowns

Materials: Many dandelion flowers with stems.

Procedure: Entwine the flowers together, as shown in the illustration, to make a crown.

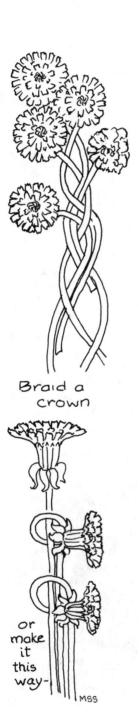

Braid a crown

or make it this way–

MSS

DANDELIONS

curls

chains

This technique can be used with any abundant flower that has pliable stems, such as daisies or Queen Anne's lace.

dandelion chain

Materials: Dandelion blossom stems.

Procedure: Remove the flower from the stem. Bend the stem and insert the smaller end into the larger one. Repeat, putting the next stem through the circle of the preceding one. Continue until the chain is as long as you like.

dandelion curls

Materials: Dandelion blossom stems, water.

Procedure: Make four cuts in the end of the stem; tear each cut two to three inches, dividing the stem into four sections. Dip the divided stem into the water; stem pieces usually curl up tightly.

dandelion bubbles

Materials: Dandelion blossom stems, soapy water suitable for bubble blowing.

Procedure: Remove the blossom from a stem. Dip the end of the stem into the water and blow into the other end of the stem to make bubbles.

Children also enjoy blowing through the stem into the soapy water to make a rising mountain of small bubbles.

dandelion blossom fritters & dandelion greens

These are both quite delicious. Look on pages 178–79 for cooking directions.

how many seeds?

Materials: Dandelion plants with flowers and seed heads.

Procedure: Count the number of seeds in a seed head; count the number of blossoms and/or seed heads on a typical plant. Multiply the number of seeds by the number of blossoms and/or seed heads to find how many seeds one dandelion plant may produce.

Whatever the number, it will be large. Some say there are at least 2,000 seeds per plant. No wonder dandelions are such successful weeds!

blow dandelion seeds

Materials: Dandelion seed heads.

Procedure: Pick a dandelion seed head, make a wish, and, using only three breaths, try to blow all the seeds off.

If they are all blown off, it is said that the wish will come true. Daisies also have a folklore ritual. Pull off the white petals, reciting "she (or he) loves me" with the first, "she (or he) loves me not" with the next, and so on, with the last petal giving the "loves me" or "loves me not" answer.

looking closely at plants

Stop and study a plant. Take time. Look closely. Try a sketch or two, or write down observations. Chances are you will discover features you have never noticed before. Careful viewing increases appreciation and understanding of plants and leads to identification. Knowing a plant's name will help you feel more familiar with the plant.

For general purposes, the plant's common name is sufficient, but sometimes the scientific name is necessary to ensure correct identification. Common names can be confusing. For instance, plants may be known by different common names in different localities. Sometimes two different plants share a common name, as in the case of the pigweeds. Both pigweed plants are common garden weeds that grow surprisingly tall if unchecked. However, one has the scientific name, *Chenopodium album*; the other is quite a different plant, *Amaranthus retroflexus*. Some children feel sophisticated to know a few scientific names, and any serious plant student will certainly need to know them.

plant observation activities

scientific names

Materials: Plant identification guides, pencils, paper.

Procedure: Have each student use an identification guide to identify several common plants in the school yard, recording both the common and scientific names.

Have the students look up the scientific names of other plants that they know. Do any of the students know two plants with the same common name? Explain how the scientific names help in such cases. Have the students invent some plants and their scientific names, and then draw the plants and label them as Edward Lear did in his *Nonsense Botany* many years ago.

a nonflowering plant hunt

Materials: Identification guides (optional).

Procedure: Go on a hunt to discover how many nonflowering

Manypeeplia Upsidownia. From Edward Lear's *Nonsense Botany*.

plants (algae, fungi, lichens, mosses, and ferns) may be found in the school yard. Bring in samples when possible and make a display. Use identification guides to find the plant names.

Encourage the children to observe these plants growing at school and in other habitats. Do they ever have flowers? Where do they grow? The children may discover lichens growing on rocks; could an apple tree grow out of a rock? How are nonflowering plants adapted for their habitats?

make a flower collection

Materials: Clippers, old newspapers, a weight, large index cards, clear self-adhesive plastic, scissors, pencils, identification guides.

Procedure: Collect different flowers (only pick ones that are abundant). Press them by placing them carefully between newspapers and putting the weight on top. After several days, lay each flower on a card, label it, cover with the plastic, and record pertinent data, such as date found, habitat, and a description of the plant on the back of the card. (Thinner flowers will press better than bulky ones.)

This activity can be simplified (include little or no data about the flowers, for example) or extended (collect different flowers in a particular habitat for a specific period of time). It can also be done with leaves of trees, shrubs, or other plants.

species variation mathematics

Materials: Pencils, paper, rulers (tape measures optional).

Procedure: Locate several plants of the same kind. Measure and record their heights and widths. Carefully measure and record the lengths and breadths of several leaves on each plant. Compute the average plant height, width, and leaf size.

Many other features can also be measured: size of flowers, length of stems, and so on. The students may be surprised at the variations within the species. Can they think of any explanations for these variations?

finding shapes in plants

Materials: Pencils and papers with a list or drawings of shapes: circular, rectangular, square, triangular, oval, heart, or star shaped.

Procedure: Have the children search for the shapes in the plants of an area and check off the shape on the list when they are found. At the end, have the children share their findings.

Looking for shapes is a technique to sharpen observation skills (and also helps with drawing skills).

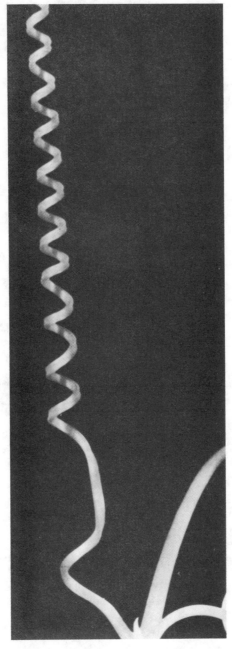

A spiral shape is seen in a tendril.

finding special features in plants

Materials: Paper and pencils.

Procedure: Make a list of the special features to be found. Then have the children hunt for plants with these features, record them, and be able to show the plants to the rest of the group.

Special features to look for might include: protections such as thorns, spines, or stinging hairs; textures such as smooth, furry, soft, bumpy, rough; or different smells of flowers and some leaves.

open nature's surprise packages— buds

Materials: Lilac twigs with spring buds beginning to swell (or other similar buds), pins, hand lenses.

Procedure: Open the buds, count the tiny leaves inside, using pins to help separate them and hand lenses for magnification.

Children are generally amazed to find so many leaves within such small buds. Try other buds. Large buds such as horse chestnuts may have flowers in them.

state flowers

Materials: Books and other reference materials about the different state flowers, pencils, paper.

Procedure: Study your state's flower. Have the children locate the plants outside and write descriptions or make sketches of them. Find out how abundant the plants are in the state and whether any other state has the same flower.

Find out the state flowers of neighboring states; do they also grow in your state? Label each state's flower on a map of the United States.

plant growth

Most flowering plants need sun, soil, water, and air for growth. Many plant growth requirements are demonstrated in the following activities. (Chapter 4 includes plant growth activities with seeds.)

plant growth activities

how fast do plants grow?

Materials: Ruler or tape measure, waterproof marking pen, colored twine, pencils, paper.

Procedure: At the start of the growing season, tie pieces of the twine around twigs of several different kinds of trees or shrubs. (The twine will help in locating the twigs later in the season.) Mark each twig with the pen just behind the bud at the end of the twig, and make several marks at 4-inch (10 c) intervals along the twig. Measure and record the heights of young wild flowers, ferns, grasses, and other appropriate plants. Revisit the same plants periodically. Notice where the growth has taken place on the twigs; measure the growth and record it. Repeat the measurements of the other plants. Record and compare the results.

Some ferns grow from the tightly curled fiddlehead stage to great height with a dramatic rapidity that will amaze the children. Graphing the comparative growth rates is an interesting followup for this project. Growth measurements can also be made with house plants. Generally, these rates will not equal those of outside plants in the spring, although the speedy growth of an amaryllis is spectacular.

Young ferns grow rapidly.

kitchen garden

Materials: Any of the following: carrots, beets, radishes, parsnips, white potatoes, sweet potatoes, yams, onions.

Procedure: Cut about an inch off the tops of the carrots, beets, radishes, and parsnips. Put the vegetable tops in shallow dishes with water in a sunny window, and watch for the leaves to grow. Cut off a piece of white potato with an eye in it, and plant it in soil in a pot. Plant an onion in a pot. Suspend the yam or sweet potato with toothpicks in a jar. Fill the jar with water so that about half of the vegetable is in the water; keep it in a warm dark place until roots grow, then put it in a moderately sunny window. Be sure to keep the kitchen garden plants well watered.

Some vegetables have been treated with chemicals and will not grow; use only untreated vegetables.

terrariums

Materials: Container suitable for a terrarium (aquarium, plastic shoe box, refrigerator dish, or wide-mouthed jar, and cover of glass or plastic film with rubber band or string to secure it), pebbles or sand, several pieces of charcoal, soil, a small rock or two, small woodland plants.

Procedure: Put a thin layer of sand or pebbles in the bottom of the aquarium, and add the charcoal, broken small. Put in a layer of soil and the small rocks for interest. Plant the plants carefully and decoratively. Water the terrarium until the soil is moist. Put the cover on and keep the terrarium out of direct sunlight and away from direct heat.

Many terrariums last indefinitely, demonstrating a truly balanced ecosystem. However, should mold or mildew appear, leave the top off for a while each day, checking that the soil does not become too dry. Use plants that do not grow tall, such as mosses, lichens, small ferns, and other short woodland plants so that they will not outgrow the terrarium.

Dish gardens, which do not have tops, are simple and fun to make. Use any suitable container, such as an aluminum pie plate, and assemble the garden in the same manner as assembling a terrarium. Keep the garden moist, but not too wet.

mold gardens

Materials: Slices of bread or fresh fruit, pencils, paper, water.

Procedure: Place some slices in a warm, dark place, some on a sunny windowsill, and some in the refrigerator. Check the slices daily and record what happens. (Molds need moisture to grow; sprinkle a little water, if the bread becomes dry.)

Mold, which grows unwanted all too easily, should grow in this experiment from the mold spores that are in the air awaiting a suitable place for growth.

plants need sun

Materials: Young seedlings or house plants, dark closet.

Procedure: Put the seedlings or house plants into the dark closet for a few days and note how and if the leaves change.

Different kinds of plants will react differently, and some may be more effective for this experiment than others. Be careful not to leave a plant in the dark too long or its health may suffer.

phototropism— plants are drawn to light

Materials: House plant (geraniums are good for this), sunny window.

Procedure: Put the plant in a sunny window. After a week or two, notice the position of the leaves. Turn the plant around and check daily to see how the leaves turn again to face the sun.

Seedlings can also be used for this activity. Almost all plants are phototropic, drawn to light. Notice this outdoors; the leaves of the plants of an area will all be positioned to catch as much of the sun's light as possible.

what kind of soil do plants like?

Procedure: Make comparative studies of plants of the same species outdoors. Find where the plants thrive and where they do not grow as well. Compare the soils of the areas as well as comparing other habitat variations.

Is there a correlation between the plant's growth and the richness of the soil, the sand content of the soil, or the compaction of the soil? (A simple way to estimate compaction is to push a pencil into the soil and judge how hard, or not, it is.) See p. 45 about growing seedlings in different types of soils.

do plants give off water vapor?

Materials: Plastic bag, short piece of string, actively growing tree or shrub.

Procedure: Place the plastic bag carefully over the end of a leafy branch and tie the opening firmly closed around the branch. What happens?

Within a period of time, water vapor should appear in the bag, an indication that the leaves are losing moisture to the air and transpiration is taking place. Make a comparison by securing a bag over the end of a twig that has no leaves.

do plants use water?

Materials: Celery stalks with different amounts of leaves, jar or glass, food coloring, water.

Procedure: Put water in the jar or glass, and color it with food coloring. Put the celery stalks in the water. Watch to see where the water goes.

As the leaves lose water by transpiration, water is pulled up the stalks into the leaves. The coloring should be apparent in the leaves. Cut open some of the stalks and notice how the veins have become colored. This kind of experiment may be done with twigs or almost any plant stem. For a variation, split the stem of a white carnation into two pieces for a couple of inches. Put one side of the stem into red-colored water and the other into green. Be prepared for a bicolored flower.

do plants need air?

Materials: Petroleum jelly, actively growing plant with leaves.

Procedure: Cover both surfaces of several leaves thickly with petroleum jelly. Also cover the upper surfaces of some and the lower surfaces of others. Check daily to see what happens.

Most plants take in air through openings known as stomates, which are located on the undersides of their leaves. Blocking these stomates should cause the leaves to fade and die.

what kind of food do plants make?

See Testing Seeds for Starch activity in Chapter 4, and then test actively growing parts of plants, such as green leaves and green stems. Also test food storage parts of plants, such as potatoes or carrots. These tests should show that the sugar made by photosynthesis turns to starch, which is the food for the plant.

pollination

Procedure: Have the children carefully touch the anthers (the pollen-bearing parts at the top of the stamens) of a flower and see if any of the dust-like yellow pollen grains are visible on their fingers. Have them gently rub the grains from their fingers onto the stigma (the top of the flower part with the ovary) of another flower of the same species.

This is a demonstration of pollination. It may be easier to do this using a small paint brush instead of fingers. For a simpler demonstration, have the children rub a little flour onto stigmas. Most stigmas are sticky, and the flour will adhere to them just as the pollen grains do. For an activity with honey bees and pollination see p. 62.

find out about galls

Materials: Clippers, pencils, paper, gall identification guide.

Procedure: Search for galls—which are strange-looking swellings or deformities on plants—at any season. Record where they were found and what they look like. Identify them, if possible. Take samples back inside for a display.

Galls are usually caused by insects and are the results of the plant's reaction to an insect having deposited an egg in the plant, as well as the growth activities of the young insect. Generally, gall-producing insects use one specific kind of plant. Galls provide their occupants with shelter, protection, and food. Open a gall; you may find the developing insect inside or a hole where the insect left the gall at maturity.

Try putting galls into zip-lock bags. Keep them until the adult insects emerge; then release them.

plant crafts

There are numerous plant crafts. Tie a bunch of pine needles onto a small twig, and you have a doll's broom. Gather plant materials and make collages or mobiles. Make a whistle from a length of hollow stem. Put a growing cucumber into a bottle when very small. Cut it off the vine when the cucumber nearly fills the bottle and you have a "ship-in-the-bottle" mystery for those who do not know the secret.

Crafts are teaching tools in that they familiarize children with the natural objects being used. Also, gathering materials for a craft often creates a goal for an outside visit, and sharpens observation as well. In an age of plastics and consumer goods, it is pleasing to find that simple natural objects still are useful. Many crafts offer clues to history, telling how things were made or done in olden days. Following are some examples of plant craft activities. For other plant crafts, see Chapter 2, especially activities about making leaf prints; Chapter 4 for seed craft activities; and Chapter 10, for seaside plant activities.

plant craft activities

decorative plant cards

Materials: Large index cards, scissors, clear self-adhesive plastic.

Procedure: Cut the plastic to match the size of the cards. Have the children gather plant materials: grasses, leaves, flowers, and so on. Arrange these on the cards and cover with the plastic.

Thick items should be pressed between newspapers under a weight for several days before using. Other items can be made: bookmarks, letter paper, postcards, place mats, window decorations (place materials between two pieces of plastic), or pencil and other holders.

Try using black flocked paper as the background. Arrange the plant materials on it, using a little glue to hold them in place. Cover the arrangement with a piece of clear kitchen plastic wrap, securing it in place with tape on the back side.

Try also to use blueprint paper for making prints.

drying flowers & seed heads for arrangements

Materials: Plants suitable for drying (everlasting, goldenrod, thistle, dock, yarrow, sea lavender, milkweed pods, cattails, phragmites, iris pods, and others), string, container to hold arrangement.

Procedure: Gather flower and seed stalks from appropriate plants. Hang them upside to dry, using the string to hold them. Once dried, arrange them decoratively in the container.

Experiment to find other plants that dry well.

dried arrangements in plaster of paris

Materials: Plaster of Paris, water, small containers, such as paper or styrofoam cups, or small aluminum pie plates.

Procedure: Collect materials to be arranged, or use materials already dried as described in the preceding activity. Mix plaster of Paris and water in the containers, and when it begins to harden, place in it the materials for the dried arrangement.

This is a particularly appropriate fall project, when the seed heads of many weeds are available. All ages can enjoy it.

mushroom spore prints

Materials: Mushrooms, white and colored papers.

Procedure: Pick mushrooms, remove stems, and place the mushroom tops right side up on a piece of paper. Cover with a glass or small bowl so that the spores will drop directly onto the paper undisturbed by drafts. In a few

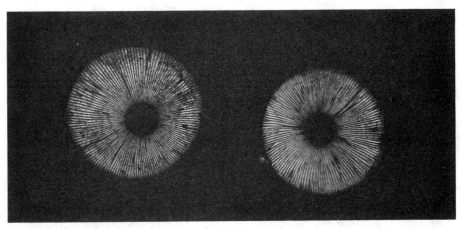

Mushroom spore prints.

hours remove the tops and enjoy the patterns the spores have left on the paper. If the spores do not show, try darker or lighter paper and fresh mushroom caps.

Use gilled mushrooms for this activity. (Remember that many mushrooms are poisonous to eat. Exercise caution, especially if working with young children, and always wash hands after handling mushrooms.)

shelf fungus drawings

Materials: Artists' shelf fungus (crescent-shaped and generally growing on dead trees; select fungi that are still growing and are soft on the underside), pencil or knitting needle.

Procedure: Draw a picture on the underside of the fungus using the pencil or knitting needle. Be careful not to touch the underside

A shelf fungus drawing. Note the young artist's fingerprints on the right-hand side made before the fungus had dried.

as fingerprints will show. When the fungus has dried, the picture can no longer be smudged, and will be permanent.

grass weaving

Materials: Piece of cardboard (not too stiff to bend; about 6 by 8 inches, or 15–20 c), scissors, string, dried grass (long, pliable pieces).

Procedure: First make a cardboard loom. Cut ¼-inch (6.5 mm) slits about ¼-inch (6.5 mm) apart in each of the narrower ends of the cardboard. Knot the end of the string, catch it in a corner slit, and thread the loom by hooking the string in the slits at each end as shown. Keep the string taut by bending the cardboard slightly. At the end, tie the string to the loop next to it. Weave the grass pieces in and out across the strings. To make a smooth edge, weave the ends back in for a short distance and cut them off. Keep the woven grasses tightly together. When there is room for no more, take the weaving off the loom.

Woven plant materials have traditionally been used for mats, baskets, and many other items. Experiment with different

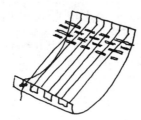

materials such as cattail leaves. Allow materials to dry before weaving; otherwise they will shrink in the woven object. Then soak the dried materials in water just before using them to make them pliable and prevent breakage.

dyeing with plants

Materials: Enamel pot, water, clean white cotton material, stove, onion skins, strainer, wooden spoon.

Procedure: Make a dyebath by simmering six loose handfuls of onion skins in a half gallon of water in the enamel pot for an hour. Strain out the onion skins and discard them. Put the material into the dyebath in the enamel pot. Simmer, stirring the material occasionally with the wooden spoon, until the material has reached the desired depth of color. Remove the material, rinse it thoroughly in cold water, let it dry, and enjoy its new color.

For a brighter color, put copper pennies into the onion skin dyebath in the enamel pot. For a darker color, put the dyebath into an iron pot (an iron frying pan, if the material is not too large) instead of the enamel pot. Try dyeing paper; dip white paper into the simmering dyebath, remove, and dry. Try coloring hard-boiled eggs this way. All dyeing used to be done with natural materials. To find out how and to experiment further, consult books on natural dyeing.

plants & people

We are dependent on plant materials for many things, from food, clothing, and shelter to items that involve almost every activity. Think of your activities in the past two hours. How many plants have you encountered, either directly or indirectly? You are looking at a material derived from plants right now, since this page is made from wood pulp, a product made from trees.

plants & people activities

what parts of plants do we eat?

Procedure: Ask the children to think of the different parts of plants that we eat, for instance: roots (carrots), tubers (potatoes), stems (celery), leaves (spinach), buds (broccoli), fruits (tomatoes). Name as many plants as possible for each category.

origins of cultivated plants

Materials: Books or articles about historic origins and uses of cultivated plants.

Procedure: Trace the history of many of our cultivated plants. For instance, onions originated in Asia and were used in religious ceremonies in ancient Egypt; in ancient Rome, celery was used for funeral wreaths and was not eaten as a vegetable until the Middle Ages.

Many of our foods originated with the Indians of the American continents: potatoes, beans, cranberries, strawberries, maple sugar, pumpkins, squash, peanuts, and perhaps the most important of all, corn. Have the students study Indian uses of these foods and how the foods were introduced into Europe.

insect repellent

Materials: Mature bracken ferns.

Procedure: Pick a bracken fern and wear it upside down on your head to help in repelling biting insects.

The bracken fern helps in several ways. One is psychological; if the insects have been annoying, balancing the fern on the head distracts from the problem and gives a positive feeling of being able to do something about it. Another way is chemical: bracken fern contains a substance that repels insects. A third way is physical. Deer flies tend to land on the highest object and will often sit on the top of the inverted fern's stem rather than on the person's head.

rushlights

Materials: Freshly cut rushes, salad oil (or bacon or other fat).

Procedure: Carefully peel the outer green layer off the rush stems, leaving the inner long column of white pith intact. Soak the pith in oil or melted fat. Ignite one end of the pith and it will burn, giving light like a candle.

Rushlights were commonly used for lighting before electricity. Devise a way to hold the

She hopes that the bracken fern will keep the insects away.

rushlights; for instance, put a branch in a bottle and thumbtack the rushlight at an angle to the branch. (You may have to change the position of the thumbtack as the light burns down.) Light several of these rushlights in a dark room to experience how it was to live long ago with rushlighting.

amusing plant uses

do you like butter?

Materials: Buttercup flowers.

Procedure: Hold a yellow buttercup flower under a person's chin to see if that person likes butter. If a yellow reflection shows, the answer is said to be yes.

grass whistles

Materials: Long blades of grass from 3/8 inch (9 mm) to 1/2 inch (13 mm) wide.

Procedure: Hold a grass blade parallel between both thumbs, held vertically and tightly pressed together. Blow through the vertical cracks between the thumbs and around the taut blade of grass. A squeaking whistling noise can be made.

popping leaves

Materials: Large green leaves without any holes in them (grape leaves work well).

Procedure: Curl one hand to make a circle with your thumb and index finger. Place a large leaf flat over the circle and hit it hard with the palm of your other hand. It should make a loud "pop."

making crowns

Materials: Maple leaves.

Procedure: Break the stems off the maple leaves. Place one leaf overlapping another and use a stem as a pin to hold them together. Pin leaves together in this fashion until the band is long enough for a crown; then pin the first leaf to the last, and the crown is ready to wear.

Flowers also make lovely crowns. Dandelions, Queen Anne's lace, or daisies are particularly effective. Make one and give it to someone special! Directions for making flower crowns appear earlier in this chapter.

A crown for her grandmother.

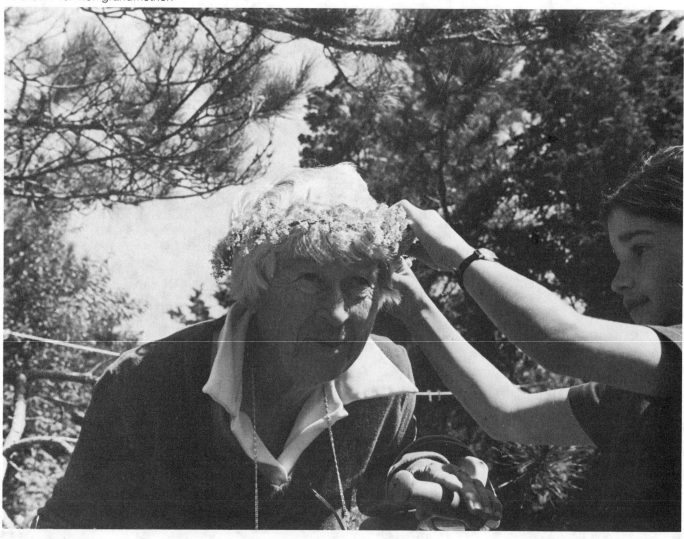

make a clover blossom necklace

Materials: Clover blossoms with stems.

Procedures: Make a slit with a fingernail through the stem of a clover blossom. Pull the stem of another blossom through the hole. Make a slit in the second stem and pull a third through. Continue and when the band is long enough, make a larger slit in the last stem, and carefully fit the blossom of the first through the slit—the necklace is complete.

froggy fiddles

Materials: Large plantain leaves.

Procedure: Use a fingernail to

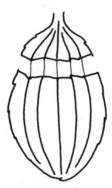

FROGGY FIDDLE

scrape partway through the top side of the base of a plantain leaf where it joins the stem. Carefully pull the leaf apart from the stem without breaking the veins, which with imagination will become the strings of the froggy fiddle.

using our noses

Procedure: Enjoy the variety of smells to be found in the plant kingdom on an outside visit. Flowers send out fragrances as they are, but many leaves need to be crushed to bring out the smell (yarrow, bayberry, tansy, sassafras, mugwort, eucalyptus, sweet fern, and others). Find as many smells as possible.

soft things

Procedure: Feel the pleasant softness of some plants. Try stems of staghorn sumac, midribs of butternut leaves, and many mosses. Mullein leaves are furry enough to make a snuggly doll's blanket.

bibliography

adults

ANDERSON, EDGAR, *Plants, Man and Life.* Berkeley: University of California Press, 1967.

BAILEY, L. H., *How Plants Get Their Names.* New York: Dover, 1963.

BLAND, JOHN, *Forests of Lilliput.* Englewood Cliffs, N.J.: Prentice-Hall, 1971.

CRAE, IDA, *Nature's Colors: Dyes from Plants.* New York: Macmillan, 1974.

GRAHAM, ADA, *Foxtails, Ferns and Fishscales.* New York: Four Winds, 1976.

GRIMM, WILLIAM C., and M. JEAN CRAIG, *The Wondrous World of Seedless Plants.* Indianapolis: Bobbs-Merrill, 1973.

HOKE, JOHN, *Terrariums.* New York: Watts, 1972.

POLING, JAMES, *Leaves.* New York: Holt, 1971.

SKELSEY, ALICE, and GLORIA HUCKABY, *Growing up Green.* New York: Workman, 1973.

children & adults

BRANLEY, FRANKLYN M., *Roots Are Food Finders.* New York: Crowell, 1975.

BUSCH, PHYLLIS S., *Lions in the Grass.* Cleveland: World, 1968.

———, *Wildflowers and the Stories behind Their Names.* New York: Scribner, 1977.

DOWDEN, ANNE OPHELIA, *Wild Green Things in the City.* New York: Crowell, 1972.

FROMAN, ROBERT, *Mushrooms and Molds.* New York: Crowell, 1972.

GUTNIK, MARTIN J., *How Plants Make Food.* Chicago: Children's Press, 1976.

HOGNER, DOROTHY CHILDS, *Endangered Plants.* New York: Crowell, 1977.

HUTCHINS, ROSS E., *Galls and Gall Insects.* New York: Dodd Mead, 1969.

LADYMAN, PHYLISS, *Learning about Flowering Plants.* New York: Young Scott, 1970.

MARTIN, ALEXANDER C., *Weeds.* New York: Golden Press, 1972.

SELSAM, MILLICENT E., and JOYCE HUNT, *A First Look at the World of Plants.* New York: Walker, 1978.

SHUTTLESWORTH, FLOYD S., and HERBERT S. ZIM, *Non-flowering Plants.* New York: Golden Press, 1967.

ZIM, HERBERT S., *Flowers.* New York: Simon & Schuster, 1950.

4

nature's life packages: seeds

Seeds are remarkable life packages, each containing a young plant in the form of an embryo and a supply of food for the plant. Most seeds are formed in flowers and most have protective covers that help them to withstand the effects of time, travel, and weather.

About 250,000 different species of plants produce these life packages, which vary greatly in size, shape, and color. One kind of coconut weighs as much as 40 pounds (18k), while the dustlike begonia seeds are so small that one million of them weigh only about an ounce (28 grams). Peas are round, grass seeds are long, pumpkin seeds are flat; other seeds are oval, pointed, triangular, hooked, diamond or otherwise shaped. Watermelon seeds are black, lima beans are white, sunflower seeds are striped; other seeds are red, yellow, orange, purple, green, blue, brown, black, mottled, shiny, or dull.

The "fruit" is what botanists call the plant structure that contains the seeds, whether it is juicy like an apple or dry like the pod of a peanut. Fruits vary. Berries are fleshy fruits in which the seeds are the only hard parts. Nuts are hard, dry fruits with one or two seeds. Nuts do not split open to release their seeds as do capsules, which are dry fruits that open down one side to release many seeds, such as witch hazel or yucca. Pods are elongated fruits that usually contain more than one seed; anyone who has shelled peas knows something about pods. Maple seeds, which many children call Pinocchio noses, are specialized fruits with flat wings to aid in wind dispersal.

Seeds are remarkably adapted for dispersal. Without dispersal they would fall directly under the parent plant, and overcrowding would prevent most of the young plants

from surviving. Coconuts and cranberries can travel like boats; they float in water and drift with currents. Burdock and beggars' ticks travel by hitchhiking; their seeds have hooks that catch on animals passing by, giving the seeds a free ride. Often seeds are caught in mud on the feet of water or shore birds; when the birds fly to another body of water, the seeds go along. Many seeds are eaten by animals; some, such as the seeds in most berries, have particularly hard coats and are indigestible. Such seeds pass right through the animal's digestive system. This transportation gives seeds not only a free ride, but also some fertilizer to help the germinating seed's growth. Dandelions and milkweed seeds have parachutes; they can drift with the wind far from the parent plants. Maple seeds have wings, which enable them to be carried by the wind, spinning as they go.

Children are intrigued by the amazing specializations of seed dispersal, especially by the pepper shakers and slingshots. Poppies, iris, and evening primrose have pepper shakers; their seeds are thrown out when the pods sway in the wind. Children delight in shaking out the seeds from the pods. Witch hazel, patient lucy, and jewelweed have slingshots; touch the ripe seed pod and the seeds are propelled out.

Seeds have other fascinating adaptations. Some have built-in timers; petunia seeds, which ripen in the summer, will not germinate until the following spring, giving the new plant the benefit of an entire growing season. Seeds of some desert plants will not germinate until a particular amount of rain has fallen. All seeds need air, water, and a certain degree of warmth to germinate. If conditions are not right, seeds will not grow.

Seeds are remarkable.

Some can remain viable for hundreds of years, awaiting proper conditions.

Seed plants are divided into two main groups, monocots (monocotyledons) and dicots (dicotyledons). Monocot plants have seeds with one food storage part, or cotyledon; grasses, corn, and coconuts are examples. Dicots have seeds with two food storage parts, or cotyledons, as with beans, walnuts, and peanuts. Have you noticed how a peanut comes apart in two halves? Those halves are the cotyledons, each with food for the new peanut plant, also a food that we eat.

Seeds offer useful learning experiences for children of all ages. Very young children can plant seeds and be rewarded in a few days with the miracle of the growth of the new plant. Older children can do a variety of experiments, technical and otherwise, to determine factors affecting germination. Seeds are small, easy for children to handle. They are easy to obtain. Perhaps, most important, their adaptations and potential powers of growth can stir our sense of wonder about the intricate designs in nature.

seed activities

activities with seed structure

seed variations

Materials: Transparent tape, paper, pencils, assorted seeds.

Procedure: Have the children collect a wide variety of seeds from home and outdoors. Combine all the seeds and give each child an assortment. Ask the children to sort their seeds by size—smallest to largest, by shapes—round, oval, triangular, and others, or by color. The children can make displays of their seed categories by attaching the seeds to paper with the tape.

Try testing the seeds for hardness. Can the seeds be opened with fingers, fingernails, a dull knife, or by using a hammer? Many seeds require the hammer, which the children enjoy using.

This activity is designed to demonstrate the great variations of seeds in size, shape, and color. Questions may arise about what is, and what is not, a seed. Try to lead the children to discover the answers themselves; doing some of the other seed activities in this chapter may be helpful for this.

what is inside a seed?

Materials: Lima bean seeds that have been soaked in water overnight.

Procedure: Give each child one of the lima bean seeds. Have the children remove the seed coats and gently pull the two cotyledons apart. Ask them to find the tiny leaves and root of the embryo.

PARTS OF A
BEAN SEED

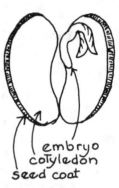

embryo
cotyledon
seed coat

This may be done with other seeds, such as other beans and sunflower seeds. Open the seeds at the outside curve to avoid damaging the embryo. Sketching the cotyledons and the embryo helps to sharpen observation techniques. To add a "tasteful" touch to this activity, open nuts such as peanuts or almonds and eat them when the experiment is through.

testing seeds for starch

Materials: Hammer, paper towels, diluted iodine solution (about one part iodine to four parts water), eyedropper, lima beans, corn kernels, bread, sugar, flour, salt.

Procedure: With the hammer, mash a lima bean and a corn kernel separately on paper towels. Put bread, flour, sugar, and salt separately on the towels. Put a drop or two of the iodine solution (iodine turns blue in the presence of starch) onto each substance to tell which ones contain starch.

Starch is a food stored inside some seeds for the young plants that grow from the seeds. All seeds contain either starch, oil, or protein. Some seeds may contain two of these foods, and others, all three. Test a variety of seeds for starch; also, test them for oil as described in the following activity.

testing seeds for oil

Materials: Hammer, brown paper bag, salad oil, peanuts, other seeds.

Procedure: Put a few drops of the salad oil on the bag and notice how it looks. Use the hammer to mash a peanut on the bag, and then rub the small pieces onto the bag. Compare the spots made by the mashed peanut with the spot made by the oil. Repeat the test with other seeds.

seed growth activities

growing seeds indoors

Materials: Seeds, soil, and suitable containers (see suggestions below).

Procedure: Punch several holes in the bottom of the containers for drainage. Fill them with soil, and plant the seeds. Keep the soil moist; and, when the plants appear, put them in a sunny window.

Seeds that are especially fail-safe are: lima bean, scarlet runner bean, kidney bean, pea, corn, sunflower, grass, and radish. Try seeds from the kitchen such as orange, grapefruit, tomato. Possible containers are: paper, styrofoam, and plastic cups, milk cartons, plastic margarine cups, tin cans, styrofoam egg cartons, flower or peat pots, and large tubs. Try putting plastic bags around the containers while the seeds germinate; the bag acts as a greenhouse and keeps in the moisture.

If it is not feasible to have individual containers for each child, try a communal tub garden. A large plastic dishpan is a suitable container; fill it with soil and have the children plant their seeds in it. The tub garden is easy to care for; children enjoy it. And because so many of the seeds that are planted usually grow, everyone feels successful. This is a particularly appropriate project for a group of very young children. (If they have planted bean seeds, don't forget to read them the story of "Jack and the Beanstalk.")

the force of germinating seeds

Materials: Beans, plastic pill vial or other small plastic container, water, tape or wire.

Procedure: Fill the plastic container with beans, then fill it with water. Tape or wire the top down securely and wait.

The rehydration and life force in the seeds will crack open the plastic container. Ask the children if this makes it easier to understand how weeds sometimes crack and grow up through weak areas in pavements.

watching seeds germinate

Materials: Plate, cotton, variety of small seeds (radish and grass seeds, for example), water, plastic bag.

Procedure: Put a layer of cotton on the plate. Have the children sprinkle a variety of seeds over the cotton, being careful not to crowd them. Moisten the cotton and the seeds. Slip the plastic bag over everything. Remove the bag daily to watch the seeds as they germinate.

Children delight in seeing each day's progress. For a variation, plant each different kind of seed on a separate plate. Try planting some of the seeds in different positions. Have the children record the differences in germination. Older children can make graphs of the results. Another way to watch seeds germinate is to line the inside of a jar with paper towels or fill it with cotton. Put some seeds between the towels or cotton and the glass. Add water to a depth of about ½ inch (about 13mm) and screw on the top to keep the moisture in. The seed's growth can easily be watched. Put the jar on its side and watch to see how the seedling's roots turn downward.

germination & growth experiments

Materials: Seeds of one kind, soil, planting containers, and other items (depending on the experiment).

Procedure: Plant one seed in each container in a variety of ways and keep them in a variety of conditions. Observe them daily and keep records of the results.

Following are some possible experiments:

• Plant seeds at different depths; leave one on the surface of the soil.
• Plant seeds in different soils, pebbles, sand, sawdust, clay, or vermiculite.
• Plant seeds all in the same soil, but water them with different liquids: water, water with fertilizer, salt water, vinegar, root beer, and so on.
• Plant seeds in the same soil and keep them under different conditions: cold, warm, hot, dry, moist, wet, sunny, moderate light, dark.
• Plant seeds that have been cut in half, heated to a desert temperature (about 130°F, or 55°C), frozen, or boiled.

• Stick a pin or nail through seeds and plant them.
• Plant seeds in a tiny container, a middle-sized one, and a large one.
• Plant six seeds in a small container, plant a dozen, or more.

Depending on the children's interest, try some or all of these experiments and encourage the children to think of experiments of their own. With older children stress the keeping of precise records, and make graphs of the results when possible.

planting wild seeds

Materials: Weed seeds, acorns, and other seeds gathered outside, soil, planting containers.

Procedure: Plant the seeds, water them, and wait to see what happens.

Some wild seeds will grow with no extra care, but many need certain conditions to germinate. Some must be cold for a period of time, which is a natural protection against germinating in the fall when a seedling would shortly

The results of a garden are rewarding.

perish in the cold weather. Some of the seeds that travel by animal express, through the alimentary tract of an animal, depend on the acids in the digestive juices to weaken the hard seed coat. These seeds will germinate if scarified with a knife before planting. If possible, find appropriate reference materials to research the needs of different wild seeds, or have the children experiment with different ways of planting wild seeds.

planting seeds outdoors

Most children enjoy having a garden of their own, even if the area is small. Assist young children in planting seeds according to directions on the seed packages. The results of a garden—flowers or vegetables—are rewarding to all gardeners. Some children may be interested in doing growth experiments; some of the activities outlined in this chapter are suitable for out-of-doors. (See Chapter 14 for more information on children and gardens.)

do cotyledons help seed growth?

Materials: Bean seeds, cotton, water, six plates, six plastic bags.

Procedure: Soak the beans in water overnight. Place a layer of cotton on each plate and moisten it. Put several bean seeds on one plate as a control, and on the other plates place the following: embryos carefully removed from the seeds, seeds with one cotyledon removed, seeds with half a cotyledon removed, seeds with one and a half cotyledons removed, and several cotyledons. Label the contents of each plate. Put the plastic bags over them. Record results daily and find out how the cotyledons affect growth.

For another experiment, plant several bean seeds in soil. When the plants appear above the surface, remove two cotyledons from several, remove one cotyledon each from several others, and leave some seeds with both cotyledons as a control. Record results.

come-to-life gardens

Materials: Soils from different outside habitats in early spring, containers, water.

Procedure: Put the different soils into different containers. Keep them moist and watch to see what hidden seeds were in the soil that will now germinate and grow.

bean sprout sandwiches

Materials: Mung beans (or alfalfa seeds or other suitable seeds for sprouts), jar, cheesecloth, rubber band, water, strainer, bread, mayonnaise.

Procedure: Soak the beans in water overnight, and drain. Place them in the jar (it should be no more than half full) and put the

cheesecloth over the top, holding it in place with the rubber band. Keep the jar in a moderately warm place (65-75°F, or 19-24°C). Rinse the beans twice daily with water, draining all excess water through the cheesecloth. After four or five days the sprouts should be ready for eating. If desired, the sprouts may be put in a sunny window for the last day to develop chlorophyll.

Sprouts, mayonnaise, and bread are all that is needed for delicious sandwiches. Or, sample the sprouts plain with a touch of salt. Wouldn't this be a tasty ending to a study of seed growth?

seed dispersal activities

how do seeds travel?

Materials: Bags, or other containers for carrying seeds.

Procedure: Collect different seeds outside. Use observation and deduction to find out how each kind is dispersed. (Fall is the best time for this activity.)

Dispersal by parachute is simple to understand. The children have only to blow dandelion or milkweed seeds to see how the parachutes work. Helicopters are also easy. Toss maple, ash, or elm seeds in the air and watch how they descend. Children like to shake the little seeds from the pepper-shaker seed heads of iris, or touch the slingshot pods of jewelweed, also uderstandably known as touch-me-not. Perhaps during the seed hunt, someone will acquire some hitchhikers. Look on clothing for tick trefoil seeds, or burs of burdock or cocklebur; remove them, throw them away, and the method of dispersal is obvious. Eat apples on the hunt, throw the cores, and

TRAVELLING SEEDS—

Jewelweed

SLING SHOTS

Witch-Hazel

Bean

HELICOPTERS

Maple

Tree of Heaven

Linden

PARACHUTES

Dandelion

Sycamore

Milkweed

again the dispersal technique is obvious. Have the children think about what may happen to some of the indigestible seeds of fruits to help them understand dispersal by animal express. Tumbleweed seeds are tossed out as the old plant is blown by the wind; if you have tumbleweed in your area,

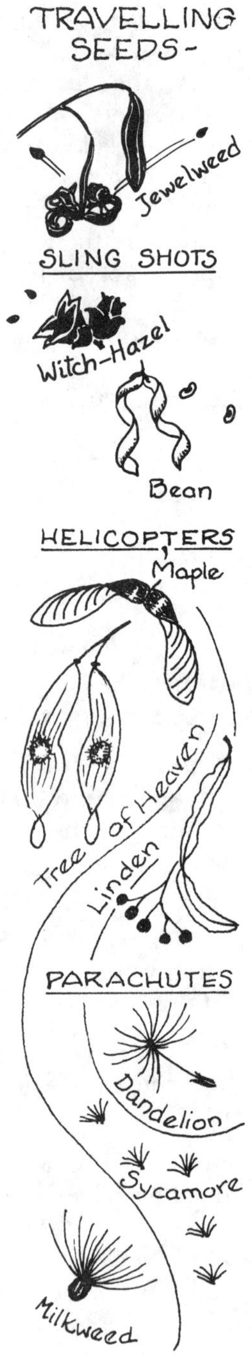

HITCH HIKERS

Burdock

Beggar-ticks

Tick Trefoil

ANIMAL EXPRESS

Cherries and Berries

Poison Ivy

BOATS

Coconut

Cranberries

The Lotus pod rots, dropping seeds as it travels

MSS

inspect one for seeds and have the children figure out how they are dispersed. You may not find any boat-traveling seeds on your hunt; ask the children about coconuts and sea beans; some may know how they float like boats. Cranberries also float. Buy some later, and have the children cut

them open to see the air spaces that give them buoyancy. If you spot a squirrel on the hunt, ask the children what squirrels do with acorns, and they may understand how some oak trees are planted. After a seed-collecting hunt, children enjoy making seed-dispersal displays; most seeds can easily be stuck to paper with transparent tape.

milkweed seed classroom game

Materials: Two to four milkweed seeds.

Procedure: Ask everyone to remain seated. Release the milkweed seeds and see how long the students can keep the seeds in the air by blowing them up. (Using hands is not allowed; ask the students to sit on their hands to help them remember.)

fly parachutes & helicopters

Materials: Seeds that travel by parachute (milkweed, thistle) and helicopter (maple, ash, elm).

Procedure: Divide the class into two groups. One group goes outside by the school building. The other group goes to windows of an upstairs classroom and releases parachutes and helicopters. The students below try to catch them, usually with great enthusiasm and excitement. Let the groups change places and repeat the fun.

goldenrod parachute math

Materials: Several goldenrod plants with seed heads.

Procedure: Count the number of parachutelike seeds on one seed head. Count the number of seed heads on a spray, the number of sprays on a branch, and the number of fruiting branches on

the plant. Multiply these numbers to find an estimate of the number of seeds produced by one plant. Repeat the process with several other plants to compute an average number per plant.

Calculate how much land would be needed if all the seeds of one goldenrod plant were to germinate and grow. If 1 square foot (.9 sq. m) is allowed for each two seeds, the average number of seeds per plant must be divided by two to find the number of square feet (or meters) needed for all the seeds to grow. Find out the area of the school yard or grounds. Compute how many goldenrod plants would be needed to produce enough seeds to populate the whole area with these plants, assuming the impossible—that every seed will grow into a new plant.

Do this kind of exercise with other plants. Along with math, it teaches how prolific nature must be in order to ensure reproduction.

johnny appleseed

Materials: Books and other materials with information about Johnny Appleseed (also see bibliography at end of this chapter).

Procedure: Have the students do research on the role of Johnny Appleseed (born John Chapman in Massachusetts, 1775–1845) in dispersing apple seeds along the frontier.

Since the beginnings of agriculture, people have been important agents in seed dispersal. The colonists carried many seeds of familiar Old World plants with them to America, and many other seeds "hitchhiked" in hay, on the bottom of boots, and in other ways. Have the students do re-search on people as seed dis-persers. The children can create a classroom play about Johnny Appleseed.

seed craft activities

seed mosaics

Materials: A variety of seeds, glue, heavy paper or cardboard.

Procedure: Glue the seeds to the paper or cardboard, making pictures, designs, or whatever else comes to mind.

Seeds for mosaics may be collected by the children outside. Beans, lentils, barley, and such can be used to augment the collection. Catalpa seeds are fun to use because they have whiskers!

percussion instruments

Materials: Large seeds (beans, squash, sunflower), cardboard containers, tin cans with plastic lids, tape.

Procedure: Put a handful of seeds into a holder; seal the top with tape. Shake the container for use as a percussion instrument.

Many gourds, when thoroughly dried out, can be used as instruments; shake them and the seeds will rattle.

seed necklaces

Materials: Assorted seeds, darning or embroidery needle, heavy duty thread or string.

ADD-A-SEED APPLESEED NECKLACE

Alternate seeds with small glass beads~
String seeds when fresh~
When you eat an apple, add the seeds.
MS/MSS

Procedure: Thread the needle and poke it through the seeds to make a necklace. If any of the seeds are too hard, pour boiling water over them and wait for them to soften.

Use imagination and all kinds of different seeds to make necklaces. For added interest, try dyeing some of the seeds before using them.

acorn snake

Materials: About twenty acorns, sandpaper, drill with small bit, vise, knife, sturdy string, large needle, acrylic or oil paint, small paintbrush.

Procedure: Smooth off the tips of the acorns with sandpaper. Use the vise to hold the acorns and bore holes lengthwise through them, being careful not to split them. On the largest acorn, paint the snake's mouth and eyes. Line the others up from largest to smallest behind the snake's head. Thread the snake together with the string; knot the string at the ends. Leave a small length at the head end for the tongue. (For perfection, split the end to make a forked tongue.)

acorn cap whistles

Materials: Sturdy acorn caps.

Procedure: Hold both thumbs over the hollow side of the acorn cap, leaving a "V"-shaped opening at the top of the thumbs. Blow at the base of the "V", and with luck a loud whistle will result.

If this doesn't work the first time, keep on trying. Needless to say, kids love making the whistles.

acorn cap puppets

Materials: Acorn caps, pen.

Procedure: Put the acorn cap on the end of a finger. Draw eyes, nose, and mouth below, and you have a finger puppet with a hat.

acorn miniatures

Materials: Acorns with caps, knife, nail, small twigs, glue, plasticine.

Procedure: Cut an acorn in half and carefully scoop out the nutmeat from the bottom half to make a doll's soup bowl. Cut the point off the bottom of the acorn cap so that the bottom is flat to make a saucer. Put the acorn half on top and the doll will have a cup and saucer. For a doll's pipe, make another acorn-half soup bowl. Make a hole in one side of the bowl with the nail. Insert a twig into the hole and cut the twig to the proper length to complete the miniature pipe. Make acorn cap mushrooms by gluing a short twig to the inside of an acorn cap; mount the little mushroom in some plasticine.

Can you think of other acorn miniatures?

applehead doll

Materials: Medium-sized apple, paring knife, black-headed pins, watercolors, paintbrush, medium-weight wire, scraps of cloth, glue, yarn or cornsilk.

Procedure: Peel off the apple skin. With the paring knife sculpt features for the doll's face: eyes, nose, mouth, cheeks, and maybe even ears. Put the apple in a warm, dry place; check it every few days and remold the features if necessary. When it is dry, insert the black-headed pins for eyes, and paint lips, cheeks, and eyebrows with the watercolors. Make a rough body outline, including arms and legs, with the wire; leave enough wire at the neck to hold the head in place. Wrap cloth around the body to give it the proper shape; make clothes with the cloth scraps and put them on. Put on the head and glue hair on from pieces of yarn or cornsilk.

Burs can be fun to play with. Notice the burry smiling face on the shirt.

bur baskets & other burry items

Materials: Burs.

Procedure: Stick the burs together to make a basket; try making animals and other items.

Warning! Watch out that burs do not get attached where they are not wanted, especially in hair.

cone birds

Materials: A variety of evergreen cones, pipe cleaners, twigs, feathers, glue, maple seeds, thin wire, felt-tipped markers, paper, scissors.

Procedure: Make a cone bird: use a cone for the body, a maple seed for the head and beak, pipe cleaners or twigs for legs, and feathers for the tail. Attach the pieces with glue or wire. Make a cone turkey: use a cone for the body, bend a pipe cleaner to make the head and neck, and color eyes, and wattles with felt-tipped markers. Attach pipe-cleaner legs. Cut a fan-shaped piece of paper for the tail and insert. Young children can make these turkeys, and if they glue the feet to cards, they will have place cards for a Thanksgiving dinner table.

You can make other kinds of cone creatures. Let the children use their imaginations, and perhaps they will make a cone menagerie.

The beginnings of a cone menagerie.

corn husk dolls

Materials: Dry corn husks, string, paints, paintbrush.

Procedure: Soak the husks in water. Fold three husks of the same length together and tie a string 1 inch (2.5 c) below the fold to make the head. Cut two husks into 5-inch (12.7 c) lengths and tie strings around them about ½ inch (13 mm) from each end to make

CORN HUSK
DOLLIES

Soak
dried
husks

3 leaves

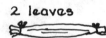

2 leaves

Paint faces,
dress them up,
use corn silk
for hair.

Use your
imagination!

hands. Insert the arms through the body husks and tie a string around the body below the arms. Use paints to give the doll a face.

Use scraps of cloth to make clothes and glue on corn silk for hair. Indian children played with corn-husk dolls and animals; the children of the early colonists quickly learned how to make these toys. Indians used corn husks for many purposes, including mats, baskets, masks, and bags. Try making some of these items yourself.

grass-haired people

Materials: Styrofoam cups, grass seed, cotton, water, felt-tipped markers, plastic bags.

Procedure: Draw a face on the cup. Fill it with cotton and wet it thoroughly. Sprinkle grass seed on top and enclose the cup in a plastic bag. When the grass hair grows, remove the bag and keep the head watered.

Don't forget a haircut if the hair becomes too long! There are other

POTATO PIG

ways to use grass for hair or fur. Try a potato pig. Find a potato shaped as much like a pig as possible. Scoop out a trough in the back. Put in cloves for eyes and four wooden matchsticks for legs. Cut triangular-shaped ears from stiff paper; make slits and insert the ears. Give the pig a curly pipe-cleaner tail. Finally, fill the trough in the back of the pig with soil, plant with grass seed, keep moist, and wait to enjoy the pig with the green hairy back.

maple seed dragonfly

Materials: Maple seeds, twig or wooden match, glue, small beads, thread.

Procedure: Glue two pairs of maple seeds to the twig or match; the maple-seed wings become wings for the dragonfly. Glue beads in place for eyes. Hang with a piece of thread. Make a number of these and use them for a mobile.

milkweed pod boat

Materials: Half of a milkweed pod, oak leaf.

Procedure: The milkweed pod half is the hull of the boat. Stick the oak leaf in (stem right through the bottom of the boat) to make a sail.

Use plasticine to hold the sail if you wish to float the boat. Milkweed pods have a multitude of other craft uses, from making them into mice to using them for wings on pine-cone angels.

MILKWEED
SEED PODS

WALNUT TURTLE

AND WHALES

walnut shell turtle

Materials: Walnut shell half, green construction paper, scissors, glue.

Procedure: Cut out the head, tail, and feet from green paper and glue to the bottom of the shell as shown.

Try making a walnut mouse; glue on paper eyes, ears, whiskers, and use a pipe cleaner for the tail. Or make a walnut boat. Cut a triangular paper sail, glue it to a wooden match, and secure the end of the match in the inside of the walnut shell with plasticine.

activities with seed uses

collecting wild bird seed

Materials: Bags or other containers for seeds.

Procedure: In the fall go on a birdseed search. Gather weed seeds, berries, and the like for use in bird feeders.

Use the wild birdseed plain or mixed with commercial birdseed in the feeders. Does it disappear? Do the birds seem to enjoy it? Wild seeds are vital foods for many species of birds, especially during winters.

squirrels & acorns

Procedure: Watch squirrels in autumn and try to see them eating acorns or burying them for later use. Look for acorns that have been nibbled on by squirrels.

Acorns are an important food for squirrels, as well as other wildlife, such as deer. Study the importance of acorns to wildlife. Other wild seeds are eaten by many different mammals, especially mice, rats, chipmunks, marmots, chickarees, squirrels, pocket gophers, raccoons, bears, and foxes. (Remember the fable of "The Fox and the Grapes"?) Find reference materials and have the children research how local mammals use seeds. Encourage them to observe the animals if possible.

grains & people

Materials: Books with information about historic and present-day uses of grains.

Procedure: Study the use of grains throughout American (or other) history.

There is much to study; the food stored in seeds for the plant embryo is also a nutritious food for people. Bread has long been called the staff of life, signifying our dependence on wheat, as well as on other grains such as rye, oats, buckwheat, barley, and rice. Corn, grown by the Indians and later hybridized by Gregor Mendel, has become a particularly important grain. We eat corn on the cob, corn chips, corn muffins; we use corn oil, corn syrup, and cornstarch; and corn products are used in industries in many ways. Make a grain display as part of the grain study. Have the students bring from home labels, box tops, or wrappers from grains and grain products and display them on a bulletin board.

kitchen seed hunt

Materials: Paper, pencils.

Procedure: Have the children make lists of all the seeds and seed products they can find in their kitchens.

The lists may be long, including grains and grain products as well as fruits, vegetables (peas, beans, tomatoes, squash, and so on), jams, jellies, nuts, many spices, coffee, cocoa. After all the lists are in, how about cooking some popcorn in class?

bibliography

adults

BROWN, LAUREN, *Weeds in Winter.* New York: Norton, 1976.

FIAROTTA, PHYLLIS, *Snips and Snails and Walnut Whales.* New York: Workman, 1975.

LOEWER, H. PETER, *Seeds and Cuttings.* New York: Walker, 1975.

SCHWANTZ, FRANZ, *The Origin of Cultivated Plants.* Cambridge, Mass.: Harvard University Press, 1966.

SKELSEY, ALICE, and GLORIA HUCKABY, *Growing up Green.* New York: Workman, 1973.

U. S. DEPARTMENT OF AGRICULTURE, *Seeds.* The Yearbook of Agriculture, 1961.

children & adults

ALIKI, *The Story of Johnny Appleseed.* Englewood Cliffs, N.J.: Prentice-Hall, 1963.

BUDLONG, WARE, and MARK H. FLEITZER, *Experimenting with Seeds and Plants.* New York: Putnam, 1970.

COOPER, ELIZABETH, *Sweet and Delicious: Fruits of Tree, Bush and Vine.* Children's Press, 1973.

EARLE, OLIVE L., and MICHAEL KANTOR, *Nuts.* New York: Morrow, 1976.

HAMMOND, WINIFRED G., *The Riddle of Seeds.* New York: Coward-McCann, 1965.

HUTCHINS, ROSS E., *The Amazing Seeds.* New York: Dodd, Mead, 1965.

JORDAN, HELENE J., *How a Seed Grows.* New York: Crowell, 1960.

LAUBER, PATRICIA, *Seeds: Pop–Stick–Glide.* New York: Crown, 1981.

PETIE, HARRIS, *The Seed the Squirrel Dropped.* Englewood Cliffs, N.J.: Prentice-Hall, 1976.

PRIME, C. T., and AARON KLEIN, *Seedlings and Soil.* New York: Doubleday, 1973.

RHAN, JOAN ELMA, *How Plants Travel.* New York: Atheneum, 1973.

SELSAM, MILLICENT, *The Apple and Other Fruits.* New York: Morrow, 1973.

SHUTTLESWORTH, DOROTHY E., *The Hidden Magic of Seeds.* Emmaus, Pa.: Rodale Press, 1976.

5

creatures small & spineless: the invertebrates

Ask a group of children or adults, "What is an animal?" and you may be greeted with blank looks. Although the question seems simple, it is not, and attempts to answer can range from equating animals as one and the same with mammals, to defining animals as all creatures that are not human beings. The fact is that the animal kingdom is vast (as is the plant kingdom) and includes humans, as well as the rest of the mammals, and all other creatures. How do animals and plants differ? Consider a dog and a tree. The dog can move about freely and react quickly to stimulations. The dog stops growing at maturity and eats meat for food. The tree cannot move or react quickly; it never stops growing (until it dies), and, most important of all, it makes its own food. Although differences between a dog and a tree seem clear, the identities of some of the very small living organisms can be confusing.

Both the animal and plant kingdoms are subdivided into the following groups (from general to specific): phylum, class, order, family, genus, species. This system of classification allows for standardization of names and of relationships between living things. If the system seems difficult to remember, learn this phrase as a memory trick: *King Philip Came Over From Geneva Switzerland.* The first letters are the clues: King, kingdom; Philip, phylum; Came, class; Over, order; From, family; Geneva, genus; Switzerland, species. Following the clues, the description of yourself as a human being is: kingdom, animal; phylum, vertebrate; class, mammal; order, primate; family, hominidae; genus, homo; species, sapiens.

Most of the animals we know well are the classes in the vertebrate (having a backbone) phylum: mammals, birds, reptiles, amphibians, and fish. The invertebrates (without a backbone) include many phyla, such as: porifera (sponges), coelenterates (hydras, jellyfish, corals), various worms (planaria, earthworms), mollusks (snails, clams, squids), arthropods (lobsters, insects, spiders), and echinoderms (starfish, sea urchins).

major phyla

porifera

The porifera, or porebearers, are the natural sponges, whose evolutionary importance lies in the fact that they were the first multicellular animals. Without tissues, a sponge consists of a colony of three different kinds of cells that perform different functions. Sponges were once thought to be plants, since they do not move from place to place. However, unlike plants, they do not make their food, but procure it by consuming tiny plants and animals from the water filtered through their pores. Porifera are interesting animals, but their sedentary nature does not recommend them as pets, and their former economic importance to humans has been subverted by the manufactured "sponges" found in modern kitchens. Although a few species of sponges are freshwater inhabitants, most of them live in salt water.

coelenterates

Coelenterates are hollow sacklike animals with stinging tentacles. They are the earliest animals to have tissues, such as mouth, digestive sac, tentacles, and nerves. The latter are especially significant, as simple nerves were followed by more complex nerve structures, then by the development of simple brains, ultimately followed by the complex human brain, which sets us apart from all other animals. However, the simple nerves of a coelenterate, such as the sea anemone, suffice for such needs as responding to the stimulus of food by sending out stinging cells from the tentacles to poison, and thereby catch, tiny animals. The digestive sac where the prey is con-

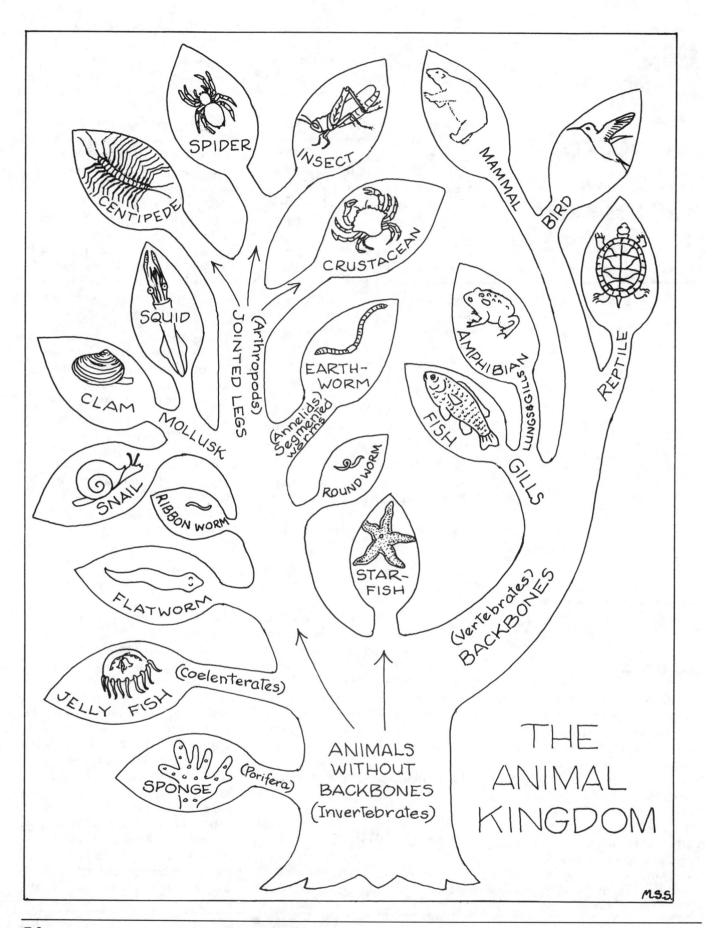

THE ANIMAL KINGDOM

SPONGE

JELLY FISH

FLATWORM

RIBBON WORM

ROUND WORM

mollusks

Mollusks are soft-bodied animals, generally enclosed in hard, protective shells. Snails, periwinkles, whelks, clams, oysters, mussels, chitons, and tooth shells are a few of the well-known members of this phylum. Squids, octopi, and slugs are also members, even though they lack protective shells. The bodies of mollusks are more highly structured than any of the worms and squids, and octopi have image-perceiving eyes that are remarkably well developed, quite similar in structure to human eyes.

Old shell heaps give evidence that Indians long ago consumed great quantities of shellfish, and today we relish meals of fried clams or oysters on the half shell. Mollusk shells have been used for utensils, money, and in the making of tools. Also, they give us aesthetic pleasure by their beauty and symmetry of design. Collecting shells on ocean beaches is one of childhood's special pleasures—one that often lingers through adulthood.

sumed represents another large evolutionary step, even though the waste products come back out through the mouth. As with the sponges, only a few coelenterates, such as hydras and some jellyfish, are freshwater dwellers; most coelenterates live in salt water.

flatworms, ribbon worms & roundworms

There are several phyla of worms. The lowest includes planaria, the flatworms so often used in zoology classes. These little worms were among the first creatures to have a right and a left side, as well as a top and a bottom. They have an incomplete digestive system (the waste products go out the mouth as with the coelenterates), simple eyes, and even a primitive brain. Look for them on rocks or vegetation in fresh water. They are enjoyable creatures to watch and their eye-spots give them a rather appealing look. The ribbon worms and round-worms are not easily found, but these animals represent further development in that they have complete digestive systems (from mouth to anus), an improvement over the digestive two-way traffic jam of coelenterates and flatworms.

segmented worms

The segmented worms (annelids) have further specializations, such as circulatory and excretory systems. Perhaps the best-known segmented worm is the earthworm, which burrows underground often by swallowing soil. The worm utilizes the organic materials in the soil for food and deposits the waste products, known as castings, at the entrance of its burrow. These "underground plows" (a name for earthworms that children enjoy) perform Herculean tasks in soil tilling; the amount of soil brought up from underground and deposited on the surface by earthworms has been estimated at 18 tons per acre (16 metric tonnes per hectare) per year. The earthworm's contribution to life in our world extends far beyond its plebian role as food for robins.

EARTH-WORM

SNAIL

CLAM

SQUID

arthropods

The phylum arthropoda includes more different kinds of animals than any other group. All arthropods have jointed legs and external skeletons. Crustaceans are arthropods with two pair of antennae and varying numbers of legs; insects have one pair of antennae and six legs; spiders have no antennae and eight legs; and centipedes and millipedes have one pair of antennae and many legs, as their names suggest. The external skeleton of arthropods serves as protection against enemies, physical injury, and drying out. It does, however, limit size, since in order to grow, the animal must molt by shedding its external skeleton and growing a larger one.

Many crustaceans, such as lobsters, shrimp, crabs, barnacles, and scores of lesser known kinds, live in salt water; crayfish and numerous small varieties live in fresh water. Sand fleas or beach hoppers are land-dwelling crustaceans, as are sow bugs, the small, gray, many-legged creatures often found under logs. Most people who have not had opportunities to meet many crustaceans face-to-face may be more familiar with them on the gourmet dinner plate as boiled lobster or crayfish, shrimp Newburg, or crabmeat salad.

CRUSTACEAN

Unlike crustaceans, you can see insects everywhere. There are more insects than all other animals in the world; in one fair-sized backyard, more than 1,000 different kinds may be found. Insects have been on earth about 200 million years, and they definitely are here to stay. On land insects are ubiquitous; in cities and the country, on mountaintops and in low areas, from arctic regions to the tropics. Also, many insects live in fresh water. The oceans, however, are almost insect free, for only a few kinds of insects can live in salt water.

INSECT

Insects have bodies divided into three main parts: head, thorax, and abdomen. They have a pair of antennae on the head and three pairs of legs on the thorax; most adult insects have two pairs of wings on the thorax. Insects are the only flying invertebrates and the only animals to have wings as such; the wings of birds and bats are modifications of forelimbs. Insects reproduce by laying eggs that hatch into insect nymphs or larvae.

The young drawer of this fly diagram writes: "The fly has six legs as any other bug. Flies stay around picnics, parties, and cookouts to get the food. When the flies are young, they are maggots and they stay around and on garbage and trash cans."

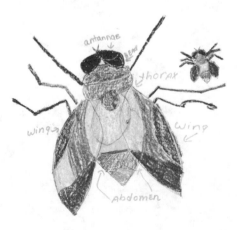

Nymphs look rather like their parents and grow by a series of molts until they reach the adult stage. This process is known as incomplete metamorphosis. With complete metamorphosis, the young insect or larva looks nothing like its parents; it grows, again by molting, until it reaches the pupal stage, when it rests while metamorphosis takes place; and ultimately the adult insect emerges. For its pupal stage, a moth larva, for instance, spins a protective cocoon in which the caterpillar changes into the moth.

The small size of most insects makes them appealing to most small children. It can be exciting for a two-year-old to discover ants for the first time. The seemingly infinite variety of insect shapes, structures, colors, and sizes certainly keeps them from being monotonous; even different species of ants vary considerably in appearance. Try lying down in the grass to get an ant's-eye view of the world.

Spiders can also be fascinating to children, despite Little Miss Muffet's experience. Although it is true that some spiders can inflict poisonous bites on humans, even these small creatures, if unmolested, generally go about their own business, such as building webs and catching prey. Spider webs are made of silken threads released from the spinnerets at the base of the abdomen, and although we may not enjoy the sight of a cobweb under a table in the living room, an orb web glistening with dew in the early morning sun invites admiration.

SPIDER

An orb web glistening in morning dew.

have one pair per segment. Millipedes are scavengers, but centipedes are carnivorous; watch out—they can bite! Here is a poem about them to share with children.

A centipede was happy quite
Until a frog in fun
Said, "Pray which leg comes after which?"
This raised her mind to such a pitch
She lay distracted in the ditch
Considering how to run.

Anonymous

echinoderms

The best-known members of the echinoderm phylum of spiny-skinned animals are the starfish, sea urchins, and sand dollars. These animals are circular in shape, symmetrical in form, and live only in salt water. Think kindly of the echinoderms because they are said to be the invertebrates that are most closely related to the vertebrates, and therefore to ourselves. Zoologists find that echinoderms' embryonic development indicates that they are derived from the same forms of animals as the vertebrate ancestors.

Unlike insects, spiders have only two body parts: the cephalothorax, which is a joining together of the head and thorax, and the abdomen. They also have eight legs, and most children who can count enjoy distinguishing spider from insect by the number of legs. Children are also intrigued to learn that spiders only eat liquid food, and through "straws" at that. A spider's mouthparts inject a toxin that liquefies the body of its prey. The spider then sucks the liquid

food through its mouth parts, leaving only skeletal remains of its meal.

Close relatives of spiders are ticks, mites, daddy longlegs, and horseshoe crabs. The latter have special appeal as they are a venerable old species, sometimes referred to as living fossils.

Millipedes and centipedes are often found under rocks or logs. Millipedes have two pairs of legs on each body segment; centipedes

activities with inverte-brates

Life originated in the sea and many invertebrates continue to live in salt water; many others live in freshwater. Activities with marine invertebrates are included in Chapter 10 and activities with freshwater invertebrates are found in Chapter 11; the activities in this chapter deal only with land invertebrates.

Some of these activities involve keeping the animals for observation. At the end of the activity, release the creatures in a suitable habitat. Practicing respect for animal life teaches children to act in a similar manner toward all life.

finding invertebrates

what's under a log?

Procedure: Carefully lift or move an old log that is on the ground and look to see who is living underneath it. Look quickly, for some animals scurry away when they are exposed. Replace the log in its original position, and try another one.

Generally, animals that live under logs prefer a dark, moist environment, and for many of them, the decaying log offers an abundant food supply. Some of the most common creatures to be found are sow bugs, millipedes, centipedes, earthworms, slugs, ants, and many other scavengers helping to recycle the log into soil. Exploring under logs is exciting; even three-year-olds enjoy

discovering the tiny dwellers of these small habitats.

finding creatures on a white sheet

Materials: Old white sheet or other white material.

Procedure: Put the sheet on the ground beside bushes or other medium-sized vegetation. Lean the plant leaves and stems over the sheet and shake them. Watch to see the creatures that fall onto the sheet.

Most of the animals on the sheet will be spiders and different varieties of insects, which are seen easily on the white sheet. When finished with this activity, put some small weights on the corners of the sheet and leave it out overnight. In the morning, lift it up to see what small animals may have crawled under it during the night. Also try putting a board or flat stone on the ground overnight and check to see what is underneath in the morning.

who lives in leaf litter?

Materials: Old tray, trowels.

Procedure: Scoop up some leaf litter with the trowel. Put it on the tray and use the trowel or fingers to sift through the litter to find what creatures may be in it.

Try this activitiy with soil; also try it with materials from different habitats. For an indoor activity, bring in a large supply of litter and soil. Use newspapers for trays and see how many creatures a group of children can find.

seeking soil creatures

Materials: Large can, circle of ½-inch (13 mm) hardware cloth slightly larger than bottom of can; piece of thin cardboard; masking

BERLESE FUNNEL

tape; wide-mouthed, large jar; gooseneck lamp with 25-watt bulb; also, paper towels, black paper, scissors, plastic bag.

Procedure: Cut the bottom off the can and push the hardware cloth through the can to the bottom. Use the cardboard and masking tape to make a funnel. The funnel should be wide enough at the top to fit around the can and wide enough at the bottom to fit into the jar, but it should not extend down to the bottom of the jar. Put several wet paper towels on the bottom of the jar and tape the black paper around the outside. Put the small end of the funnel into the jar and place the bottom of the can into the top of the funnel. Then go outside and gather some damp leaf litter and underlying soil in the plastic bag.

Put a handful or two into the can. Position the lamp directly over the top of the can and wait. Carefully remove the paper from the jar from time to time to look for the soil creatures.

It may take a day for the light and heat from the bulb to drive the small creatures in the litter and soil down through the funnel to the dark, moist environment of the jar. Use this funnel with different materials: garden soil, compost, leaf litter, and soils from different habitats. If possible, identify and record the creatures found in the different materials.

using insect nets

Materials: Insect nets, plastic containers (such as oleomargarine containers) with clear tops with small holes in them.

Procedure: Sweep the nets through grass in a field, through leaves of shrubs, and other areas where insects or spiders may be found. Put the creatures caught in the net into the containers for observation, and release them when through.

Often insects can easily be caught without nets by using the plastic containers. This is especially effective with young children, who may have difficulty using nets.

activities with earthworms

digging for worms

Materials: Shovels or trowels.

Procedure: Look for earthworm castings on the soil surface and dig underneath to find the worms. Also dig for worms in different soils.

What soils have the most worms? What kind of habitat do they seem to prefer?

watching earthworms

Materials: Earthworms, paper towels, clear glass plate, piece of paper, magnifying glass, ruler, water.

Procedure: Place an earthworm on a damp paper towel and watch how it moves. Turn it upside down and see how it rights itself.

Use the magnifying glass for a closer look. Notice, if possible, the four small pairs of bristles at the sides and bottom of each segment. Pick the worm up and feel the bristles; put it on a piece of paper and listen for the scratching sound made by the bristles. Put the earthworm on the clear glass plate. Hold it up to light and look at the worm through the bottom of the plate to see the intestinal tract, blood vessels, and the pulsating heart. Measure the extended length of different earthworms and compute the average length.

Always keep the worms moist. Earthworms absorb oxygen through their damp skin. If the skin dries out, oxygen cannot be absorbed, and the worm suffocates.

what habitat do earthworms like?

Materials: Two equal-sized jars, moist soil, dry sand, six earthworms, spoons.

Procedure: Fill one jar half full with soil, the other with sand. Place three earthworms in each jar. Cover the earthworms on the soil surface with sand and those on the sandy surface with soil. Wait a day, then dig carefully with the spoons to find where the earthworms are; which habitat do they prefer, the soil or the sand?

Repeat this experiment using many other habitat materials, such as wet and dry leaves, wet leaves and wet soil, or wet oatmeal and wet sand.

earthworm race

Materials: Earthworms, one for each child.

Procedure: Find a shady area of bare, hard ground and scratch onto it a circle about 2 feet (.6 m) in diameter. Put the worms into the center of the circle. The first worm to crawl to the outside of the circle is the winner.

Believe it or not, worm races can be exciting. But be sure not to let the entrants dry out. Bury the worms comfortably under soil when the race is over.

activities with land snails & slugs

enjoy watching land snails

Materials: Land snails and terrarium or aquarium with a top (a piece of plastic material with holes punched in it and elastic band to hold it in place serves well).

Procedure: Put a little moist sand or soil in the bottom of the container, put in the land snails, and cover the container. Feed the snails lettuce, green leaves, pieces of apple, or experiment with other plant materials to find out what they do or do not like. Remove uneaten food after several days. Keep the sand or soil moist.

Use a hand lens for close observations of the snails. Note the two pairs of tentacles that look like horns on the head; the longer pair has eyes at the ends; the shorter pair has the sense of smell.

Draw the spiral shape of the shell. This shape is repeated in nature (whirlpools, storms, orb spider webs) and is used by people as a motif for design. Try to find examples of the use of this motif.

amazing slug accomplishment

Materials: Slug, razor blade.

Procedure: Put the slug on the razor blade facing one of the sharp edges. Watch the slug move over the sharp edge without harming itself.

How does the slug do it? Slugs secrete slime, which is lubricating and protective as they glide on it. It is this slime that protects them from the harmful sharp edge of the blade.

activities with sow bugs

keep sow bugs for observation

Materials: Sow bugs, open-topped container, soil, small pieces of decaying wood, half a potato.

Procedure: Set up a habitat suitable for sow bugs in the container. Put in the soil and on top put the

SOW BUG

pieces of wood and the potato half. Put in the sow bugs. Add water every few days; sow bugs must have a moist environment. (You may wish to return the sow bugs as described in the following activity.)

find a home for a sow bug

Materials: White plastic oleo (or similar) containers, sow bugs.

Procedure: Give each child a container with a sow bug in it. Spend time observing the sow bugs. Ask if any of the children know where sow bugs live and discuss the sow bug's need for moist, dark conditions. Hunt for a suitable sow bug home, under a log perhaps, and have each child carefully release the sow bug from the container into its new home.

As outlined, this is a simple activity designed for young children. Sow bugs are appealing little animals. They show up well against the white of the plastic containers, and children enjoy the opportunity for close-up viewing, as well as the happy ending of finding a nice new home for their creatures.

To adapt this activity for older children, try experiments to determine the habitat preferences of sow bugs, which are land-dwelling crustaceans. Put some sow bugs into a container with dry soil at one end and wet soil at the other; find which end the sow bugs prefer. Design other experiments to determine preferences for light or darkness, open areas or areas with something the sow bugs can go

underneath, and other conditions the children may suggest. Then release the sow bugs in an outdoor habitat that suits the conclusions drawn from the experiments. Treat the sow bugs with care, a suggestion based on an unfortunate experience. We had left some sow bugs in a sunny window as part of an experiment, and we found out, too late, that the sun was too hot—all the sow bugs had expired.

activities with insects

insects: helpers or harmers?

Procedure: Have the children think of as many ways as possible that insects are helpful and harmful to people. Make a list of each category.

It may be surprising to find out how long both lists become. Some ways in which insects are helpful are:

- Pollination (especially fruit trees)
- Role in food chains (food for frogs, birds)
- Products (honey, wax, shellac, silk)
- Serving as fishing bait
- Eating harmful insects
- Aesthetics (beautiful butterflies)
- Scavenging (breaking down decaying materials)
- Food for humans (in some parts of the world)

Some ways in which insects are harmful are:

- Biting and stinging people and other beings
- Spreading diseases (to people, other animals, and plants)
- Being parasites (on people, other animals, and plants)
- Causing insecticide use (may be harmful to the environment)

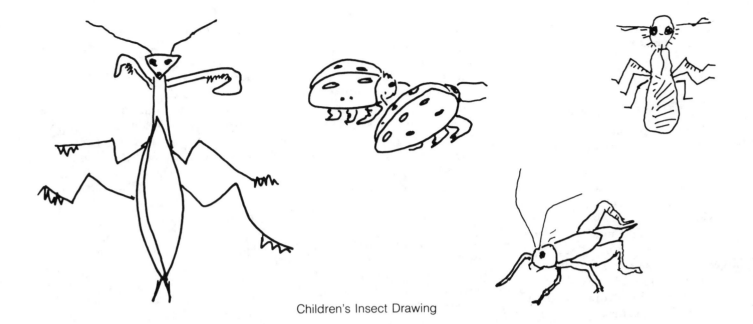

Children's Insect Drawing

- Destroying crops
- Eating houses, clothing, books, beeswax, food supplies, and whatever else insects eat that they shouldn't (from our point of view)

Take a walk and find as many examples as possible of insect helpfulness and harmfulness.

milk carton insect cage

Materials: Half-gallon milk carton, scissors, glue, small piece of screening, clear plastic wrap, masking tape.

Procedure: Cut large "windows" on adjoining sides of the carton. Glue the small piece of screening over one "window" hole, glue clear plastic wrap over the other, and

A Child's Insect Drawing

the cage is ready to use. Use masking tape to close the top opening.

This cage is especially good for caterpillars. Different caterpillars require different food plants. Bring in foliage of the same kind as the caterpillar was eating when found, or identify the caterpillar in a field guide and bring in the proper foliage as described in the guide. Insert the stems of the foliage into a narrow-necked bottle filled with water, and place foil around the top of the bottle if there is any chance that the caterpillar could drop into the water. Put the caterpillar and the bottle with the foliage into the carton cage. Close the top with masking tape and watch to see what happens. Open the top to replenish the food supply if necessary. Hopefully the caterpillar will pupate and undergo metamorphosis to the adult stage. Release the butterfly or moth after it has emerged and is ready to fly.

cake pan insect cage

Materials: Two straight-sided, equal-sized, round cake pans, piece

of window screening 2 inches (5 c) longer than the circumference of the cake pan and 1 foot (.3m) wide, large needle, and heavy thread.

Procedure: Bend the screening to fit into the cake pans, sew the edges of the screening together, and assemble.

Vary the dimensions of this type of cage to suit the needs. For added stability, secure the screening into the bottom cake pan with plaster of Paris.

This type of cage is suitable for many insects. Crickets and grasshoppers are particularly easy to keep. Use a small bottle cap for water and keep a continual supply of fresh food in the cage. The grasshoppers will require grass, while crickets enjoy a varied fare, such as small pieces of apple, bread, or potato. Experiment with different foods to see which the insects prefer. Collect fireflies, put them in the cage, and watch them in darkness. However, release them in a short time because they do not do well in captivity.

Wide-mouthed jars or almost any other closed container made at least in part with clear material for viewing make suitable insect cages. Be sure to make holes to allow air to enter inside the containers.

ant farms

Materials: Commercial ant farm and books with information about ants.

Procedure: Observe the activities of the ants, their life cycle (as evidenced by eggs, larvae, pupae, and adults), and how the colony functions as a whole. Use reference materials for further understanding of the colony. Be sure to provide proper food and adequate moisture.

The social insects, such as ants and certain bees and wasps are fascinating to study, especially since parallels often can be made between the insect society and our own. Ant farms can be made by using a wide-mouthed jar filled with soil. To dig up an ant colony is difficult; make every effort possible to find and include a queen. Sometimes, when splitting wood for instance, a colony of carpenter ants can be found. Put them with some of the wood of their home and a few drops of water for moisture in a large jar for close-up viewing.

honey bees & pollination

Procedure: Watch honey bees visit different flowers; keep still and maintain a safe distance.

Before observing bees, be absolutely certain that the children will be able to remain quiet while watching.

Pollen grains often adhere to bees' bodies as they take nectar from flowers. When the bees visit different flowers, pollen grains may rub off onto the stigmas, pollinating the flowers. To take pollen back for use in the hive, bees brush the pollen on their bodies into "baskets" composed of stiff hairs on their hind legs. Look for these baskets full of pollen, which show as blobs of yellow material on bees' last pair of legs.

Try an experiment in spring with a fruit tree. Secure a piece of mosquito netting around a branch before the buds open. This should keep the bees from pollinating the flowers. Remove the netting after the petals drop. Do any fruits develop on the branch?

feed honey bees

Materials: Honey and plate or flat stone.

Procedure: Find flowers or an area where honey bees are visiting and leave nearby the stone or plate with a few drops of honey on it. From a safe distance, observe what happens.

The best time to do this activity is in the fall when honey bees are desperately searching for food before cold weather sets in. It should not be long before a bee discovers the honey supply, drinks some, and returns with it to the hive, where the bee will communicate to the other bees just where this marvelous food supply is located. Note the time between when the first bee leaves the honey and when others arrive. Try to keep track of the times and the number of bees that come to feed. Find appropriate books on bees and read about the theory of the "bee dance" to understand how the other bees are able to find the honey. To learn more about honey bees, visit a beekeeper willing to demonstrate beekeeping, or an observation hive, which will allow for close-up viewing of the bees.

insect musicians

Materials: Tape recorder, insect field guide, recording of insect sounds (optional).

Procedure: Use the tape recorder outdoors to record sounds of insects. If possible, identify the makers of the sounds, using the field guide, or play a recording of insect sounds to determine the

A student watches the beekeeper at work.

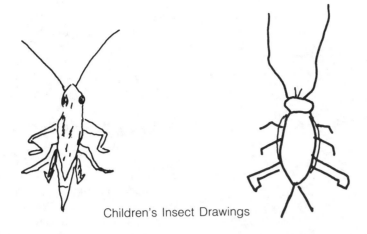

Children's Insect Drawings

kinds of insects recorded on the tape.

It is often difficult to see insects as they make sounds, but hearing them, particularly toward the end of summer, is easy. Stop with a group of children in the middle of a field on a warm end-of-summer day and just listen. You may be surprised to discover how noisy the field is. You might hear buzzes and other noises of wings, like the all-too-well-known hum of mosquitoes. To add a further dimension to this activity, play a recording of Rimsky-Korsakov's *Flight of the Bumblebee* or Mendelssohn's *Bee Wedding*.

cricket thermometer

Materials: Timepiece that indicates seconds.

Procedure: On a summer evening listen for the chirps of the snowy

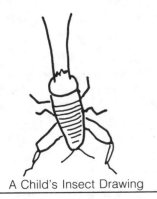

A Child's Insect Drawing

tree cricket. (If you cannot hear the snowy tree cricket in your region, experiment with other crickets' chirps.) Count the number of chirps in fourteen seconds, add forty to that number, and the result will be a close approximation of the temperature in degrees Fahrenheit. (To find the temperature in degrees Celsius, subtract 32 from the Fahrenheit number and multiply by 5/9ths.)

Insects, like other cold-blooded animals, can move more rapidly in warm weather than in cold, when they are sluggish. Crickets chirp more rapidly as the temperature goes up. Honey bees are so temperature-sensitive that they stay inside their hives when the outside temperature is below 54°F (12°C); so, if you see a bee flying on a winter's day, you know that the temperature is at least 54°F (12°C).

insect activity hunt

Materials: Paper, pencils.

Procedure: Divide the children into pairs or small groups. Have each pair or group search outside for as many signs of insect activities as possible and record the type of activity and where it was located. Afterward, share the interesting findings with all the groups.

Signs of activities may include

holes in leaves (since there may be so many, have the children record this sign only once, or only when the type of hole seems markedly different), anthills, tunnelings in logs, empty tent caterpillar nests, fall webworm nests, plant galls, and insect egg cases. Bring in a sampling of the different insect signs to make a classroom display.

Remember that given the right conditions, egg cases may hatch. You may suddenly find tiny caterpillars crawling on the display, as happened once with a gypsy moth exhibit at the local library (much to the consternation of the librarians). However, a controlled hatching can be an interesting lesson in itself, but be prepared either to release the young soon after hatching or to provide suitable food. For instance, a praying mantis egg case found in early spring may easily hatch indoors, but the young are hungry carnivores, and unless you release them immediately, they will eat each other until only one is left.

insect reports

Materials: Insects for observation, magnifying glasses, appropriate reference materials, information from any previously done insect activity.

Procedure: Observe some insects as closely as possible. Record how they move, how fast they go, what and how they eat, how they clean themselves and when they are active. Measure them and record sizes; compare different insects of the same species as well as insects of different species. Include data from previous insect activities. Use reference materials to include further information, such as life cycles, geographic distribution, and influences on the environment. Make sketches to illustrate the finished report.

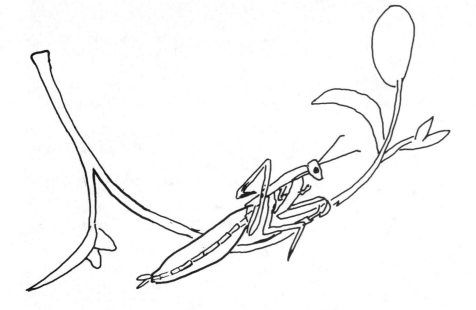

Ask the children to write insect poems. Here is one by a thirteen-year old.

HUNGRY MOSQUITOES

Like nimble-footed dancers
  On hair thin legs
  And gowns of finest lace
Twirling 'round a stage,
The mosquitoes on my screen.

clay insects

Materials: Modeling clay, toothpicks, paper, scissors, paints, paintbrushes.

Procedure: Have the children make clay insects with three body parts (head, thorax, and abdomen) using toothpicks for the six legs, pipe cleaners for the two antennae and two pairs of paper wings. When the clay is dry, paint the insect.

For a simple variation, have the children draw pictures of real or invented insects. Have them label the body parts and any specializations, like the pollen baskets of honey bees.

insecticides

Materials: Books or articles with information on insecticide use.

Procedure: Have the students study aspects of insecticide use: past uses, present uses, needs for insecticides, effectiveness in accomplishing the needs, past and present effects of insecticides on the environment, and possible alternatives to insecticide use.

While some insects were becoming resistant to the DDT insecticide, many other animals were being poisoned by DDT. How many available alternatives to such destructiveness does society have?

activities with spiders

First, a warning—spiders are *not* loved by everybody. If they do not appeal to you, consider teaching about some other animal. It is likely that both you and the children will have a more beneficial experience. If a child is wary of spiders, a teacher's genuine enthusiasm for them can help the child to appreciate and maybe even to like them!

Do not forget songs or stories about spiders. Very young children enjoy the traditional song, "The Eeensy Beensy Spider." The Greek myth about the spinning contest between a goddess, Athena, and a girl, Arachne, explains the derivation of the word *arachid* for the class of arthropods that includes spiders. E.B. White's book, *Charlotte's Web*, is a particular treasure of children's literature.

spraying spider webs

Materials: Small plant sprayer filled with water.

Procedure: Hunt for spider webs with the children. When a web is found, spray it carefully with a fine mist of water, and it will become more visible and almost glisten as if with morning dew.

catching an orb spider web

Materials: Heavy, dark-colored paper, spray paint (without fluorocarbons).

Procedure: Find an orb web that will fit on the paper. Gently shoo the spider aside, spray the web with the paint from both sides, hold the paper vertically, and catch the web onto the paper. Wait for the paper to dry, and you will have a preserved web.

Does the spider mind? Well, maybe—but orb web spiders construct a new web every morning, first consuming the old one in order to reuse the protein materials contained in the silk.

observing spiders

Materials: Spiders in containers (most of the containers described in insect activities are suitable for spiders), identification guides, hand lenses.

Procedure: Have the children closely observe spiders, noticing their eyes (many spiders have eight), how they move, how they clean themselves, and other aspects of their structure and activities. Use identification guides to identify the spiders.

A spider spinning.

bibliography

adults

BUCHSBAUM, RALPH, *Animals Without Backbones*. Chicago: University of Chicago Press, 1976.

GERTSCH, WILLIA J., *American Spiders*. New York: Van Nostrand, 1979.

HUTCHINS, ROSS E., *Insects*. Englewood Cliffs, N.J.: Prentice-Hall, 1966.

MILNE, LORUS, and MARGERY MILNE, *Invertebrates of North America*. New York: Doubleday.

MONEY, SALI, *The Animal Kingdom*. New York: Bantam, 1972.

NEWMAN, L.H., *Man and Insects*. New York: Natural History Press, 1966.

children & adults

BEHNKE, FRANCES L., *What We Find When We Look under Rocks*. New York: McGraw-Hill, 1971.

COLE, JOANNA, and JEROME WEXLER, *Find the Hidden Insect*. New York: Morrow, 1979.

FORD, BARBARA, *Can Invertebrates Learn?* New York: Messner, 1972.

HEADSTROM, RICHARD, *Adventures with Insects*. Philadelphia: Lippincott, 1963.

HESS, LILO, *The Amazing Earthworm*. New York: Scribner, 1979.

SCIENCE 5/13, *Minibeasts*. Milwaukee: McDonald-Raintree, 1973.

KELLIN, SALLY MOFFET, *A Book of Snails*. New York: Young Scott, 1968.

MITCHELL, ROBERT T., and HERBERT S. ZIM, *Butterflies and Moths*. New York: Golden Press, 1964.

OXFORD SCIENTIFIC FILMS, *Bees and Honey*. New York: Putnam, 1977.

PATENT, DOROTHY HINSHAW, *How Insects Communicate*. New York: Holiday House, 1975.

———, *The World of Worms*. New York: Holiday House, 1978.

PFADT, ROBERT E., *Animals without Backbones*. Chicago: Follett, 1967.

SELSAM, MILLICENT E., and JOYCE HUNT, *A First Look at Insects.* New York: Walker, 1974.

SMITH, HOWARD, *Hunting Big Game in City Parks*. Nashville, Tenn.: Abingdon, 1969.

WALTHER, TOM, *A Spider Might*. New York: Scribner, 1978.

6

mostly wet & scaly: fish, amphibians & reptiles

"This fish has too many bones!" That often-heard children's dinner table lament unintentionally points up how fish are set apart from invertebrates: fish were the first animals to develop bones.

Bones have several distinct advantages for animals. They support the body and give it shape. They help in movement by serving as counterbalances, against which the muscles pull. Bones protect soft, vulnerable parts of the body, as, for instance, the skull protects the brain. Animals with bones make up the phylum of the vertebrates; fishes are a class of vertebrate. The more primitive fishes (sharks, rays, and skates) have cartilaginous skeletons, but all the rest have bones, as most children already know.

Bony fish obtain oxygen through paired gills, which were the first paired respiratory organs and the forerunners of our paired lungs. Our paired nostrils may have originated with fish, but fish use theirs for smelling only, not breathing. Our arms and legs also have their counterparts in the two sets of paired fish fins, pectoral and pelvic. Most bony fish also have other fins: dorsal, caudal, and anal. Fish have a scaly skin with a protective coat of slime for streamlining and for disease prevention. Fish also have an air bladder, which is an inner hydrostatic organ that maintains the fish's buoyancy in water, and a lateral line, a kind of liquid-filled tube under the skin that serves as a sense organ. Look for it as a line running midway along the side of the body of a fish.

Amphibians were the first vertebrates to develop legs. They developed from the paired fins of the fish, giving amphibians a means of emerging from the water. As their name suggests (*amphi* means dual, and *bios* means life), amphibians live two lives: an aquatic larval stage during which respiration is by means of gills, and after a period of metamorphosis, a terrestrial air-breathing adult stage. The adults, however, generally have moist skin and live in damp habitats; they are further tied to water in that they must return to a watery area to lay their eggs.

Salamanders, frogs, and toads are amphibians. Salamanders are seemingly shy creatures because on land they generally live underneath things, such as rocks and logs, in order to keep their moist skin from drying out. Frogs are particularly popular creatures with people; perhaps this is due to the genial smiling look on their faces, especially noticeable on bullfrogs. Even very young children know about hopping like a frog or playing leapfrog.

Toads, however, are associated with warts and witches, which is unfair indeed. Although their lumpy skin includes glands that secrete an unpalatable substance as a protection against predators, toads do not cause warts, and their helpfulness in consuming harmful garden insects should redeem them from being consigned to witches' brews. Toads live in dryer habitats than their frog relatives.

Reptiles moved further from water than the amphibians. The eggshell of the reptiles marked a big evolutionary step; their eggs can be laid on land and not dry out. Their scaly skins help to prevent moisture loss, further freeing them from having to live in damp habitats. Unlike amphibians, reptiles generally have claws (except snakes); their young breathe air and look like the adults.

Reptiles have an illustrious past. Not only have they been on earth some 300 million years, but there was once a time when life on earth was dominated by notorious reptiles—the dinosaurs. Most children have heard about dinosaurs, but how many know that alligators, crocodiles, turtles, snakes, and lizards are present-day relatives of those famous creatures?

Turtles were around even before the age of the dinosaurs. They are the only reptiles with shells, made of fused ribs and other bones covered with a thin fingernail-like material. The carapace above the body and the plastron below are protective coverings that contributed to the turtle's longevity. Turtles are popular animals; most children know of the famous race with the hare. "Slow and steady wins the race" admirably describes turtles on land; in the water, however, they are not slow. All turtles, including aquatic ones, lay their eggs on land, generally buried in a hole dug by the female. Alligators and crocodiles, who are aquatic, also come onto land to lay their eggs, and despite their menacing appearance, their maternal instinct runs relatively high—for a reptile. Mother alligator not only constructs a nest for the eggs and guards it, but also assists the young to emerge and cares for them until they are able to live on their own.

Lizards are land-dwelling reptiles. They have scales, and most have four legs with five clawed toes on each foot. Salamanders, who resemble lizards, have smooth moist skin, no claws, and fewer than five toes on their front feet. Lizards

An exciting discovery.

are often rapid runners, unlike their turtle relatives; and some, the anoles, can change color from green to brown and vice versa, a feat that intrigues children (and adults, too). Some lizards lose their tails with ease, a protective device that may leave a predator with only a tail instead of a whole creature; this ability can be dismaying, however, for a child who discovers it firsthand. A few lizards are legless, appearing snakelike. However, they have eyelids and ears, which snakes lack, and on their undersides they have several rows of scales, where snakes have only one row. Both lizards and snakes shed their skins as they grow, and although most reptiles are egg layers, a few lizards and some snakes (the garter snake, for example) bear their young alive.

Snakes, perhaps the best-known reptilian order, have remarkable adaptations for swallowing food whole. Their slender teeth point backward to hold the prey while it is swallowed. The lower jaw, esophagus, and stomach can stretch wide to encompass surprisingly large prey, and the glottis (windpipe opening) is far forward so that the snake can breathe while the swallowing process goes on.

Once I was with a group of urban parents and their young children as we passed near a snake that was just starting to swallow a toad. Re-

SNAKE

alizing that many people dislike and fear snakes and that many might feel repulsed by the idea of swallowing food whole and alive, my reaction was to divert the group's attention to something in the opposite direction. A bright-eyed child, however, pointed out the snake, and to my dismay all eyes immediately turned in that direction. Flexibility is a must for outdoor teachers, so in an effort to make the group feel at ease and to overcome fear, dislike, and revulsion, I explained some of the snake's marvelous adaptations that allowed it to consume that toad, whole. The remarkable nature of the event captured the interest of all, and I like to think that each one of us came away with an added sense of wonder about the workings of the natural world.

activities with fish

Almost any body of water, except those that are toxic or polluted, supports a variety of fish. We cannot, however, go on a fish hike in the same way we go on a bird walk or an insect hunt because we are not able to see very far under water. Furthermore, fish are masters of camouflage, which makes it all the more difficult to spot them. Sometimes individual fish can be seen under the surface; notice how well suited their shape is for moving through water. Sunfish (so common that they have a variety of other names, such as blue gills, bream, or pumpkin seeds) may at

times be seen near the edge of a pond guarding the nests that contain their eggs. Occasionally one sees schools of small fish or minnows; clustering together in this manner is generally a protective behavior. Although for the most part unseen, the role of fish in ecosystems is great. Fish consume countless smaller creatures, including smaller fish, and in turn are consumed by other animals, particularly by birds and mammals, humans included.

Since fish live in water, its various properties are important to them. Activities with the properties of water are given in Chapter 9 (salt water) and Chapter 11 (freshwater).

fishing

Materials: Appropriate fishing gear (homemade with a stick, string, and hook, or more sophisticated store-bought equipment) and bait.

Procedure: Use equipment suited for the habitat. Good luck, and don't forget to come back with stories of the really big ones that got away!

A freshly caught fish almost always tastes delicious, especially when cooked outdoors. Cleaning the fish is an opportunity for a simple zoology lesson. Even if many of the parts cannot be identified, it is always a wonder to see how neatly the various organs fit within the body cavity. It is not difficult to locate the stomach. What has the fish been eating? Don't overlook the gills, whose red color shows how very close the blood vessels are to the surface in order to draw oxygen from the water.

If catching fish for food is not the goal, try feeding the fish. Debarb the hooks with wire cutters, leaving enough hook to hold the bait. Drop these in and watch the fish enjoy their meals; this is particularly effective with sunfish.

fish prints

Materials: Fish (caught or bought), poster paint, ½-inch (13 mm) paintbrush, paper (rice paper or newsprint, if possible).

Procedure: Cover the fish with a thin coat of paint. Place the paper carefully over the fish and press down firmly with fingers over the entire body. Lift the paper off. Reapply paint to make another print.

If desired, paint in the eye by hand. The flatter the fish, the easier the fish print is to make.

fish casts

Materials: Fish (caught or bought), shoe box (or any other box slightly larger than the fish), modeling clay that stays soft, plaster of Paris, water, mixing can, stick for stirring, paints, brushes, paper clip.

Procedure: Put a layer of the soft clay thicker than the fish into the box. Press the fish into the clay so that it is half buried. Mix plaster of Paris and water until the mixture is as thick as medium cream. Carefully remove the fish and pour the plaster into the impression left by the fish in the clay. Bend the paper clip into a hook and stick the ends into the hardening plaster for use as a hanger. When the plaster is dry, peel away the box and the soft clay. Use the fish as a model to paint the cast.

fish hatcheries

Procedure: Visit or study about a fish hatchery. Find out how the fish are grown and when and where they are released.

How many of these fish are caught? Why do most states require fishing licenses? How might overstocking or overfishing affect ecological balances?

how temperature affects cold-blooded animals

Materials: Goldfish in an aquarium, ice cubes in a jar, water thermometer.

Procedure: Take the temperature of the water in the aquarium. Observe how rapidly the fish swims about and count the number of times in a minute that the fish opens its mouth to breathe by forcing water through its gills. (Counting may be difficult; count several times and take the average.) Allow the jar of ice cubes to float in the aquarium. When the temperature in the aquarium has gone down 10 degrees F (about 5.5° C), remove the jar and again observe how rapidly the fish moves and how many times it opens its mouth to breathe in one minute.

Did the fish move and breathe more slowly in the colder water? (It should have.) Although this experiment may make the fish slightly uncomfortable, if carefully done it will cause no harm.

activities with amphibians

Look for amphibians in wet places. Generally, tadpoles, many frogs, and salamanders in aquatic stages will be found in water. Although frogs will sit on shore or lily pads awaiting hapless insects flying by, when something larger threatens the frog, it will dive into the water, usually disappearing among the mud or debris on the bottom. Many frogs may be found in damp meadows or on woodland floors; and the tree frogs, as their name indicates, are often found on trees. To find salamanders, look under logs, especially those in moist areas. Toads are the only amphibians that can tolerate dry conditions, although they often burrow down into soil, either for protection or to keep their skin from becoming too dry.

amphibian hunt

Materials: Identification guides, pencils, paper.

Procedure: Take a walk and see how many amphibians the group can spot. Look on the shore and in ponds for frogs; often only the eyes and a small portion of the head can be seen poking through the surface of the water. Frogs are also found in damp woods; in the same woods look under logs for salamanders. Use field guides to identify them and record the different kinds, as well as date and location.

Repeat the hunt at monthly intervals and compare the results. Do not expect to find many amphibians in cold weather. These cold-blooded animals become very sluggish at such times and hibernate during the cold winter weather.

record frog & toad choruses

Materials: Tape recorder.

Procedure: On a spring evening visit a pond where frogs or toads are calling and record the chorus. Try to identify the different sounds made by toads and the species of frogs.

Obtain a recording of frog and toad calls; use it to learn to distinguish the different calls and to identify the callers.

tadpoles

Materials: Frog or toad eggs, large jar, pond water, aquarium, algae or cornmeal.

Procedure: In spring find either a jellylike mass of frog eggs or a long thin string of toad eggs. Take only a few eggs; they are living and need to breathe, which they cannot do if overcrowded. Use a large jar to transport them from the pond to the aquarium. Put them in the pond water in the aquarium and watch to see the eggs develop and the tadpoles emerge. Notice the external gills on the tadpoles that will become internal after a few days. At this time return most of the tadpoles to the water where their eggs were found, if overcrowding occurs. Leave algae in the aquarium, or sprinkle small amounts of cornmeal on the surface of the water for the tadpoles to eat. Observe the tadpoles closely to see when the legs begin to appear, the hind legs first, then the front legs. It is extremely difficult to raise tadpoles in captivity through their complete metamorphosis into adults. After the legs appear, return all the tadpoles to their pond of origin. If repeated trips can be made to the pond, perhaps the last stage of metamorphosis into the young adults can be observed.

Have some of the children keep tadpole diaries. Record and date observations of tadpole development; include sketches.

activities with reptiles

Turtles are common in every region, but most other reptiles are more common in southern states than in northern ones. Alligators are found in fresh water areas in the southeastern states; crocodiles are found only in a few salt marsh areas in southern Florida. Many reptiles are harmless, but some are dangerous, notably snapping turtles, alligators, crocodiles, a few lizards, and the poisonous snakes. Learn to identify those that you may encounter in your area and how to avoid risks with these animals. Since all reptiles are cold-blooded, they are most active when it is hot. They slow down in cool weather and become inactive in the cold. Reptiles that live in areas with cold winter weather generally hibernate.

Snakes are often disliked and feared. Becoming better acquainted with them sometimes

Become acquainted with a snake.

relatively streamlined for swimming, when compared with the boxlike appearance of their land cousins. Determine the "scare distance"—how near a person can get to the reptile before it moves away. Look also on your walk for shed skins of snakes and lizards.

24-hour guest

Procedure: Capture a harmless turtle, lizard, or snake. Keep it in an appropriate container for a day, then release it in the place where it was found.

Feeding reptiles can be difficult; the guest will be fine without food during the brief visit. Use the time to observe the animal, to identify it (if its species is unknown), and to make sketches of it. Remember to release it exactly where it was found. The home territory of reptiles is important to them, and they generally do not thrive in unfamiliar surroundings.

turtle shell paper bags

Materials: Large supermarket-style paper bags, scissors, crayons or marking pens.

Procedure: Cut a hole in the bottom of the bag large enough for a child's head to go through; on each side of the bag near the bottom cut holes for the arms. Have the child color one side of the bag to look like a turtle's top shell, the carapace, and the other side to look like the bottom shell, the plastron.

Put the bag on the child, who will enjoy wearing the turtle shells and playing at being a turtle. It is fun to turn a whole classful of kindergarteners into turtles in this way.

how do snakes move?

Procedure: Put your bare foot on the ground and try to make it move forward by wiggling the toes.

brings more positive feelings. However, if you are reluctant to teach about snakes, don't. Choose another subject that you will enjoy.

sun bath walk

Procedure: Take a walk on a warm sunny day to hunt for reptile sunbathers. Have the children bask in the sun themselves and imagine how it would feel to a cold-blooded reptile.

Reptiles are enthusiastic sunbathers: turtles on logs in ponds, alligators on shores, and snakes and lizards on rocks or sandy areas. Use identification guides to identify the animals. Make sketches of them. Note how well a reptile may blend with its background; this is camouflage, a protective device for many. With aquatic reptiles, notice how they are adapted for living in the water. The eyes and the nostrils of alligators are the first parts of the animal to appear when it surfaces. This adaptation allows them to breathe and see what is around before they come into fuller view. Aquatic turtles have body shapes

This gives an idea of how snakes move by using their muscles. On smooth and flat ground, snakes move in a straight line by pushing their muscles against the ground. On rougher ground, snakes move in a wavy line, pushing their bodies from side to side against small objects such as pebbles or plants.

dinosaur diorama

Materials: Shoe box (without lid), white construction paper, large index cards, crayons, scissors, glue, masking tape, pebbles, small model dinosaurs (optional), book on dinosaurs.

Procedure: Lay the shoe box on its side. Cut a piece of the construction paper to fit inside the box as the background for the diorama. Use the dinosaur book as a reference and draw a prehistoric swamp on the paper. Glue the picture into place in the box. Draw some prehistoric ferns on the index cards; cut them out and attach to the bottom of the box with masking tape so that they will stand up. Draw dinosaurs and add them to the diorama in the same way (or use small model dinosaurs). Add a few pebbles and whatever else is needed to make the diorama look realistic.

Children enjoy painting dinosaur pictures and making clay models of dinosaurs. These fantastic reptiles appeal to a child's imagination; capitalize on this appeal by helping children learn about them and compare them with modern reptiles. How are they similar? How are they different?

amphibians & reptiles in legends, fables, songs & poems

Materials: Appropriate source materials.

Procedure: Have the children learn about amphibian and reptile lore, legends, and fables. Sing songs and read poems.

There is much available material. Frogs are major characters in several of Aesop's fables, and an older belief accorded salamanders the awesome ability to withstand the heat of fire. According to an ancient legend, a turtle holds up the earth. Snakes have had a bad reputation ever since the days of Adam and Eve, and rattlesnakes were depicted on several flags of the colonial states as symbols of belligerence with the saying "Don't tread on me." An especially appealing poem for young children is *The Little Turtle*.

An alligator sunbath.

There was a little turtle.
He lived in a box.
He swam in a puddle.
He climbed on the rocks.

He snapped at a mosquito.
He snapped at a flea.
He snapped at a minnow.
And he snapped at me.

He caught the mosquito.
He caught the flea.
He caught the minnow.
But he didn't catch me.

Vachel Lindsay

people's uses of reptiles & amphibians

Materials: Books and articles about uses of these animals.

Procedure: Study historic and modern uses, as well as different culture's uses of reptiles and amphibians.

Frog legs and turtle soup are known as special foods; some cultures use lizards for food. Skins of alligators, lizards, and snakes are made into leather goods, and before plastics tortoise shell was commonly used for eyeglasses and other objects. Frogs are often used as laboratory animals, and venoms of poisonous snakes are used in medicine. The students may discover many other ways that humans have used reptiles and amphibians. They may also discover that some of these animals are endangered and that states have regulations protecting some of them, such as alligators, Gila monsters, Texas tortoises, and bog turtles. And don't forget, when leaving a group of young children at the conclusion of a study of reptiles, many will think it fun to hear you say, "See you later, alligator!"

bibliography

adults

CARR, ARCHIE, *The Reptiles* (Life Nature Library). New York: Time-Life, 1963.

HERALD, EARL S., *Fishes of North America*. New York: Doubleday, n.d.

MARSHALL, N.B., *The Life of Fishes*. Cleveland, Ohio: World, 1966.

OULAHAN, RICHARD, *Reptiles and Amphibians* (Wild, Wild World of Animals). Time-Life Films, 1976.

PARKER, H. W., and A. G. C. GRANDISON, *Snakes: A Natural History*. Ithaca, N.Y.: Cornell University Press, 1977.

PORTER, GEORGE, *The World of the Frog and the Toad*. Philadelphia: Lippincott, 1967.

REEVES, MARTHA EMILIE, *The Total Turtle*. New York: Crowell, 1975.

children & adults

BARE, COLLEEN STANLEY, *The Durable Desert Tortoise*. New York: Dodd, Mead & Co., 1979.

BLASSINGAME, WYATT, *Wonders of Frogs and Toads*. N.Y.: Dodd, Mead, 1975.

BRENNER, BARBARA, *We're Off to See the Lizard*. Milwaukee: Raintree, 1977.

COLE, JOANNA, *A Frog's Body*. New York: Morrow, 1980.

COLE, JOANNA, and JEROME WEXLER, *A Fish Hatches*. New York: Morrow, 1978.

HUNTINGTON, HARRIET E., *Let's Look at Reptiles*. New York: Doubleday, 1973.

ISPEN, D.C., *Rattlesnakes and Scientists*. Reading, Mass.: Addison-Wesley, 1970.

LEEN, NINA, *Snakes*. New York: Holt, 1978.

LIVAUDAIS, MADELEINE, and ROBERT DUNNE, *The Skeleton Book*. New York: Walker, 1972.

RICCIUTI, EDWARD R., *The American Alligator*. New York: Harper, 1972.

SELSAM, MILLICENT E., and JOYCE HUNT, *A First Look at Frogs, Toads and Salamanders*. New York: Walker, 1976.

SIMON, SEYMOUR, *Discovering What Goldfish Do*. New York: McGraw-Hill, 1970.

WHITAKER, GEORGE O., and JOAN MEYERS, *Dinosaur Hunt*. New York: Harcourt, 1965.

ZIM, HERBERT S., and HOBART M. SMITH, *Reptiles and Amphibians*. New York: Golden Press, 1956.

7 our feathered friends: birds

Birds are easy to recognize; they are the only animals with feathers. Birds are warm-blooded, and their feathers help to keep them warm. Down feathers, especially, provide good insulation, as anyone who has a down jacket or sleeping bag knows.

Also, birds' feathers assist with flight. Contour feathers contribute to streamlining the shape of birds' bodies, while the primary flight feathers, the outer feathers along the end of the wings, are used for flying. The secondary flight feathers, which are the inner feathers along the wings, together with the shorter feathers covering the wings, give wings an airfoil shape. This is a highly effective shape for flight, used in designing wings of planes.

Birds have other adaptations for flying. Their ears are mere holes on the sides of the head. Ask children if they think birds could fly effectively if they had ears like those of a donkey or a rabbit, and they will understand the reason for the simple holes. Many bird bones are hollow, thus light—an aid for flying. Have you heard the expression "scarce as hen's teeth?" Birds have no teeth; teeth are heavy. Instead, birds have light horny beaks and, inside their bodies, a gizzard where food is broken apart and ground down with the aid of small pebbles that the bird has swallowed. Ask children if they can recognize the gizzard, which comes with the heart and liver in the little package inside supermarket chickens.

Not all birds, however, have all these adaptations for flight. Ostriches have wings, but they cannot fly, and they rely on running instead of flight for moving about and escaping from danger. Penguins also have wings and do not fly. Their bodies are streamlined for swimming and their wings serve as paddles.

Wet feathers would be heavy on a bird, as well as cold. However, a bird can waterproof its feathers by using its oil gland. When a bird preens, it takes oil with its beak from the gland, located on its back where the tail begins, and spreads the oil on its feathers, waterproofing them as well as keeping them in good condition for flying and for maintaining body warmth. Waterfowl use their oil glands a great deal because dry feathers are essential for maintaining buoyancy in water. This is the explanation behind the old expression "as easy as water running off a duck's back."

Birds' eggs are unique in having a hard shell, unlike the leathery covering of reptile eggs. Birds lay their eggs in nests, which may be high in a tree and elaborately constructed, or on the ground and simply made.

Sometimes in nesting season children find a baby bird, seemingly lost or orphaned, and are tempted to bring the bird home to take care of it. Help the child to understand that the best care for such a baby is that of its own parents. Finding a suitable substitute for the bird's natural diet is difficult, and feeding a baby bird every twenty minutes (as its parents do) from dawn to dusk is even more so. Furthermore, young birds need to learn many things from their own parents that humans cannot teach them. Fortunately, the "lost" baby is generally not an orphan. More than likely it is feathered, can fly a little, and is an adolescent, able to leave the nest but still needing parental care. Leave such a fledging alone and its parents will come shortly to feed it. Sometimes the young bird may be unfeathered and indeed too young to leave the nest, but has somehow fallen out of it. If at all possible, locate the nest and return the baby to it, where the parents will re-

Characteristics of Birds

All birds:
1. Have bills, but no teeth
2. Have feathers
3. ~~Hate~~ Hatch out of eggs
4. Have wings
5. Have hollow bones
6. Have two legs and two feet
7. Have lungs and breathe oxygen
8. Are warm blooded

By a fifth-grader.

sume their care. If the nest is too high, put the young bird in a small, open box and place it as near to the nest as possible. Handling the bird will not cause its parents to stay away.

Most birds that are caring for their young have well-defined territories

for gathering food. The territory was established by the male before the nest was built. His song, for all its beauty, has a practical purpose.

Romantic notions to the contrary, the male bird is saying "this is mine, this is mine," a straightforward message to other birds of the

same species that the singer is staking his claim to his territory.

In the late summer and early fall, when the young have matured enough to be on their own, many species of birds migrate south. Migration is complex, still with unsolved mysteries. Perhaps a child whose curiosity about bird behavior was stimulated by you will grow up to solve another portion of the migration puzzle. Certainly for many birds, especially those that eat insects, there is a far greater food supply available in the warm South than in the cold winter weather of the North. In spring these birds migrate northward and find long summer days that give them a greater number of hours for finding food and feeding their young.

activities with birds

Bird study and activities do not require rare birds or wilderness areas. Some of the common birds, such as starlings, pigeons, house sparrows, jays, and robins, are ideal for studying since they coexist well with people and can be observed easily in their daily activities.

birdwatching activities

Birdwatching can be done by children of all ages anywhere and at almost any hour during daylight. Birdwatching can be simple or involved; from sitting on a park bench and looking at the pigeons strutting by, to spotting migratory warblers through binoculars on a spring walk at dawn. Birdwatching often becomes an engrossing lifetime hobby.

What features of a bird help a

young birdwatcher to identify it? First is color. "Robin redbreasts" are easy to identify, as are bluejays, because of their coloration. A flash of red disappearing into the trees might indicate a cardinal or a scarlet tanager. Also indicative are color patterns and field marks, such as a streaked breast or light bars on the wings. Size is important. Compare the bird with other common birds. Is it about the size of a crow? A robin? A sparrow? Observe the bird's shape. Is it chunky? Long and slender? Tall and thin? An experienced birder

will also regard the shape of the bird's beak, wings, tail, and legs, and whether the head has a crest. The bird's behavior is also significant. Does it hop or walk? How does it fly? Does it sing or call? Sound often helps to identify the bird before it is seen. Habitat is another consideration, for, like all animals, different species of birds have their preferred habitats.

For close-up pigeon watching, feed the pigeons. Here a father shows how—to his little girl and two interested bystanders.

NOTICE SHAPE

of beak

crest?

Of wings

of tail

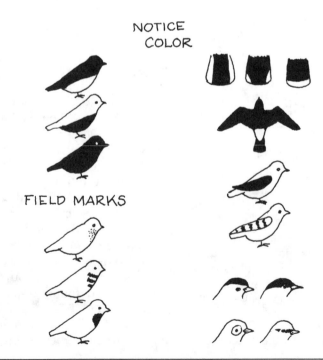

NOTICE COLOR

FIELD MARKS

When looking for birds outside, remember to move slowly and quietly, especially with a group, although admittedly this can be difficult with a number of enthusiastic children. Sometimes sitting down to watch and listen has an effective calming influence. When a bird is located, look at it carefully and note as many features as possible; then turn to the guide book while the information is fresh in mind. Although birdwatching

WHERE WAS IT?

water

marsh

field

conifers

deciduous

suburbs

city

HOW DOES IT FLY?

can be done at any hour of the day, early morning and shortly before dusk are the times when birds are most active and easily seen.

Are binoculars helpful? Yes, they are extremely useful for observing birds that are either small, far away, or both. However, young children, unless they have had experience, may have difficulty in using binoculars. Also, unless every member of the group has binoculars, difficulties may arise with sharing the equipment. Use your own judgment. Binoculars are not an absolute necessity, especially with young beginning birders.

keep a bird list

Materials: Field guide, paper, pencils, binoculars (optional).

Procedure: Identify and record the different species of birds found by birdwatching.

The ability to identify different birds is a tool that can be used for developing further understanding of birds. Include on the bird list the date, time of day, location, weather conditions, and what the bird was doing. Take extra time to observe as much about the bird as possible. This is the way to learn about birds, not merely their names.

Another approach is to keep a bird calendar. Record on it the first time a bird of a species is seen. A long-term project is possible by comparing the bird calendar from one year with that of the preceding year.

mystery bird descriptions

Materials: Pictures of birds, paper, pencils.

Procedure: Have each child write a description of a bird in a picture. (They can all describe the same bird, or different ones.) Read the

descriptions aloud and compare them. Then use a simple field guide to discover the names of the mystery birds.

Repeat this activity several times, and the children will begin to learn from their own experiences the features, such as shape, color, and field marks, that are useful for identification purposes. This can lay the groundwork for a birdwatching trip outside.

school yard bird survey

Procedure: Divide the students into groups and give each group the name of a commonly seen local bird. Have them draw pictures from field guides of their bird to learn identifying characteristics. Then have each group look for its bird in the school yard and count how many were seen in fifteen minutes. Record the results on a chart in the classroom. Repeat the survey at periodic intervals and compare the data.

bird behavior hunt

Materials: Bird behavior checklists, pencils.

Procedure: Divide the students into pairs of small groups. Give each pair or group a behavior checklist. Have each pair or group find and check off as many of the activities on the list as possible. Afterward, have the children describe and compare behaviors they have seen.

Suggestions for a bird behavior checklist:

LOCATION OF BIRD	MOVEMENT
Ground	Walking
Tree branch	Hopping
Tree trunk	Running
Shrub	Flapping flight
Water	Gliding flight
Air	Wading
Other?	Swimming
	Sitting
	Sleeping
	Other?

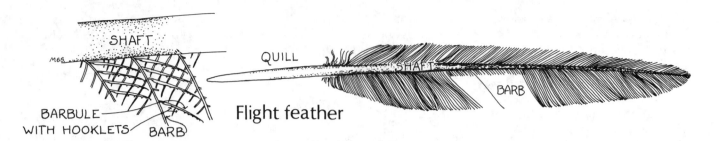

SHAFT

QUILL

SHAFT

BARB

BARBULE WITH HOOKLETS

BARB

Flight feather

COMMUNICATION	MAINTENANCE
Singing	Preening
Courting	Using oil glands
Warning call	Feeding on
Aggressive by	plants
pecking	Feeding on
Aggressive by	insects
chasing	Feeding on
Flocking with	other animals
others	Other?
Other?	

If it is nesting season, add a nesting behavior category and list nest building, incubating eggs, feeding young in nest, and caring for young out of the nest.

Do the children know what preening is? As we discussed earlier, a bird preens to keep its feathers in good order both by oiling them with oil from its oil gland and by mending small breaks in the feathers. This mending process works much like zipping a zipper. A bird's outer feathers have barbs that are attached to each other by tiny hooks called barbules. Find a feather, make a break between the barbs, and look at the barbules with a magnifying glass. To mend the break, run your fingers over it and the barbules will "zip" the break together. Children love to "zip up" breaks in feathers.

nesting mathematics

Materials: An observable nest with incubating eggs (or young hatchlings), watch, paper, pencils.

Procedure: After the eggs have hatched, make daily half-hour counts of the number of trips the parent birds make to feed their young early in the morning, in the middle of the day, and in the evening. (Shorter and fewer counting periods may be used, if necessary, but the resulting estimates will not be as reliable.) Monitor the nest in this way until the young leave. Record all the data and also the number of young and the length of the days from sunrise to sunset. Then use the information to solve problems, such as the ones that follow. How many trips did the parent birds make during the first day to feed the young? (Assume that the average of the visits during the day's counting periods was an average number for each half-hour during the daylight hours.) How many times was each baby fed? How often was each baby fed? How many trips did the parents make during one week? How many trips did the parents make in all? If the parents brought four insects on each trip, how many insects did they bring to feed their young while they were in the nest?

You and the children may be astonished to discover what constant care is given by parent birds to their young.

signs of birds

Procedure: Combine a hunt for signs of birds with a birdwatching walk. Look for feathers, nests, droppings, woodpecker and sapsucker holes in trees, footprints (in mud or sand), and other clues of bird activity.

Owls leave a particularly interesting sign—owl pellets. Owls do not pick meat off the bones, as we do when eating, for instance, a chicken drumstick. Instead, owls swallow every part of their prey—fur or feathers, skin, bones, and all. Later, the indigestible parts are regurgitated in a pellet. If you have the luck to find one on the ground, take it apart carefully. You may discover the tiny skull of a mouse or of some other animal, and you will have an idea of what the owl had for its meal.

beak & feet adaptations

Materials: Field guides, paper, pencils, binoculars (optional).

Procedure: Go birdwatching for the express purpose of noticing specializations of birds' beaks and feet. Try to find out how they help the different birds in their modes of life.

Much can be told about a bird's way of life from the shape of its feet and beak. Webbed feet, as even most young children know, are for swimming (and are rather clumsy for walking). Pheasants, partridge, chickens, and other ground birds have feet useful for running, as well as for scratching the ground to find seeds or insects. Hawks, owls, and other birds of prey have strong feet with sharp, curved talons for grasping prey. Most songbirds have perching feet, three toes in front, one behind, which automatically clasp the perch when the leg is relaxed. Woodpeckers have feet adapted for climbing, two toes in front and two in back, with sharp claws for

YOU CAN TELL WHAT THEY EAT
BY THEIR BILLS AND THEIR FEET

caterpillars, beetles & crawling insects

flying insects

rats, mice, snakes & grasshoppers

insects in wood

small water plants

nectar

frogs & fish

not to scale

M.S.S/M.A.S

seeds

"A wonderful bird is the pelican, his beak holds as much as his belly can."

A BIRD CAME DOWN THE WALK

A bird came down the walk:
He did not know I saw:
He bit an angle-worm in halves
And ate the fellow, raw.

And then he drank a dew
From a convenient grass,
And then hopped sidewise to the wall
To let a beetle pass.

He glanced with rapid eyes
That hurried all abroad,–
They looked like frightened beads, I thought
He stirred his velvet head

Like one in danger; cautious,
I offered him a crumb,
And he unrolled his feathers
And rowed him softer home

Than oars divide the ocean,
Too silver for a seam,
Or butterflies, off banks of noon,
Leap, plashless, as they swim.

Emily Dickinson

activities with feeding birds

Bird feeders near windows allow for indoor birdwatching. They give opportunities for close-up observation and identification of different species of birds, as well as for studying bird behavior. When one jay aggressively chases another away, it may be a demonstration that the first jay is higher in the "peck order" than the second. Other dramas make the bird feeder an exciting place to watch. As a bonus—or not, depending on your point of view—there is often the squirrel sideshow as squirrels try to share in the free meal offered by the feeder.

drumlin farm bird pudding

Materials: One pound lard (or leftover cooking fat), one cup hot water, two cups oatmeal, one cup flour, four cups wild birdseed, large pan, mixing spoons.

Procedure: Soften the lard or fat over warm heat in the large pan. Add remaining ingredients and mix well.

---

clinging to upright surfaces. Wading birds, such as herons, have long legs with long slender toes to keep the bird from sinking into the mud.

Also, bird beaks vary widely. Ducks and geese have broad, flat beaks with serrated edges for straining food from water. Ground birds have short, stout beaks for ground feeding. Birds of prey (owls, for instance) tear flesh apart with their strong, hooked beaks and their talons. Imagine having a mouse for dinner: You would cut it up with a knife and fork, wouldn't you? We often call the beaks and talons of birds of prey their knives and forks because they serve the same purpose. Seed-

eating birds have short, thick bills for crushing seeds, while the beaks of insect-eaters are slender and pointed, useful for picking up insects. Herons have beaks like long spears for catching fish, and pelicans have a flexible pouch underneath for holding fish.

bird poems

Materials: Paper, pencils.

Procedure: Have the children write poems about birds they have observed. Encourage them to describe in the poem how the bird looked and what it was doing.

Read the following poem to show how one poet describes a personal encounter with a bird.

Children like to add the ingredients and take turns mixing. Other ingredients can be added, such as seeds that the children may have gathered themselves on a walk, and the proportions of the ingredients may be changed to suit your fancy, or what you have available. Bird pudding can be slathered into any kind of container-type feeder. This is a messy, globby activity that delights most young children.

easy feeders for young children

Materials: Pine cones, peanut butter, birdseed, string, plastic disposable-type bowls, hole puncher, bird pudding, spoons.

Procedure: Have the children make pine cone feeders by smooshing peanut butter with spoons onto the pine cones. Then roll the cone in birdseed, tie a string to the top end, and it is ready to hang outside. To make a bowl feeder, punch three holes evenly spaced around the top edge of the plastic bowl, fill the bowl with bird pudding, and tie strings through the holes for hanging.

Three-, four-, and five-year-olds enjoy making these winter treats for the birds, with some assistance from adults. Use your imagination for other easy ones suitable for young children. For instance, try using empty grapefruit or orange halves instead of bowls. The illustration will give suggestions for feeders that older children may enjoy building.

Recycle an old Christmas tree for bird use by standing it in the backyard. Hang simple feeders from its branches. Attach other items, such as stale doughnuts or sprigs from local shrubs and plants with berries or seed heads. String popcorn and cranberries together and drape the strings around the tree for an aesthetic effect and for

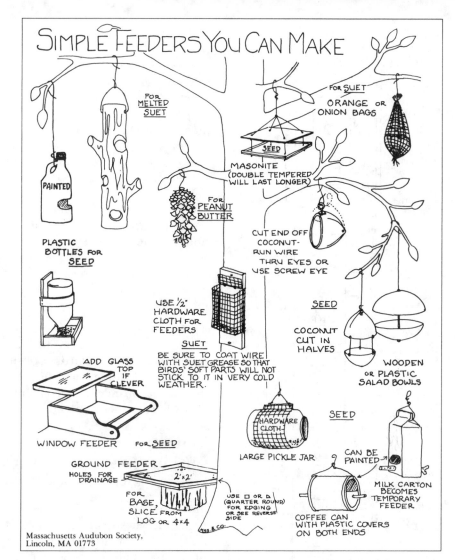

SIMPLE FEEDERS YOU CAN MAKE

FOR MELTED SUET

PAINTED

PLASTIC BOTTLES FOR SEED

ADD GLASS TOP IF CLEVER

WINDOW FEEDER — FOR SEED

GROUND FEEDER
HOLES FOR DRAINAGE
2'×2'
FOR BASE, SLICE FROM LOG OR 4×4
USE ⬜ OR ◗ (QUARTER ROUND) FOR EDGING OR SEE REVERSE SIDE

FOR PEANUT BUTTER

USE ½" HARDWARE CLOTH FOR FEEDERS
SUET
BE SURE TO COAT WIRE WITH SUET GREASE SO THAT BIRDS' SOFT PARTS WILL NOT STICK TO IT IN VERY COLD WEATHER.

FOR SUET
ORANGE OR ONION BAGS

SEED
MASONITE (DOUBLE TEMPERED) WILL LAST LONGER)

CUT END OFF COCONUT-RUN WIRE THRU EYES OR USE SCREW EYE

COCONUT CUT IN HALVES

SEED

WOODEN OR PLASTIC SALAD BOWLS

HARDWARE CLOTH
LARGE PICKLE JAR

SEED

CAN BE PAINTED

COFFEE CAN WITH PLASTIC COVERS ON BOTH ENDS

MILK CARTON BECOMES TEMPORARY FEEDER

Massachusetts Audubon Society, Lincoln, MA 01773

edibility by the birds. Soften some bird pudding and smear it onto the branches. Add your own innovations, and your tree may become the gourmet bird restaurant of the area!

bird garden

Procedure: Plant flowers, shrubs, and trees that will produce seeds and fruits that birds particularly like to eat.

The types of plants depend on the climate, weather conditions, and species of birds of the area. Some general suggestions are: sunflowers, honeysuckle, climbing roses, bittersweet, buckthorn, flowering cherries and crabapples, sumac, red cedar, and mountain ash. Certain red flowers attract hummingbirds. Find information from a local source to learn about

the recommended plants for birds in your area.

Birds need water to drink and many enjoy the availability of a birdbath. A simple birdbath can be made using the lid of a garbage can upside down, or line a shallow basin with concrete so that the water in it will be between ½–2 inches (1.2–5c) deep.

activities with bird houses, nests & eggs

build a bluebird house

Materials: 1-inch (2.5 c) unplaned pine, 2-inch (5 c) galvanized nails, carpentry tools.

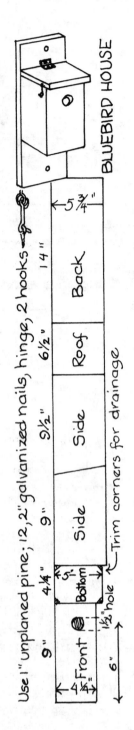

BLUEBIRD HOUSE

Use 1" unplaned pine; 12, 2" galvanized nails, hinge, 2 hooks

Back — 5¾" — 14"

Roof 6½"

Side 9½"

Side 9"

Bottom 5" 4½"

Front ½" hole 6" 4¼"

9" 4¼"

Trim corners for drainage

Procedure: Assemble the bluebird house as indicated in the diagram. Place the house in an open field or abandoned orchard on a tree or post about 6 feet (1.8 m) above the ground.

Bluebirds generally nest in woodpecker holes, but land development has eliminated many bluebird nesting areas, and starling and house sparrows use many of the tree cavities that remain. To discourage starlings from using the bluebird house, be certain to cut the entrance hole exactly 1½ inches (3.8 c) in diameter, and the starlings cannot get in. Starlings and house sparrows generally nest earlier than bluebirds. Block the entrance hole until the bluebirds are seen and they will have a better chance of using the bird house. Bluebirds prefer rustic houses, so do not paint the house. A temporary bluebird nest box can be made by using a half-gallon milk carton.

Tree swallows may also use this house. Nesting boxes can be made for other species of birds. Consult birdhouse building references to determine proper measurements and where to place the box.

identifying bird nests

Materials: Field guide to bird nests.

Procedure: Take a walk to see how many bird nests can be found. Note details of their construction (if not too high up) and try to identify the makers by using the field guide.

It may be surprising how many bird nests can be found in an area once sharp-eyed children start looking for them. Be careful not to disturb any active nests and leave empty ones where you find them; sometimes they are used again.

nesting materials for the birds

Materials: Yarn, string, thread, small strips of cloth, small piece of hardware cloth or empty mesh onion bag.

Procedure: Cut the yarn and other materials into pieces about 6–8 inches (15–25 c) long. Put them through the holes in the hardware cloth or into the mesh bag so that ends hang out. Hang the hardware cloth or bag on a low branch outside and watch to see if any of the materials are taken by birds to be used in nest building.

can you make a nest?

Materials: Mud, twigs, pieces of hay, and other possible nest-building materials.

Procedure: Have each child try to make a nest.

Children enjoy trying, and they find that nest building (even with the benefit of hands and fingers instead of beaks and feet) is no easy matter—something birds can do well, but we cannot.

experiments with eggs

Materials: Chicken eggs, 2 books, pencils, paper, 2-cup (500 ml) measuring cup, water, pot, stove, flashlight.

Procedure: What shape is an egg? Put an egg on paper and draw around it with a pencil. What is its length? Place it endwise between the books; the distance between the books is the egg's length. To measure the width, place the egg sidewise between the books. What is the egg's volume? Put one cup (250 ml) of water into the measuring cup. Put in the egg; the amount the water rises in the cup is equal to the volume of the egg. Hardboil the egg; hold it up in front of a flashlight and compare it with an uncooked egg. More light should be seen through the raw egg. Spin the hardboiled egg and the raw egg. The loose liquid in the raw egg should act as a brake, causing it to spin more slowly. Open a raw egg. Notice the yolk, the albumen (the white), the chalazae (which look like two whitish, twisted ropes and which keep the yolk centered in the albumen) and the tiny white spot on the top of the yolk (which is where the embryo chick could start to develop in the egg if the egg were fertile).

Almost all chicken eggs bought at the supermarket are not fertile, because chicken farmers do not keep roosters in with egg-laying flocks. Hens will ovulate and lay eggs without mating, just as female mammals ovulate whether they have mated or not. Hens that have mated with a rooster are likely to produce fertile eggs. Inside the hen, near the ovary, the sperm joins with the microscopic egg nucleus, which is in the center of the tiny white spot on the surface of the yolk. This fertilization occurs before the layers of the egg white, the membrane, and the shell have been added around the yolk. The fertile egg, when it is laid, will look no different from an infertile egg (and will taste no different), but if both eggs are incubated, only the fertile egg can grow a chick.

These experiments with chicken eggs help to familiarize children with the unique features of bird eggs in general. Some of the children may already know that many wild bird eggs are spotted in order to blend with their surroundings (just as many hatchlings are also spotted). Generally, these are the eggs that are laid in unconcealed nests. Eggs that are laid in burrows, tree holes, or other concealed places, or those eggs that are incubated by both parents and thus seldom exposed, are generally plain colored.

hatching chicken eggs

Materials: Incubator, incubator thermometer, fertile chicken eggs, water, and an available person to turn the eggs two to four times daily.

Procedure: Establish the incubator according to the directions that come with it several days in advance of putting in the eggs, to be certain that the temperature has stabilized at about 100°–101°F (37.4 C). Put the eggs in and turn them at least two times daily (four times if possible); turning prevents the embryo from adhering to the side of the egg. Maintain moisture in the incubator according to the directions. Never count your chickens before they hatch, but be hopeful, and maybe on the nineteenth or twentieth day, pecking and occasional cheeps can be heard from within the eggs, and the chicks will hatch on the twenty-first day.

Hatching eggs demonstrates the miracle of new life and growth, and, although the incubator is artificial, children can understand how mother hens or wild birds provide the warmth necessary for incubation of the eggs.

A friendly chicken in the classroom allows for touching and close-up viewing of a bird.

Before starting to incubate the eggs, be sure to have made plans for the future care of any chickens that may be the result of the project. It is important that children understand that creating life brings with it the responsibility of caring for that life.

activities with bird songs

Of all the forms of animal communication, bird songs and calls are probably the most familiar to us. The male's song declaring his territory not only warns other males to stay away, but also advertises to females that he has a fine area with plenty of food available for raising a family. Birds also have other songs and calls used for signaling danger, keeping the flock together, and announcing the presence of food. Some birds have many different songs and calls. Do not forget to try to identify birds by their songs and calls when birdwatching.

introduction to indoor learning of bird songs

Materials: Recording of bird songs, tape recorder.

Procedure: Make a birdsong tape to use with the children. Play the recording and tape one-minute segments of five common, locally heard bird songs. Introduce each segment by giving the name of the bird singing in the segment. Then record on the tape short segments of the five different bird songs, in different order from the beginning segments. Include each bird's song three times, and the tape is ready to use. Divide the children into five groups and assign one of the birds on the tape to each group. First play to the class the five beginning segments on the tape, so that each group can learn its bird's song. Then play the portion of the tape with the songs in different order and have the members of each group raise their hands when they hear the song of their bird.

This is an activity that can have many variations, including learning more and more bird songs by this technique or going outside to try to hear those songs learned on the tape.

birdsong chairs

Materials: Recording of bird songs, chairs.

Procedure: Play this game in the usual manner of musical chairs, substituting bird songs for music. Line up the chairs, one facing one direction, the next facing the other. Start with one fewer chairs than the number of children in the group. Play the bird songs and have the children go around the chairs until the bird songs stop. Then every child tries to find a chair to sit on. The one child without a seat leaves the game; remove a chair and repeat the process until only one chair is left, and the child who sits in it when the song stops is the winner.

This game can be made more sophisticated by substituting a specific bird's song as the signal to sit down.

activities with bird migration

spring arrivals

Materials: Mural-sized piece of paper, crayons, paper, scissors, glue.

Procedure: In early spring have the students draw on the large paper a scene showing a deciduous and an evergreen tree, a field, shrubs, a pond, and a swamp. Put the picture up in the classroom. Each time a new bird that has migrated back from the south is seen by the class (or perhaps by individual students at home) have a student draw, label, and cut out a picture of the bird and glue it on the picture in its appropriate habitat.

When outside with the class, do not forget to watch for migrating birds overhead. If the school is in the area of one of the waterfowl flyways, listen for the calls of ducks and geese as they fly over. Also notice the large "V"-shaped flight pattern common to many species of migratory waterfowl.

migration reports

Materials: Books with information about bird migration.

Procedure: Have each child study the migration habit of a different bird and write a report about it. Encourage the children to include information about when the bird migrates, how fast and how high it travels, whether it travels by day or by night, the route it follows, and where it stays in winter and in summer.

In the fourth century B.C., Aristotle speculated that some birds flew to warm areas in winter, but others wintered sleeping in holes in trees, caves, or underneath mud in swamps. Although we know that no bird is going to winter under mud in a swamp, there are still unanswered questions about some aspects of migration. Discuss this with the children, because they should be aware that there are many facets of the natural world that we cannot explain.

migration geography

Materials: Books with information about bird migration.

Procedure: Have the students study

the physical geography of the areas one species of bird occupies during the winter and during the summer. What foods might be available to the bird in both areas? Study also the areas the bird may visit on its migratory route. Make maps to show the location of the areas.

birds & people activities

how are birds helpful or harmful to us?

Procedure: Consider with the children ways that birds are helpful and useful to us, and ways in which they can be harmful.

Birds are helpful, for instance, by providing eggs and meat, and also feathers for down jackets or sleeping bags, and by eating bothersome insects, mice and other unwanted animals. Birds are harmful by eating planted seeds or crops, and sometimes in populated areas their droppings are unsanitary. Have the sudents heard of quill pens or feather dusters? They certainly know how Indians used feathers in headdresses. What else can they add?

How have people used and domesticated birds? Have the students study falconry or the domestication of chickens, turkeys, and other birds.

bird immigrants

Materials: Books with information about birds imported into the United States.

Procedure: Learn about the different birds (especially pigeons, house sparrows, and starlings) brought to this country, why they were brought, and what has happened to them since their arrival.

Pigeons were brought over by the colonists. House sparrows were imported in the middle of the nineteenth century to control insects, and at the end of the century, 120 starlings were brought in and released in New York City's Central Park. Evidently each of these immigrant species found the new world to be a land of golden opportunity, as evidenced by the millions of their progeny living today in all parts of the country.

Starlings, pigeons, and house sparrows have adapted well to life in cities and provide urbanites with opportunities for close-up studies of bird behavior, since these birds are accustomed to existing in close proximity with humans. It is said that pigeons can even recognize individual persons who feed them.

endangered species of birds

Materials: Reference materials with information on endangered bird species, birds that have become extinct, and about the evolution of birds.

Procedure: Have the students study endangered species of birds and

Pigeons have adapted to city living.

what is being done to help them. Our national symbol, the bald eagle, is a particularly important bird to study.

For helpful background material, learn about the evolution of birds from reptiles (the scales on birds' legs are leftover features from their reptilian past) and the ancestral birds. Studies of birds, such as the dodo and the passenger pigeon, which have become extinct because of human activities, underscore the need for action to protect present-day endangered species. Hunting regulations, bird and wildlife refuges, restrictions on the release of toxic materials into the environment, and studies by bird-banding are among the many actions that may be useful in aiding endangered species.

bird symbols

Procedure: Compile a collection of bird symbols and sayings.

Here are some examples. The bluebird is a symbol of happiness; the dove, peace and gentleness; the eagle, bravery and courage; the goose, stupidity; the owl, wisdom; and the peacock, pride and vanity. Sayings include describing a person as "crazy as a coot," "chicken-hearted," or "bird-brained." "Birds of a feather flock together" is well known, as is the expression "to eat like a bird." The latter, however, is misleading since many birds eat great amounts in comparison to their body size. Study bird behavior to find if the other statements are accurate or not.

state birds

Materials: Books with lists and information on state birds, map of the United States.

Procedure: Look up the official bird of each state and put its name in the proper state on the map.

bird stamps

Procedure: Make a collection of stamps that have birds on them.

Preschoolers glued on this bird's feathers.

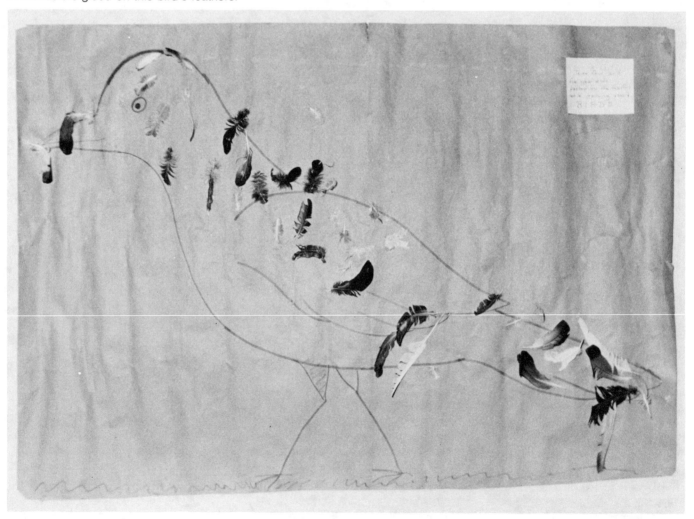

The first bird shown on an adhesive postage stamp is reported to be a dove on a stamp issued by Switzerland in 1845. Hundreds of birds have been depicted on stamps since then, and it is an interesting hobby to collect them.

bird mobiles & other art projects

Materials: Stiff paper, scissors, crayons or paint, fine string, thin sticks.

Procedure: Draw, color or paint, and cut out life-sized pictures of different common local birds. Attach a piece of string to each picture, hang them from sticks, and assemble the whole into a mobile.

Obtain a collection of feathers from a chicken farm if possible. Glue feathers onto the birds for a mobile instead of coloring or painting them. Or use fish-line filament and make a mobile with feathers alone. Young children enjoy gluing feathers onto a large outline drawing of a bird.

Sketching birds seen outside increases observation. Afterward, when more time is available, complete sketches into drawings inside. Use field guides for references and color or paint the birds. Show the children reproductions of some of Audubon's bird prints.

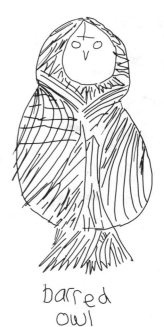

barred owl

By a fourth-grader.

bibliography

adults

ARMSTRONG, EDWARD A., *The Life and Lore of the Bird.* New York: Crown, 1975.

EISERER, LEN. *The American Robin.* Chicago: Nelson Hall, 1976.

HARRISON, COLLIN, *Field Guide to Nests, Eggs, and Nestlings of North American Birds.* New York: Collins, 1978.

HARRISON, GEORGE, *The Backyard Birdwatcher.* New York: Simon & Schuster, 1979.

NATIONAL WILDLIFE FEDERATION, *The Gift of Birds.* Washington, D.C.: National Wildlife Federation, 1979.

ROBBINS, CHANDLER S., BERTEL BRUUN, and HERBERT S. ZIM, *Birds of North America.* Racine, Wis.: Western, 1966.

SCHUTZ, WALTER, *How to Attract, House, and Feed Birds.* New York: Macmillan, 1970.

STOKES, DONALD W., *A Guide to the Behavior of Common Birds.* Boston: Little, Brown, 1979.

children & adults

COLE, JOANNA, and JEROME WEXLER, *A Chick Hatches.* New York: Morrow, 1976.

FLANAGAN, GERALDINE LUX, *Window into a Nest.* Boston: Houghton Mifflin, 1957.

FORD, BARBARA, *How Birds Learn to Sing.* New York: Messner, 1975.

FREEDMAN, RUSSELL, *How Birds Fly.* New York: Holiday House, 1977.

FRESCHET, BERNICE, *Biography of a Buzzard.* New York: Putnam, 1976.

GANS, ROMA, *When Birds Change Their Feathers.* New York: Crowell, 1980.

GARELICK, MAY, *It's About Birds.* New York: Holt, 1979.

GOINS, ELLEN H., and JOHN L. TVETEN, *Treasures of the Nest.* New York: McKay, 1978.

MAY, JULIAN, *Why Birds Migrate.* New York: Holiday House, 1970.

PARNALL, PETER, *A Dog's Book of Birds.* New York: Scribner, 1973.

PETERSON, ROGER TORY, *The Birds.* New York: Time, 1967.

PETTIT, TED S., *Bird Feeders and Shelters You Can Make.* New York: Putnam, 1970.

ZIM, HERBERT S., and IRA N. GABRIELSON, *Birds* (Golden Nature Guide). Racine, Wis.: Western, 1956.

8
warm & furry: mammals

Of all the members of the animal kingdom, mammals are understandably popular with humans—we are mammals, too. Like humans, our mammal relatives are warm-blooded, have hair, and feed milk to their young. In fact, mammals are the only animals to have hair. Rabbits, sheep, porcupines, bats, seals, armadillos, and even some whales, all have hair in some form. Hair, especially in the form of fur, provides effective insulation that aids the warm-blooded mammals to maintain a constant body temperature. To protect themselves against the cold of winter, many mammals grow an extra heavy coat in the fall and many also add a layer of fat under the skin. When the cold is extreme and the insulating hair is not adequate, blood vessels in the skin constrict, the metabolic rate increases, and muscular action, such as shivering, takes place, all of which help to maintain the required internal temperature. In hot weather, panting, perspiring, salivating, and dilating of blood vessels in the skin cause heat loss and assist in maintaining a constant body temperature.

Most children know that kittens, puppies, calves, fawns, and human babies drink milk. Milk is the universal mammal baby food. The composition of milk varies with different species, and many humans are particularly familiar with cow's milk. All mammal milk, however, is highly nutritious.

The process of nourishing young mammals with milk means that a mammal baby must depend on its mother for a relatively long period. This also means an emphasis on parental care in mammals and a time of learning for the young mammals—kittens learn to wash, wolf pups learn to hunt, little squirrels learn how to leap and climb, and beaver kits are introduced to dam building. Could this be why mammal brains are larger and more developed than those of other animals? With humans the period of childhood dependency and education is especially long; in fact, to some school-age children, it seems endless.

Mammals are relatively large-sized animals and, therefore, unavoidably noticeable. However, their numbers are limited. There are only about 12,000 species of mammals, as compared to more than 900,000 species of insects—and new insect species are being discovered all the time. Imagine how overwhelming it might seem if mosquitoes were the size of bats, or if ants were as big as mice, or as big as dogs, or horses, or even elephants! Perhaps some enterprising math student could figure out how much, if any, free groundspace would be left if elephant-sized ants took over!

Mammals are conspicuous because of their large size, worldwide distribution, and diversity of structure. There are a number of orders in the class of mammals and great varieties of sizes and shapes between, for example, a mouse and an elephant.

The most primitive mammal order in North America is the marsupial, with one representative, the opossum (Australia's kangaroo is probably the best-known marsupial.) Mother opossum carries her babies in her pouch. When born, the babies look like embryos and are about the size of a rubber eraser on a pencil. They must find their way to the pouch, where they latch onto a nipple, and continue to grow and develop until mature enough to emerge from the pouch. Opossums are notoriously dimwitted, scarcely sharing the mammalian penchant for large brains. They have, however, a clever survival trick, known to most children as "playing possum,"

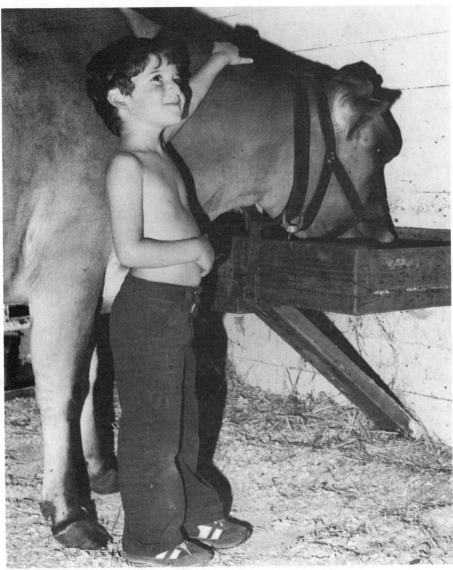

Nate and Daisy are both mammals.

Characteristics of Mammals

1. Have hair
2. Have lungs and breath oxygen
3. Young are born live
4. Have milk and feed their young
5. Are warm-blooded
6. Have backbones
7. Have four appendages

By a fifth-grader.

that is, seeming to feign death when attacked.

Shrews and moles are insectivores. Although the use of shrews as symbols for ill-tempered persons has been immortalized by Shakespeare's play, *The Taming of the Shrew*, it is a fact that shrews, and moles also, are helpful to us because they consume large numbers of insects, many of which humans consider harmful.

Bats also consume insects. How do bats catch insects if they are "as blind as bats"? They use echo-location, which works much like sonar, but they used it long before we did. Bats emit a series of high-pitched squeaks. The sound waves from the squeaks bounce off objects, such as flying insects, and these are heard by the bat's ears with such precision that the bat locates and consumes the insect in far less time than it took you to read this explanation.

Carnivores, as their name suggests, are adapted for meat-eating. Bears, raccoons, ringtails, martens, fishers, weasels, ferrets, mink, otters, wolverines, badgers, skunks, dogs, coyotes, wolves, foxes, and all members of the cat family are carnivores. Although all the carnivores eat flesh, many are actually omnivorous—they eat plants as well as meat. Bears, for instance, eat berries, nuts, fruits, and honey, and raccoons love sweet corn, as many a gardener can testify.

The largest of all the mammal orders is that of the rodents, the gnawing mammals. Rodents have two pairs of prominent, chisel-shaped, incisor teeth. These teeth grow and maintain their sharp edges continuously; they must be used frequently for gnawing or they will become too long. Mice, rats, voles, woodchucks, marmots, prairie dogs, squirrels, chipmunks, chickarees, gophers, beavers, lemmings, muskrats, and porcupines

A display of the strength of rodent teeth. A beaver has been gnawing here.

are all members of this chisel-toothed tribe. The lagomorphs, which include pikas, hares, and rabbits, have front teeth that look like those of a rodent from the front. Remember Bugs Bunny's buck teeth? If he would open his mouth wide for us, we could see that his top pair of incisors have a smaller pair just behind them, unlike rodents, which have but one top pair.

There are many hoofed mammals in North America. These animals once had five toes on each foot, but some of the toes disappeared through evolution. The earliest-known ancestor of the modern horse, eohippus, or dawn horse, had only four toes on the front feet and three on the hind. Gradually, as speed out in the open became an effective means of protection, the descendants of eohippus evolved into the modern horse, which normally has one hoof on each foot. This one hoof is a modification of the toenail of the original middle toe of that foot. The horse runs on the tips of its middle toes (an image that intrigues children) with hooves that are an adaptation for speed. Hooved animals are divided into two groups: those with an odd number of toes, such as horses and donkeys; and those with an even number of toes, such as deer and goats, which have two hooves per foot. This is an adaptation for speed, as well as for surefootedness in rough country. Children are fascinated to feel the center of a goat's hoof and to find that it feels like the rubber on sneakers.

Horses, which are fast runners, are odd-toed, hooved mammals.

The speedy, sure-footed mountain sheep are even-toed, hooved mammals.

gestive process. Point out to a child how a cow lying down in the pasture may look as if she is chewing gum. Watch closely, and you and the child will see a lump being swallowed down her throat. Keep on watching; you will see the lump of another cud come back up into her mouth, and she will resume her cud-chewing.

A number of mammals live in the sea: sea lions, seals, sea otters, manatees, dolphins, and whales. It is interesting to consider how these animals have evolved from terrestrial mammal ancestors to aquatic animals with many specializations, such as a streamlined shape and flippers. All their young nurse— even baby whales drink milk from their mothers while in the water. Baby blue whales are said to drink 130 gallons (491 l) of milk a day, gaining up to 200 pounds (90k) in weight daily. Adult blue whales weigh up to 150 tons (136 metric tonnes); they are the largest known animals, past or present.

Sometimes you may find orphaned young mammals, especially in the spring. What should be done for them? The most important first step is to ascertain if the baby is truly an orphan, because the absence of visible parents does not mean that the baby has been abandoned. A mother rabbit, for instance, leaves her babies alone as much as possible, so that she will not betray their presence to predators. Generally, she nurses them only at dawn and dusk. As a natural protection against predators, small fawns are scentless and lie still for long periods of time on the forest floor, camouflaged by their white spots. The mother is never far away. If you have any doubts as to whether the baby is

It acts as effectively, too, especially with mountain goats and sheep. Other even-toed mammals are pigs, elks, moose, caribou, antelopes, buffalo, sheep, and cattle.

All these even-toed mammals, except pigs, are grazers or browsers that chew cuds, a protective adaptation. A typical cud-chewer, a deer for example, has no top front teeth; it swallows its food whole, without taking time to chew it while it is moving about to eat and

is vulnerable to predators. Later on, the deer lies down, generally concealed from its predators by camouflage, and in relative safety takes time for chewing. The food has passed through two sections of its stomach and is brought back up into the mouth in small lumps, called cuds. The deer chews one cud at a time with its back molars, both top and bottom; when the cud is swallowed, it goes on to the third and fourth portions of its stomach for completion of the digestive process.

The fawn's white spots help to camouflage it.

orphaned, leave it and retreat. The parent will not come while you are there, unless it is capable of attacking a human, and if that is the case, you are advised to retreat even more quickly!

A baby mammal, however, that has lost its parents cannot survive alone without its mother's milk. Small, cuddly, soft, and furry babies are appealing and may make nature's "survival of the fittest" law seem overly harsh. It is tempting to try to raise the baby, and sometimes, with care and luck, it can be done. Remember, however, that federal, state, or local regulations may be in effect, such as the need for a proper permit to keep the animal. Remember that the baby's own mother's milk may differ significantly from cow's milk, and that an acceptable substitute may be hard or impossible to find. Most of all, remember that the baby—no matter how small and helpless—is a wild animal and will act in ways that its own instinct dictates. Even at an early age, the friendliest of wild babies may attempt to bite if it feels threatened. The ultimate goal in rearing a wildling should be to return it to the natural world where it belongs. Try to teach it independence as it grows and realize that it will be happier living in its natural home than in yours; wild mammals are not domestic mammals and they do not make good pets. If you have an attitude of care and concern for a young creature, beginning with the decision as to whether it was abandoned, to following the goal of returning it to its own home, your attitude will be noted by any children with you, thereby increasing their own feelings of care and responsibility for the natural world.

activities with mammals

mammal watching

It is not as easy to watch mammals as it is to watch birds. In the first place, there usually are many more bird species and individuals of different species in a given area than there are mammals. Second, mammals are secretive. If they hear, smell, or see a human, most will hide. Third, many mammals are nocturnal, a fact that obviously limits the potential number that can be seen on a field trip during the school day.

But do not feel daunted by the challenges of mammal watching. Since you know how shy mammals can be, make it a point to move quietly when you hope to see them. If you are with a group, it is a great help to have a silent signal that says *freeze*. Many groups I have been with have had rewarding long views of cottontail rabbits while standing "frozen" in place. When nearing a place where a mammal is suspected to be, approach from the downwind side (with the wind blowing toward you) to lessen the likelihood that the animal will smell you and depart before you have seen it. Also, use any available cover to hide behind; this lessens the chance that you will be spotted first by the animal.

Knowing the likely habitats to find mammals is helpful. For instance, look for woodchucks in or at the edges of fields; if you know where a beaver pond is, that is the place to watch for beavers. If you wish to see raccoons, possibly the best place is the garbage pail by your kitchen door at night, for those little masked bandits are notorious garbage thieves.

Many national, state, and local parks and wildlife refuges support a wide variety of mammals that have become tolerant of human presence. These animals can be observed and photographed far more easily than their wilder relatives. Remember, however, that these friendly looking animals are by no means tame. The innocent-appearing raccoon that approaches the picnic table for a free handout can easily deliver a severe bite to a hand that is offering to share a sandwich. Once in a state park, I went to our tent to fetch a flashlight, and, fortunately, at the entrance I saw that the tent was not unoccupied and that the occupant was distinctly black and white. My immediate reversal of direction averted catastrophe! I have often wondered since how, or if, we could have cleansed the tent of the smell of skunk.

Remember to exercise caution in the presence of wild mammals. Also, remember to take precautions if you are going into the woods during a hunting season; wear a hat or vest of fluorescent orange.

plan for night mammal watching

Materials: Flashlight, red cellophane, string, camouflage head net, camouflage clothing (optional), ladder (optional).

Procedure: By day select a tree limb that is comfortable to sit on, accessible by climbing (or ladder), and in a place suitable for night mammal watching. Tie the red cellophane with the string over the bulb end of the flashlight. When it is dark, put on the camouflage head net (and clothing), take the flashlight, and climb up to the selected tree limb. Make yourself as comfortable as possible and quietly wait and watch, using the red light from the flashlight for better visibility.

Mammals smell the air at nose level. Since air near the ground tends to rise, if you sit above the animal you decrease the possibility that it will detect you by scent. The eyes of most nocturnal animals do not respond to the red end of the spectrum; hence, the red light that enables you to see the animal is virtually unseen by the animal itself. Therefore, the animal is not frightened away by it. The author of this mammal-watching plan, a veteran mammal watcher himself, also suggests the use of a hammock. Set it up during the day, and it should provide the ultimate in night watching comfort. Another suggestion is to use a head lamp instead of an ordinary flashlight, which would leave both hands free. He also suggests "varmint callers" and other aids that hunters use to lure their quarry.

Leaving attractive bait on the ground may attract mammals. Try leaving dog or cat food, table scraps, pieces of fruit, or peanut butter spread on bread or crackers.

squirrel watching

Materials: Paper, pencils, tape recorder (optional).

Procedure: Observe squirrels closely for half an hour. Try to follow the activity and behavior of one squirrel and write down the observations. Also, observe and write down the activity and behavior of other squirrels that come into view. Use the recorder to tape any chatterings or other noises the squirrels may make.

Things that are commonplace often tend to be overlooked. Squirrels may be common, but

Get to know a squirrel.

studying them can be as revealing as studying rarer creatures. Furthermore, squirrels are generally easy to find and observe in cities, suburbs, and rural, wooded areas. How does the squirrel move? If it finds food, where does it take the food and how does it eat it? What happens when another squirrel approaches? Look closely and find ways to distinguish one squirrel from another.

Repeat the activity and make a tail study. Tree squirrels have beautiful tails, which they use for a variety of purposes. Tails are useful as balancers, as parachutes in case of falls, as umbrellas in the rain, and as blankets in the cold. These tails are also meaningful signalers. Try to decipher the message in short rapid flips, slow wavings, or whatever other signals

may be observed. Sometimes, when approaching an unknown object, a squirrel holds its tail forward along the side of its body; perhaps it feels the tail can protect it from potential danger. In any event, if the unknown object should bite, it might get only a "mouthful of tail" rather than a "body of squirrel."

watching from automobiles

Procedure: Watch for mammals while on an automobile trip and keep a record of those seen.

You can spot wild mammals from cars more often than you might think, for example, woodchucks eating grass at the side of a superhighway, or deer in fields at dusk. At night look in the light

from the car headlights for the luminous eye reflections of mammals by the side of the road. Wild carnivores are attracted to the sides of roads, since they often find animals that have been run over by cars there.

Play "mammal watch." Assign points for different kinds of mammals based on the relative ease of seeing them from an automobile in the area. For instance, dogs, cats, and cows might score 1 point each; squirrels, goats, or horses, 3 each; rabbits or deer, 10 each; and 25 for a moose. Those sitting on the same side of the car, front and back, are a team; keep score of the mammals they see and count on their side of the road. Those sitting in the middle have to choose one side or another, or possibly be the scorekeeper.

activities with mammal signs

Signs of mammals are often more frequently seen than the mammals themselves. Practice looking for these clues to mammal activity.

mammal detectives

Materials: Pencils, paper.

Procedure: Divide the group into pairs of detectives. Have each pair hunt for, record, and describe the following mammal clues: tracks, homes, food leftovers, sounds, smells, and scat (fecal droppings). Decide on a specified length of time for the hunt, and afterward compare the results to see how much information the detectives discovered about mammal activity in the area.

Animal tracks are often found in mud, by shores, or in puddles. Food leftovers may include evidences of a kill made by a carnivore, nuts that have been opened by rodents, bark gnawed by rodents, pieces of evergreen cones dropped by squirrels, or twigs nibbled by deer or rabbits. Homes are built in trees as well as on the ground. Squirrels make nests in trees, and many animals use holes in trees for dens. Woodchucks, chipmunks, gophers, foxes, and other mammals use burrows in the ground; you can find mole holes and mouse tunnels in grass.

Scat is one of the most common mammal signs and can be identified in field guides. Some people may feel squeamish about scat, but most scat left by herbivores has little or no odor. The scat of meateaters may smell; however, it is interesting because just looking at it sometimes reveals what the animal has eaten. Generally, once the children have entered into the spirit of being detectives, they accept the idea of looking for scat as clues as quite normal, with no embarrassed giggles.

Mammal smells and sounds are less common clues. You might notice the smell of skunk remaining from an earlier encounter between the skunk and another animal. Foxes have scent glands on their feet, which leave a smell that resembles a skunk's smell; sniffing at a large burrow hole can reveal whether a fox family lives there. Mammal sounds may include squirrels scolding, prairie dogs whistling, coyotes (or even wolves) howling, rodents gnawing, running noises (mice, squirrels, chipmunks), the distinctive snarls of the cat family, or the slaps of beaver tails.

who ate the "goodies"?

Materials: "Goodies" (bits of dog or cat food, pieces of fruit, peanut butter spread on bread or crackers, table scraps), flour.

Procedure: At evening time leave the "goodies" outside on a flat, bare surface. Sprinkle flour lightly on the ground around them. Go to bed, and first thing in the morning go out to see if the "goodies" have been eaten. If so, try to identify the eater by the tracks left in the flour.

how to collect animal tracks

Materials: Half-gallon milk carton, scissors, plaster of Paris, water, mixing stick or spoon, petroleum jelly, pencil.

Procedure: Find a clear animal track and make a plaster cast of it by following the directions in the illustration. When it is finished, on the bottom write the date, location, and, if known, the kind of animal that made the track.

It can be fun and informative to make a collection of track casts.

PLASTER CASTS

Extra

Use for barriers

½ gal. milk carton

Use for mixing

Put barrier around track.

Sift plaster into water. Stir it gently. Pour onto tracks & into molds. Leave it to harden.

Reproducing original or making a positive.
Place a barrier around mold. Grease mold & barrier. Pour in plaster. Separate when hard.

Positive   Negative

Drawing tracks is another way to keep track records; include measurements of the tracks themselves, as well as the distance between the prints. Photographing tracks also is effective.

activities with mammal adaptations

Animals are adapted for obtaining food, protection, and reproduction. Mountain lions have teeth for tearing flesh, and squirrels have teeth that can be used for gnawing nuts. Porcupines have quills for defense against predators, and foxes grow extra heavy coats in winter to protect themselves against the cold weather. Colts can stand and walk shortly after birth so that they can move with their mothers as they graze. Fawns have white spots to aid in camouflage. Humans have many adaptations; our opposable thumbs, for instance, give our hands a dexterity that they otherwise would not have. To show how handy this adaptation is, try taping students' thumbs to their hands with masking tape, and then have them attempt to pick things up, to write, and do other activities.

Describe cows' or horses' tails as flyswatters, or the gnawing teeth of beavers and other rodents as chisels, and the students have a clear understanding of the adaptation, as well as a trick for remembering it. Some other comparisons that appeal to children are: the tail of a fox as a nose muff; the tail of the beaver as a rudder; moles' forelegs or pigs' noses as shovels; or the tusks of a walrus as a clam rake. Children will discover many other comparisons for themselves.

invent a carnivore

Materials: Cardboard, scissors, pins, pipe cleaners, toothpicks, glue, masking tape, buttons, string, felt-tipped pens, and other small items for use in making animals.

Procedure: Have each child invent and construct a mammal that has adaptations for catching and eating other animals.

Perhaps the animal has a tail with a spearlike mechanism at the end for stabbing and holding prey. Children have good imaginations for this activity. They can invent all kinds of animals—maybe even mammals adapted for life in spaceships. Make drawings of invented animals instead of creating them with materials.

camouflaged toothpicks

Materials: Assortment of colored toothpicks.

Procedure: Scatter the toothpicks over a green lawn. Allow the children a specified time to find as many toothpicks as possible.

Camouflage is a protective device of many animals, and this activity demonstrates its effectiveness. Count the number of each color toothpick found by the students. Which colors did they find most easily? Which color was the most difficult—green perhaps?

hiding animals by camouflage

Materials: Paints or crayons, stiff paper, scissors.

Procedure: Ask the children to draw, color, and cut out animals (real or imaginary). Go outside and have half the group place their animals in plain sight, but where they will be concealed by camouflage. How many of these animals can the other half of the group find? Repeat, swapping the roles of the groups.

Which animals were the easiest to find? Which were the most difficult and why? This activity can also be done indoors.

adaptations of domestic animals

Materials: Various domestic animals.

Procedure: Study adaptations of

domestic animals to understand similar adaptations of their wild relatives.

Watching a pig push food around with its nose gives an idea of how wild pigs may use their noses as shovels. Feeling the bottoms of the hooves of goats or sheep gives an understanding of how these paired hooves help with surefootedness because of their "nonskid" bottoms. Watching a cow being milked is surely a demonstration of the effectiveness of the mammary glands from which mammals get their name. Dogs and cats are also useful to study, as well as many smaller animals such as mice, hamsters, gerbils, rabbits, and guinea pigs, all of which can be kept in a classroom.

understanding dog "talk"

Materials: A dog, pencils, paper.

Procedure: Watch the dog and notice any communication it may make. Keep a record.

Most children will already know the meaning of a wagging tail, panting, or a growl with teeth bared and ears back. Other signals to watch for are: tail between the legs (shame), hair raised up on the back of the neck (readiness to fight), sniffing around another dog (finding out if it is male or female), and front legs down on ground out front and the rear up ("let's play"). It is likely that the children will observe other kinds of signals. This activity helps children to understand that mammals have many means of communication and that communication is an important aspect of mammal behavior.

cat watching

Materials: A cat, paper, and pencils.

Procedure: Observe the cat closely

and watch for signs of its hunting instinct. Record the observations.

Cats often look like miniature tigers. Try dangling a lure in front of the cat; it may respond by stalking quietly, one foot at a time, with its tail twitching, and its eyes staring steadily at the lure. Then, suddenly, it may pounce with its claws extended. These observations show how mountain lions, lynxes, and bobcats catch their prey. Look (carefully) in the cat's mouth and notice how effectively the teeth are shaped and placed for tearing flesh.

mammals & people activities

usefulness of mammals to people

Procedure: Think of as many ways as possible that mammals are helpful to humans.

Some wild and domestic mammals provide us with meat, skins, and leather. Wool and milk are also important products. Many mammals, from elephants to oxen, help carry loads; seeing-eye dogs, sheep dogs, fox hounds, and many other dogs are trained to be useful to people. Not all mammals are helpful, however; some attack humans and their livestock, and others spread diseases and parasites.

history of domestic mammals

Materials: Books with information on the history of domestic animals.

Procedure: Study when and how certain mammals became domesticated and how they were used.

Sheep, goats, and pigs are believed to have been domesticated as far back as 9,000 years ago; cattle have been domesticated for 6,000 years, and horses for 4,000. What "old" animal friends we have!

endangered species

Materials: Books and articles on endangered species.

Procedure: Study mammals that are endangered, why they are endangered, and what can be done to protect them.

mammals in children's literature

Procedure: Have the children read, or read to the children, stories about mammals.

There is much to choose from. Very young children enjoy such stories as *The Three Bears* or *Peter Rabbit*. *Winnie-the-Pooh* and *The Wind in the Willows* are classics for slightly older children. Books by Thornton W. Burgess and Ernest Thompson Seton are widely read by children, and Rudyard Kipling's *Just So Stories* appeal to young imaginations. Many of Aesop's fables include mammals as the main characters.

noah's ark game

Materials: Paper, pencils.

Procedure: Count the number of children, divide by two, and make a list of that many animals. Write the name of each animal twice, on separate pieces of paper, and let each child choose a paper. The child reads the name of the animal, gives back the paper, and then acts the way that his or her animal behaves in order to find a mate—the other child that received the same animal name.

"The Cow" by Alexander Calder—clearly a mammal.

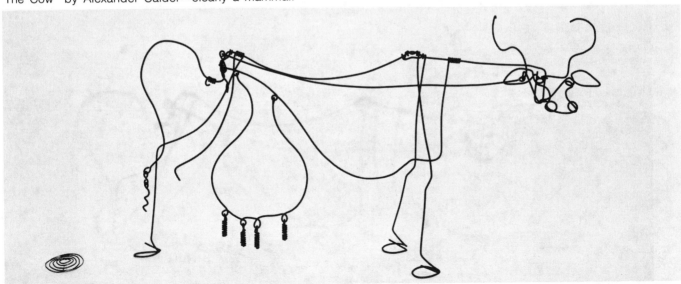

bibliography

adults

BARKALOW, FREDERICK S., JR., and MONICA SHORTEN, *The World of the Gray Squirrel*. Philadelphia: Lippincott, 1973.

BURT, WILLIAM H., and RICHARD P. GROSSENHEIDER, *A Field Guide to the Mammals*. Boston: Houghton Mifflin, 1976.

CAHALANE, VICTOR H., *Mammals of North America*. New York: Macmillan, 1961.

CARRINGTON, RICHARD, *The Mammals*, Life Nature Library. New York: Time, 1963.

HALMI, ROBERT, *In the Wilds of North America*. New York: Four Winds, 1971.

LOPEZ, BARRY HOLSTUN, *Of Wolves and Men*. New York: Scribner, 1978.

MURIE, OLAUS J., *A Field Guide to Animal Tracks*. Boston: Houghton Mifflin, 1975.

RYDEN, HOPE, *Mustangs*. New York: Viking, 1972.

VAN GELDER, RICHARD G., *Biology of Mammals*. New York: Scribner, 1969.

children & adults

ARONSKY, JIM, *Crinkleroot's Book of Animal Tracks and Wildlife Signs*. New York: Putnam, 1979.

DAY, JENIFER W., *What Is a Mammal?* Racine, Wis.: Western, 1978.

HENRY, MARGUERITE, *Mustang*. Chicago: Rand McNally, 1966.

HESS, LILO, *The Curious Raccoons*. New York: Scribner, 1968.

LaBASTILLE, ANNE, *The Opossums*. Washington, D.C.: National Wildlife Federation, 1973.

PATENT, DOROTHY HINSHAW, *Weasels, Otters, Skunks, and Their Family*. New York: Holiday House, 1973.

POLING, JAMES, *Beavers*. New York: Watts, 1976.

SCOTT, JACK DENTON, and OZZIE SWEET, *Return of the Buffalo*. New York: Putnam, 1976.

SHUTTLESWORTH, DOROTHY, *The Story of Rodents*. New York: Doubleday, 1971.

Tee-VAN, HELEN DAMROSCH, *Small Mammals Are Where You Find Them*. New York: Knopf, 1966.

WILLIAMSON, MARGARET, *The First Book of Mammals*. New York: Watts, 1957.

9

by the sea I: salt water, tides, waves & shorelines

Let's take a trip to the seashore. What shall we take? A picnic lunch, perhaps. A bathing suit if it's warm enough. A towel and an extra sweater; sometimes the ocean shore becomes colder than you might think. And wear old sneakers that you don't mind getting wet. If it is very cold, wear warm boots. Are you concerned about biting insects? Bring along an insect repellent. You may also want to bring suntan oil. Take lots of containers—plastic bags, pails, jars, and maybe a bag for trash; it's always good to leave the shore cleaner than when you came. Also, tuck in a magnifying glass, a field guide to seashore life, and perhaps a guide to shells. If there is still room, a trowel can be handy, and so can a pocketknife; remember to carry one. If you have a mask and snorkel, or a water glass for viewing, bring them. Gather the children, and you are ready to go.

The seashore always promises discoveries. Some hints, suggestions, and activities for finding and studying them are described in this chapter and in Chapter 10. There is perhaps no other environment with such a number and variety of plants and animals for children of all ages to enjoy.

salt water

How well John Masefield describes the lure of the sea in this line from his poem: "I must go down to the seas again, to the lonely sea and the sky." Something deep within all of us seems to respond to the sea. Perhaps it is a subconscious recognition that long, long ago the sea was where we belonged; along with all other life on earth, we, too, trace our evolutionary origins back to the sea.

During the hundred million or so years since life evolved from the oceans to the land, the water of the sea has become saltier. Erosion on land continually washes salts and other elements into the oceans. Near the sea the air may smell salty. Try a small taste of seawater (from an unpolluted area); it is decidedly salty. Drinking seawater will never slake a thirst because the salinity takes more water from the body than it adds to it (and, furthermore, it can make you ill.)

The salinity of seawater varies. It is lower in areas where freshwater rivers empty into the ocean, and higher where the rate of evaporation is great. Coastal waters are said to average approximately 32 parts salt per 1,000 parts water. This salt is primarily comprised of common table salt (sodium chloride), along with other salts and traces of minerals and other elements.

activities with seawater

Some of the activities with freshwater in Chapter 11 can also be done with salt water.

how salty is salt water?

Materials: Seawater, measuring cups and spoons, pot, stove.

Procedure: Measure an amount of seawater, put it in the pot, and boil it until evaporation has left the salts, a very small amount of which will be trace elements. Measure the amount of these solids. Find the ratio between these solids and the original amount of seawater.

Experiment with water from different shore areas: beach, tidepool, salt marsh, harbor, tidal estuary, and, if possible, an area some distance offshore. Make a comparative chart of the results. Repeat the experiments at different seasons. Another way to measure salinity is to use a hydrometer.

using sea salt

Materials: Salts evaporated from seawater. (Be certain the water came from a nonpolluted area.)

Procedure: If the crystals are large, break them with the back of a spoon or grind them in a blender. Then use the salt on your food as you would ordinary table salt.

Tastes good, doesn't it? Something about having made it yourself may give it a special quality. Also, it contains many trace elements that are lacking in ordinary table salt. Because of these trace elements, many health food stores sell sea salt.

freezing salt water

Materials: Salt water, freshwater, two equal-sized containers, freezer.

Procedure: Put equal amounts of salt water and freshwater into different containers. Let them sit for a few hours to ensure that their temperatures are the same. Then place the two containers in the same area of a freezer. Check them periodically.

The freshwater will freeze first. Why? What does this indicate about shore areas in winter? Try this experiment using salt water from different areas.

Sometimes, if the water is salty enough, an egg will float in seawater. Try it; children are intrigued.

tides

The tides of the ocean are caused by the gravitational pull of the moon, and to a lesser degree that of the sun. In the Atlantic Ocean, the tide rises and falls about the same amount twice daily. There are two daily tides along the Pacific coast, but the heights of these tides vary; one tide rises and falls far less than the other. The Gulf of Mexico has but one small tide a day. Wave motion dynamics and the size of the ocean basins are among the factors that cause these variations. Differences in the heights of tides may be caused by the configuration of the shore. In Canada's Bay of Fundy, which becomes narrower as the land converges on each side, the tidal wave reaches a height of 50 feet (15 m), whereas along the neighboring coast of Maine, the tide rises about 8 feet (2.4 m). The height of tides is also influenced by the relative positions of the sun and the moon. The greatest tides, known as the spring tides, occur at the times of the full and the new moon. At these times the earth and the sun are aligned; thus, the gravitational pull is greater. The smallest, or neap, tides occur about midway between the full and new moon, when the sun and the moon are at right angles to one another.

activities with tides

when will the tide be high?

Materials: Tide table for your general area.

Procedure: Use the tide table to forecast the tides. You may have to adjust for a difference between the times on the tide table and your

Morning			Afternoon	
High	2:51	**SUNDAY** **31**	High	3:17
Height	10.5		Height	10.9
Low	9:00		Low	9:34
Height	−0.8		Height	−0.8
Sunrise	5:08		Sunset	6:19
High	3:49	**MONDAY** **1**	High	4:14
Height	9.9		Height	10.6
Low	9:55		Low	10:35
Height	−0.2		Height	−0.4
Sunrise	5:10		Sunset	6:17
High	4:50	**TUESDAY** **2**	High	5:15
Height	9.4		Height	10.2
Low	10:56		Low	11:40
Height	0.3		Height	−0.1
Sunrise	5:11		Sunset	6:15
High	5:55	**WEDNESDAY** **3**	High	6:18
Height	9.0		Height	10.0
Low	11:57		Low	—
Height	0.6		Height	—
Sunrise	5:12		Sunset	6:13
High	7:01	**THURSDAY** **4**	High	7:21
Height	8.8		Height	9.9
Low	12:43		Low	1:02
Height	0.0		Height	0.8
Sunrise	5:13		Sunset	6:12
High	8:05	**FRIDAY** **5**	High	8:21
Height	8.8		Height	9.9
Low	1:46		Low	2:02
Height	0.0		Height	0.7
Sunrise	5:14		Sunset	6:10
High	8:58	**SATURDAY** **6**	High	9:14
Height	9.0		Height	10.0
Low	2:43		Low	2:56
Height	0.0		Height	0.5
Sunrise	5:15		Sunset	6:05

A tide table.

specific location. Note the time when the tide reaches its highest point and calculate the difference between that time and the time on the tide table. Then, when using the tide table, remember to adjust for the difference.

guess the tide's progress

Procedure: When the tide is coming in, have the children guess where the water will be in one hour, two hours, or longer, depending on your time schedule. On a rocky shore the guesses may have to be described in relation to specific objects; on a sandy beach the guesses can easily be marked in the sand.

Sometimes the tide rises or falls more quickly than you might think. Don't forget and leave an article in an intertidal area too long when the tide is coming in; the water may take it away. Remember the old saying, "Time and tide wait for no man."

tidal power

Procedure: Study historical uses of tidal power and the potential uses of this energy source.

"The Great Wave" by Katsushika Hokusai.

waves

Ocean waves are continually sculpturing the shores. Surf pounding on a rocky shore little by little erodes rock fragments, especially the less-resistant rock types. Beaches of smooth water-worn rocks are often found along rocky shores. Sand is made by further wave action on small rocks and pebbles. Waves on a sandy beach continue the erosion process, as well as move the sand and alter the shape and contours of the beach. The strong backwash of winter storm waves produces a beach with a steep incline; the gentler summer waves cause a gradual slope.

The action of waves is an important factor for ocean plants and animals. Seaweeds must be flexible, while animals on the shore must either maintain a firm grip or burrow in sand or mud to prevent themselves from being washed away. Shore plants above the high-tide line must be able to withstand salt spray.

activities with waves

your own bottle of waves

Materials: Bottle (a small beverage bottle with a screw-on top will do), white vinegar, salad oil, food coloring.

Procedure: Fill the bottle about one-third full of salad oil. Add drops of food coloring (blue with a touch of green is effective). Fill the rest of the bottle with vinegar. Gently rock the bottle; it is fun to watch the salad oil waves.

play tag with waves on a beach

Procedure: As a wave on a beach recedes, run down to the water's edge. As the next wave comes in, run away from it, and see who gets "caught."

If the waves seem at all threatening, try another game. Guess the highest point on the beach that water from the waves will reach in a five-minute period. Large waves are awesome; sit and watch them. Listen to them, breathe deeply, and smell them. You will feel the ocean's power in many ways.

rocky shores

Waves on a rocky coast are dramatic; be cautious about them. Also, be careful of your footing on rocky shores, which can be both rough and slippery. Wear old sneakers.

Plants and animals on rocky coasts can withstand the onslaught of surf. These are fascinating places to explore at low tide. Look on the rocks for snails and all the other animals that can cling to the exposed surface. Look under seaweed and explore tide pools. (See Chapter 10 for what you might find and ways to go about it.)

Rocky shores usually have beaches of stones and pebbles. My family calls one such area Skipping Stone Beach. Why? The beach is made almost entirely of flat, rounded stones, just right for skipping. If you are unfamiliar with them, read the following activity.

rocky shore stone & pebble activities

skipping stones

Materials: Flat, rounded stones.

Procedure: Throw a skipping stone with a sidewise twist so that it skims along the top of the water, bouncing on the water until it slows and finally sinks.

To skip a stone requires a slight knack, rather like throwing a frisbee. Who can skip a stone so that it gives the greatest number of skips on the water?

pebble number games

Materials: Rocky or pebbly beach, driftwood.

Procedure: Float the driftwood, then put stones on it. How many stones can it hold before sinking or tipping over? Who can find a piece of driftwood and gather the correct number of stones needed to sink it? Who can float out a piece of driftwood and toss stones onto it to sink it the most quickly? Lacking driftwood, who can throw a stone so that the first wave from the ripples caused by the stone reaches the shore in five seconds?

Ingenuity can help in inventing many other "number" activities with stones and water.

rock collections

Procedure: Collect pretty, odd-shaped, or otherwise interesting rocks. Indoors arrange them aesthetically on a shelf, or by categories such as color, size, shape, and texture. A little mineral or baby oil rubbed on the rocks will add to their luster.

Another way to display beach stones and pebbles is to put them in a jar and then fill the jar with water, which will bring out the luster of the pebbles. This makes a decorative souvenir of a trip to the shore. Shells or beach glass can also be included.

pebble mosaics

Materials: Variously colored pebbles, a surface for gluing them on (heavy paper, cardboard, flat piece of wood, or driftwood), model glue, pencil.

Procedure: Draw a design or picture on the flat surface. Glue the pebbles on by colors to show the design or picture.

If the backing is wood, screw in two hook-eyes so the mosaic can be hung with string or picture wire. Pebbles can also be glued onto other items such as boxes, juice cans, or the wooden edges of picture frames. What ideas can you think of? Broken bits of shell can also be used along with or instead of the pebbles.

stone animals

Materials: Stones of various shapes and sizes, model cement, and odd items such as pipe cleaners, string, yarn, buttons, toothpicks, shells, and felt-tipped pens.

Procedure: Glue stones together to create animals. The odd items are useful for noses, eyes, ears, tails, claws, and other features.

Stone people or abstract sculptures can also be made. Some rocks, or several glued together, are useful bookends. Try decorating them with acrylic paints.

sandy shores

Sandy beach ecology differs markedly from that of the rocky shore. A sandy beach does not have firm surfaces for plants and animals to cling to, no seaweed shelter for vulnerable creatures, and no tide pools as refuges. Most small animals on a sandy beach must burrow and dig to escape being carried out to sea with the backwash of waves. Notice the number of small holes on a sandy beach; they are the doorways of many creatures' homes. Look under the dried seaweed and other debris at the high-tide line; sand fleas and other small beings find homes in the protective covering. Although almost no plants can anchor themselves to live in the water off a sandy beach, plants can live at the back of a beach, and they become progressively more common as the distance from the water increases. These plants are adapted for a salty, sandy environment. They are extremely important to beaches and dunes as their roots hold the sand, thus preventing erosion. Nevertheless, sand dunes especially are fragile. Avoid walking on them as much as possible.

activities with beach sand

sand collections

Materials: Small containers (clear pill vials, plastic bags, or small jars), hand lenses.

Procedure: Collect samples of different sands. Color, size, and shape of the grains are factors to be considered.

Very young children enjoy collecting sands that are obviously different. Older children can use hand lenses to discern less obvious variations between different sands. Have them put each different-looking sand in a separate container; label each container, including name of beach, location on the beach, and date. How many different kinds of sand can be found on one beach? Why are there different sands at varied locations on the beach?

Another method for keeping a sand collection is to put a small amount of sand on a blank index card and spread it out thinly. Cover the sand with clear self-adhesive plastic.

sand grains come in different sizes

Materials: Small containers for sand, hand lens, ruler for fine measurements, masking tape, pencil, paper.

Procedure: Collect small samples of sand from varied locations, such as the edge of the water, at the high-tide line, at the back of the beach, and at the top and bottom of sand dunes. On pieces of masking tape, label the sands with name of beach, location on beach, and date. Randomly pick fifteen grains from a sample and put them on the paper. Use the hand lens and ruler to measure the grains. Calculate the average size of the fifteen grains and record the size on the label. Repeat the measuring with each sample.

Sand grains measure between 1/500 and 1/8 inches (.05 and 2 mm). The eroding agents, wind and water, drop larger particles first, carrying the lighter ones the farthest. An onshore wind, for instance, leaves coarser sand on the beach near the water, blowing the finer sand to the dunes. Explain the reasons why your sand samples may be of different-sized grains.

sand grains come in different shapes

Materials: Small containers for sand, hand lens, masking tape, pencil, paper.

Procedure: Collect and label sand samples as described in the previous activity. Take a few grains of sand from a sample. Hold them near your ear and grind them together. Rough and angular grains sound scratchy; smoother grains sound softer. Record on the labels how each sample sounds. Take five randomly picked grains from each sample. Use a hand lens and carefully sketch the shapes of the grains; use a separate piece of paper for each sample, labeling each one. Do the samples that sound scratchiest coincide with the sketches of the most angular-looking grains?

Wind and water action make sand grains angular, and wind action is far more abrasive than that of water. Chemical action of ions in solution in water leaves grains with smoother, rounder, and more polished surfaces. With this information, can you guess which erosion force has most recently

been at work with the different sand samples?

how much does sand weigh?

Materials: Scales, containers for sand, teaspoon, pencil, paper.

Procedure: Weigh one teaspoon of sand from each of the samples gathered before, or from new samples, including wet sand and dry sand from different areas. Record the results.

Can any conclusions be drawn from the variations in the weights? Correlate this information with any from other sand studies. Repeat sand studies at different seasons. The results may be interesting to compare or graph.

what minerals are in sand?

Materials: Hand lens, pencil, graph paper, sand samples.

Procedure: Use the same samples as in the previous sand studies, or take new samples. Spread about thirty grains of sand from a sample on the paper. Use the point of the pencil to separate the grains into the following categories: (1) clear and glassy in texture with uneven fractures (probably quartz); (2) milky grains of red, pink, and white hues with flat cleavage planes (probably feldspar); (3) flakes, not rounded grains, of clearish white or black shades (probably mica); (4) dark minerals (probably hornblende family); and (5) others (the commonest are jasper, garnet, amethyst, hematite, and glauconite). Put each category into a square on the graph paper. Compare the amounts in each square and estimate the percentages of each mineral in the sand sample. To check the results, repeat the process using sand from the same sample. Repeat, using

sand from another sample. How do the results compare with the first sample?

Try putting a magnet into some of the sand from a sample. If any grains stick to it, it may seem like magic to young children. Help them to figure out that the grains that stick contain iron.

Sometimes sands include ground-up shells. Test for this by putting a small amount of sand in a vial, and carefully add a weak solution of hydrochloric acid. (With young children, adult assistance is essential, as the acid can be dangerous.) If shell pieces are present, the acid will react with the calcium carbonate of the shells by giving off bubbles of carbon dioxide.

temperatures at the beach

Materials: Thermometer, paper, pencil.

Procedure: Take and record temperatures of the water, surface of the wet sand, 2 inches (5 c) under the surface of the wet sand, the surface of dry sand, 2 inches (5 c) under the dry sand surface, and 1 foot (.3 m) under the dry surface. Compare the results.

What do the results indicate for plant and animal life on the sandy shore? One time we found the temperature of the surface sand on a dune to be 110° F (43.3° C); 2 inches (5 c) below it was 82° F (27.8° C); while 1 foot (.3 m) down it was 66° F (18.8° C). A 44° (24.4° C) change in 1 short foot (.3 m) seems quite a challenge for any plant or animal.

sand castles, forts & holes to china

Materials: Anything from two hands to shovels, pails, and cups.

Procedure: Build and/or excavate as the spirit moves.

Sand castles may take as many forms as there are builders. Walls are best made by hand, but wet sand in cups, turned out carefully upside down, make nice turrets. A moat at the seaward side with a large wall behind can change the castle into a fort against rising tide. Protecting the fort from the oncoming water can be an exciting battle, even though ultimately the waves and tide always win.

"Holes to China" also lose to water. Dig a hole on a beach, and sooner or later you will find water. No matter how hard you try, you will go no deeper—walls cave in and sand continually fills in the watery bottom of the hole.

These kinds of beach activities are enjoyed by almost any age, and elemental as they may seem, they teach about waves, tides, erosion, water tables, and maybe even a few engineering principles.

drawing on sand

Procedure: Use fingers, or perhaps a stick, to draw pictures on the sand.

The sandy "drawing board" is also useful for such games as tic-tac-toe or for writing messages. Try using it as a base for sand bas-reliefs or figure out how to use it for a sundial.

sand casting crafts

Materials: Plaster of Paris, mixing container, spoon, decorative seaside items (shells, pebbles, beach glass, dried seed heads, sea lavender).

Procedure: Dig a small hole about the dimension of half a tennis ball in damp sand. Line the hole with shells, pebbles, or other items. Mix plaster of Paris according to directions (seawater may be used) and, when it is the consistency of thick cream, pour it carefully into the sand mold. Allow it to harden, take it out, turn it upside down, and you have a fine paperweight. Dried plant arrangements may be created by making a hole in the sand and lining it with appropriate items for the outside of the "vase." Pour in the mixed plaster of Paris. Allow it to harden slightly. Then arrange in it seed heads, sea lavender, or other materials for a dried arrangement. This makes an ornamental seaside memento.

There are many other possibilities for sand casting; use your own imagination. Tina, a ten-year-old who helped me with sand casting, solved a sudden problem of what to do with extra plaster; it was mixed and nearly ready to harden. She put her foot down into the sand, withdrew it quickly, and poured the extra plaster into the foot mold. Shortly thereafter, we had a casting of Tina's foot.

sand clay is fun

Materials: One cup of fine beach sand, one-half cup corn starch, one-half cup (and maybe a little more) boiling water, double boiler, stove, flat pan or cookie sheet.

Procedure: Mix the sand and

Tina adds a last sprig to her sand-casted dried arrangement.

cornstarch thoroughly in the top of the double boiler. Pour in the boiling water and mix well (but carefully, so as not to scratch the pot). Cook in double boiler briefly until mixture has thickened. Should it be too thick, add a little boiling water. Wait a moment for cooling and the clay is ready for modeling. Let your imagination guide you, and when your piece is finished, put it on a flat pan or cookie sheet in a 275°F (132.2°C) oven until dry. It can be dried without the oven, but it will take longer.

Tina and I tried some modeling together. Mine turned out to be a prosaic turtle, whereas Tina made a mouse with shells for ears, small pebbles for eyes, pieces of broom straw for whiskers, and yarn for his tail. He looked good enough to squeak!

salt marshes

The environments of salt marshes are vastly different from those of the rocky and sandy shores. The beauty of the ocean against rocks or surf on an expanse of white beach is generally undisputed. Salt marshes, however, have a more quiet beauty; creeks meander through a flat topography where vegetational changes seem gradual and possibly even dull, lacking bushes and trees. But just pause for a moment. Sit quietly. Relax. Let the gentle colors and the soft motion of the marsh grasses in the wind bring a pleasant feeling of serenity.

The peaceful scene, however, belies itself, for underneath the calm, tremendous productivity goes on. The gently moving grasses produce basic nutrients at an incredible rate. The sun's energy combined with materials washed into the marsh from land and ocean is converted by photosynthesis to sugars, starches, and ultimately plant material. When these substances decay, they become detritus (decayed organic material), which is food for innumerable marine organisms. Some salt marshes are said to produce as much as 10 tons (9 metric tonnes) of organic material per acre per year, whereas a good inland hayfield may produce only 4 tons (3.6 met-

ric tonnes). Much marine life is either directly or indirectly dependent on the fertility of salt marshes. It is reported that about two-thirds of commercially caught fish off the Atlantic and Gulf coasts, and about half of those caught off the Pacific coast, depend on the marshes and adjacent estuaries for nutrition, as well as for spawning. Salt marshes also fulfill another vital ecological role; they protect coastal areas against erosion and storm damage.

Visitors to a salt marsh should be prepared for muck and mire. Old clothes are advisable and also old sneakers, if it is warm enough. At the marsh, do not hurry; take time to watch, to smell, to feel, and to listen. Salt marshes are subtle places, and patience is required in learning to understand them.

salt marsh activities

velocity of water in a salt marsh creek

Materials: Small pieces of wood of uniform size, stop watch, pencil, paper.

Procedure: Determine the velocity of the water at various locations along the creek. Measure 5 yards (4.5 m) downstream along the creek, marking the beginning and end of the measurement. Drop a piece of wood in the stream at the

beginning. Time how long it takes for the wood to travel the five yards (4.5 m). Divide the number of seconds by 5 (or by 4.5). The answer will be the number of seconds per yard (or meter) that the water is flowing. To ensure accuracy, repeat the test at each location several times. Record the average times for each location.

This method may remind the children of how Winnie-the-Pooh used "Pooh sticks" in one of A.A. Milne's books. Do you have extra time? Let the children choose "boats" from materials at hand in the marsh and hold boat races down the 5 yard (4.5 m) course. Many ages enjoy this game, and it subtly teaches about how things float and how water flows. Repeat the water velocity tests at different tides and seasons. Do not forget that at different tides the creeks will flow in opposite directions. The flooding of the salt marsh by the incoming tide is important, as it brings with it valuable nutrients from the ocean.

water temperature & salinity in a salt marsh

Materials: Thermometer, hydrometer, pencil, paper.

Procedure: Take the water temperature, and use the hydrometer to determine water salinity at various points in the salt marsh, such as the head of a creek, specific locations along the creek, at the point where the creek reaches open water, and in several "pannes," brackish pools of water in the marsh. Water salinity may also be determined by evaporation as explained earlier in this chapter. Take the temperature of the air and on the ground at the base of the salt marsh grass. Record all the data.

Repeat these salt marsh studies at different tides and seasons. Study the information about salinity, temperature, and creek flow velocity (if that activity has been done), and perhaps make a graph using all the data. It may give clues about problems that plants and animals face living in a salt marsh, as well as clues about salt marsh ecology. Drought over several seasons can cause increased salinity in the marsh, which can be fatal to some species of animals. Yet, heavy rainfalls may dilute the salt marsh water to the point that other species suffer.

historical value of salt marshes

Materials: Books with information on Indians' and colonists' uses of salt marshes.

Procedure: Study historical uses of salt marshes by the Indians and the colonists.

Indians found that salt marshes offered abundant supplies of food, including birds and mammals that also dined on marsh inhabitants. The Indians used surplus fish, along with salt marsh seaweed, as fertilizer for crops. Do you remember reading how the Indians taught the Pilgrims to fertilize corn by putting a fish at the bottom of each hole when sowing the seeds? Salt marsh hay was another very important product from salt marshes. Have the children research other historical uses of salt marshes and their significance to the communities involved.

a salt marsh debate

Materials: Reference materials (books, pamphlets, newspaper, and magazine articles) with information on salt marsh ecology, modern fishing and shellfishing practices, and industrial building expansion.

Procedure: Have the children study how salt marshes contribute to the functioning of saltwater ecosystems and the resulting significance to commerical fishing and

shellfishing. Also, have them do research on how salt marshes act as buffers against erosion, protecting properties against storm damage. Then divide the children into three groups: conservationists, fishermen, and builders. If interviews are possible, have the first group interview salt marsh conservationists; the next interview fishermen; and the last interview industrial builders. Also, have them use the reference materials on modern fishing and industrial building.

Stage a debate in which the conservationists try to convince the fishermen that salt marshes miles away may influence the volume of their catch as well as the sizes of individual fish or shellfish. The conservationists try to explain to the builders that salt marshes should not be filled in, but that they should be protected. Fishermen and builders explain their points of view on the issues. Perhaps one builder may want to put up a much-needed hospital on land that is partially salt marsh. Try to have fair representations for all sides of the issues of ecological needs versus pressing human needs.

harbors

Most major coastal cities in the world are situated on harbors. Transportation by boat has been a major factor in human societies and continues to be important, although to a lesser degree because of competition from planes, trains, trucks, buses, and cars. A visit to an urban harbor, however, will still show many, many boats: freighters, tugs, fishing boats, coast guard boats, and pleasure craft. The smell of the sea is there too,

although perhaps somewhat mitigated by exhaust fumes and other pollutants. An urban harbor is both nostalgic and exciting. The boats themselves suggest stories of trips on the open ocean. The fish piers testify to the bounty of the sea, which humans have enjoyed since earliest days. And the gulls and the ocean water are welcome sights at the edge of a busy city.

harbor activities

Explore a harbor with children.

history of a harbor

Materials: Reference materials including historical information on the harbor.

Procedure: Study the history of your area's harbor. Find out the main articles of trade during the harbor's history and changes as they developed. Compare past and present figures on numbers of boats using the harbor, amount of trade conducted, or tons of fish brought in.

This is a project that can lead in

There is always something of interest in an urban harbor.

many directions: economics of trade, political history (as evidenced by the Boston Tea Party and the uses of harbors by naval boats during times of war), or social history (what items did the early settlers have shipped by boat from the Old World?). Perhaps interviews can be arranged with some of the "old-timers" who can give personal anecdotes about happenings in the harbor many

years ago. Whatever the history of the harbor, much of it has been dictated by the forces of the ocean.

influences on harbor ecology

Materials: Map of city and harbor, tide table, hydrometer, appropriate reference materials.

Procedure: Study the map of the

city and the harbor. Is the harbor protected? Will storm waves and winds be held to a minimum? Find out from the tide table the height of the tides; how much water flows in and out daily? Measure the salinity of the water with the hydrometer. (Water salinity may also be determined by evaporation, as explained earlier in this chapter.) Find out from reference materials where the city's sewer system discharges. Into the harbor? What other city wastes might be finding their way into the harbor?

Waves, tidal flow, salinity, and pollutants from sewage or other wastes can affect plant and animal life in the harbor. What changes may these factors have caused in your city's harbor?

harbor plant & animal life

Procedure: Look on pilings under piers and other places to see what kind of marine plants and animals you can find. Keep a list; if you do not know a name, describe or sketch the plant or animal. If possible, compare your findings with life at a nearby coastal area free from the factors that may influence life in the harbor.

bibliography

adults

AMOS, WILLIAM A., *The Life of the Seashore.* New York: McGraw-Hill, 1966.

BERRILL, N.J., and JACQUELYN BERRILL, *1001 Questions Answered about the Seashore.* New York: Dover, 1976.

CARSON, RACHEL L., *The Edge of the Sea.* Boston: Houghton Mifflin, 1955.

———, *The Sea Around Us.* New York: Oxford University Press, 1961.

KAUFMAN, WALLACE, and ORRIN PIL-

KEY, *The Beaches Are Moving.* New York: Doubleday, 1979.

KOPPER, PHILLIP, *The Wild Edge.* New York: Quadrangle, 1979.

TEAL, JOHN, and MILDRED TEAL, *Life and Death of the Salt Marsh.* New York: Audubon/Ballantine, 1969.

WYLIE, FRANCIS E., *Tides and the Pull of the Moon.* Brattleboro, Vt.: Stephen Green, 1979.

children & adults

BLASSINGAME, WYATT, *The First Book of the Seashore.* New York: Watts, 1964.

CARTWRIGHT, SALLY, *Sand.* New York: Coward-McCann, 1975.

———, *The Tide.* New York: Coward-McCann, 1970.

CLEMENS, ELIZABETH, *Waves, Tides and Currents.* New York: Knopf, 1967.

ENGEL, LEONARD, *The Sea.* New York: Time, 1967.

GREENHOOD, DAVID, *Watch the Tides.* New York: Holiday House, 1961.

LAMBERT, DAVID, *Sea Shore.* New York: Warick, 1977.

10

by the sea II: sea plants & animals

Have you ever wished you could see a sea serpent? Long, long ago mariners used to report finding many kinds of these fabulous beasts with dragonlike heads, bodies long and sinuous, lashing tails, strange fins or webbed feet, and covered all over with great, green scales. Nowadays we generally disclaim such fantastic beings, but imaginative minds can restore them, in spirit at least. Try it sometime.

Although lacking in those sea serpents of long ago, the oceans contain many creatures almost as strange. Barnacles live by standing on their heads, and starfish feed by sending their stomachs out to their food, rather than the other way around. There are strange plants, too. One seaweed is punctured all over with holes, and one green alga in long strands looks as if it should be the hair of a mermaid.

plankton

The plankton community includes the myriad forms of life drifting with the ocean's currents and tides, from unicellular plants and animals to the large jellyfish. Important members of this community are the diatoms. These bizarre-shaped microscopic plants use energy from the sun and minerals from the water to make food through the process of photosynthesis. Diatoms constitute the basic green pastures of the sea and support many microscopic plankton animals, which in turn are consumed by larger creatures. This food chain continues with all marine life, and when we eat an ocean fish for dinner, we too are eating plankton, at least indirectly.

The abundance of plankton is seasonal. During the winter plankton supplies diminish. Spring, however, brings a renewal of the growth of plant plankton, increasing the water's fertility. Green indicates vegetation in the sea as well as on the land. Ocean waters that are green are far richer in nutrients than those that are clear blue. Also, waters that are cold contain more oxygen than warmer waters, and thus are able to support more animal life.

activities with plankton

plankton net

Materials: Fine meshed conical net of silk, muslin, or nylon with a collecting jar at the end of it, hand lens, boat (optional), microscope (optional).

Procedure: Draw the plankton net through the water until you can see a slime (usually greenish). Look for individual plants and animals in the slime with the hand lens or microscope.

A crude plankton net made out of an old sheet and a bent wire coat hanger (it resembled an overgrown baker's hat) gave me my first face-to-face contact with the green slime of the plankton community—exciting, as I had never seen it before.

phosphorescence

Procedure: At night go to the shore to look for phosphorescence. Moving the water with an oar or stick, or traveling in a boat, may cause flashes of phosphorescent light.

Noctiluca, a one-celled plankton organism, is one of the most common producers of phosphorescence. Other plankton beings are also capable of producing this "cold light"; seeing this light is another way of verifying the presence of the normally unseen plankton.

the role of plankton in food chains

Materials: Reference materials about ocean food chains.

Procedure: Study food chains from plankton to the larger animals of the sea and calculate the amount of plankton needed to support some of these animals.

It is reported that for one species of whale, *four hundred billion* diatoms are required to sustain a medium-sized individual for a few hours. The whale makes a meal of a ton of herring, about 5,000 of these fish. Each of these herring may have about 6,500 small crustaceans in its stomach, and each of these small crustaceans may contain 130,000 diatoms. What an opportunity for math problems!

The gull—for many a symbol of life by the sea.

seaside plants

Seaside plants include those growing on shores as well as those growing in water. The water plants are seaweeds, which are marine algae. Seaweeds tend to grow in separate zones. The highest zone of the rocky shore where salt spray easily reaches the plants is the area of the blue-green algae, which look like a black crust. The next zone is where the green algae find their niches, and below that the brown rockweeds take over. Deeper still is the zone of Irish moss and other red algae. Then the kelp zone extends from the low-tide mark to deep water. Seaweeds have no roots; they anchor themselves with holdfasts. Kelp holdfasts offer protection for a variety of creatures not commonly seen elsewhere, such as brittle stars, intriguing relatives of the starfish.

Seaweeds have many interesting adaptations for living in water and coping with tides and waves. Many have air bladders, which help them to float when submerged. Most are very flexible, a necessity for withstanding surf or strong tidal currents. Many are divided into a number of fronds, which further increases their flexibility. One kelp's fronds are punctured with holes, and the species is aptly called sea colander. The algin of brown seaweeds can absorb water, or dry up without deteriorating. Therefore, they are well suited for life in the intertidal zone, which is exposed as the tide goes out. At low tide, the brown rockweeds lie out on the rocks, providing a shielding blanket of moisture for multitudes of small creatures. Just as trees on land can be called nature's motels and restaurants, so can the seaweeds of the ocean. They offer shelter when the tide is out; when the tide is in, they provide a perfect protective forest for small creatures. Sea urchins and many sea snails feed on various seaweeds. The great kelp beds of the Pacific shore are the well-known homes and bedding for sea otters. Sargassum or gulfweed is host to many kinds of creatures, a number of which live permanently in this weed. Some kinds of fish lay their eggs in sargassum which then serves as a nursery for the young. Unlike other seaweeds,

and the force of storm waves. The list does not indicate an easy life! However, no one species of plant endures all of these harsh environmental conditions. For instance, glasswort easily withstands inundation at high tide, but could not live in the dryer areas where beach peas may be found. Because seawater's salinity draws water out of plants, glasswort has thickened stems, which, like those of the cactus, help to keep moisture in. Other shore plants have leaves that are rolled, folded, thickened, waxy, or hairy. These are all adaptations for maintaining a moisture level in a salty environment.

Many seaside plants, especially grasses on dunes, protect their habitat against erosion; their roots hold and stabilize soil and sand. Respect the work such plants are doing by leaving them undisturbed and by walking as little as possible on sand dunes.

activities with seaside plants

seaweed prints

Materials: Seaweed, shallow pan, freshwater or seawater, heavy paper, wax paper or plastic film, old newspapers, waterproof marking pen.

Procedure: Fill the pan with water and put the paper in the pan. Then place the seaweed on top of the paper and carefully lift out paper and seaweed. An alternative method is to put the paper in an empty pan, place the seaweed on top, and then, using water from a bulb syringe, arrange the seaweed in a natural configuration. With either method, lay the wet paper on several thicknesses of newspaper. Cover the paper and seaweed with wax paper or thin plastic film and use the waterproof

sargassum does not attach itself, but floats freely.

Eelgrass also provides a safe haven for many animals, and innumerable spiral tube worms live in their coiled coverings directly on the surfaces of the long filamentous leaves of the grass. Although eelgrass may look like a seaweed, it is not. It is one of the few flower-

ing plants that can live in the ocean.

Shore plants, which grow near the ocean, have their own special adaptations to withstand occasional inundation by salt water, salt spray, glaring sun, intense heat, evaporation-causing winds, abrasion of shifting sands, lack of moisture, rocky and sandy soils,

Dune grasses protect against erosion.

Algae prints. The wreath is an artistic creation of Victorian times. Try making one, and perhaps you can bring back an old art.

Notice the air bladders in the seaweed by these crabs.

pen to note on the wax paper or plastic film the date, the location where the seaweed was found, and the type of seaweed, if known. Repeat this process with other seaweeds, placing them on top of the first. Next, put the whole pile in a flat place with some weight on top. (I just slip mine under a rug.) Change the newspapers daily until the seaweed is dry.

These seaweed prints lend themselves to many purposes. They are often decorative enough to frame and hang on a wall. They can be used for letter paper, bookmarks, or place mats. The mucilage of the seaweed usually bonds it to the paper, but clear self-adhesive plastic can be put over the print, if necessary, to keep it in place. A serious collector can make a seaweed herbarium. Label all specimens carefully, including such details as the position of the plant in relation to mean low tide, precise location, and details of the habitat, as well as date and name of seaweed.

seaweed collection

Materials: Plastic bags, pail, paper, pencil, bottles or jars with screw tops.

Procedure: Collect different seaweeds in the bags; take typical pieces of each different kind or, if the seaweed is small, take the entire plant. Try to include samples from green, brown, and red seaweeds. Fill the pail with seawater. After collecting, put each different seaweed in a bottle or jar and fill it with seawater. Label each with location where seaweed was found, date, and the kind of seaweed. Discard the seaweeds when the study is completed, as they will begin to disintegrate if kept too long.

If some of the seaweeds are unknown, have the collectors identify them in a field guide. Also, have them add on the labels any other pertinent information they may find. Sketching always increases observation. Make a seaweed picture garden; label and

give information about each kind. Seaweeds also can be collected, dried, and later reconstituted by soaking them in water, which is a useful alternative if it is not possible to take your group to the shore. Repeat seaweed collecting during the year to note seasonal changes in the seaweeds.

drying seaweeds

Procedure: Arrange seaweeds on a suitable surface and put them in a warm place until dry.

Put the seaweeds on anything from trays and cookie sheets to screening. Large kelp can be hung over railings or on laundry lines. Suitable warm places are in the sun, a hot attic, or a slightly warm oven. (Sometimes I have used a wicker laundry basket, put over a hot water heater. It works well, although some family members comment about the smell.)

As already mentioned above, dried seaweeds can be soaked in water and used for study. Add salt to the water for the seaweeds in the amount of 3½ percent of the weight of the water. Keep them in a cool place or in the refrigerator and they will last longer.

Dried rockweed has bladders that are fun to pop; try them! Dried Irish moss, a seaweed found in tide pools and other rocky low tide areas, can be used in making pudding. You can find the recipe for this seaside dessert by looking in the index under Irish moss pudding.

our uses of seaweed

Materials: Appropriate reference books and articles on seaweed.

Procedure: Research past and present uses of seaweeds.

Seaweed pudding is not the only use for the emulsifying property of Irish moss. This material, known as carragheen, has become commercially important. Irish moss and other seaweeds containing carragheen are harvested; the carragheen is extracted and used in many items from chocolate milk and ice cream to toothpaste. Algin, another seaweed product, is also used commercially. What other chemicals and products of seaweed are being used? Which seaweeds can be eaten as vegetables in their own right or used for condiments? Japanese cooking often calls for seaweeds. Is it possible that we may become more dependent on seaweeds as a source of food? Why? Seaweeds have also been used for fertilizer. Should we make more use of them for fertilizer in the future?

make a simple water glass for viewing sea life

Materials: Large tin can or pipe (number 10 tin can open at both ends, or a one- to three-foot (.3–.9m) length of stove, ventilating, or heating system pipe), waterproof tape, clear, strong plastic bag (large enough to go over pipe), two large elastic bands.

Procedure: Put waterproof tape around top and bottom edges of can or pipe. Slip plastic bag over one end. Pull bag taut and hold it firmly in place with elastic bands; put one around can or pipe at top end of bag and put the other an inch or so from the covered end of can or pipe.

A water glass allows clear viewing in water in the same way that a face mask does. It is useful for viewing seaweed and other sea life underwater. For viewing from a boat, use a long water glass; otherwise the short one will do. An even simpler version of a water glass can be made using a frozen juice can open at both ends, plastic wrap, and rubber bands. I was introduced to this version by a class of kindergarteners on a field trip; each child was carrying the little water glass made at school.

activities with driftwood

Many shores abound with twisted, gnarled, or smooth pieces of driftwood; they are scoured by the sea and bleached into gentle silvery tones by the sun. Some pieces are ready-made fantastic creatures of abstract sculptures. Others lend themselves to a variety of crafts.

driftwood mobile

Materials: Driftwood pieces, fine wire or string, small drill.

Procedure: Plan the mobile so that the longer pieces will be near the top and the smaller pieces near the bottom. Drill holes in the driftwood where required for hanging. Hang the pieces carefully so that they will balance.

candle holders, lamps & vases of driftwood

Materials: Pieces of driftwood, small metal candle holders, electric sockets and cords for lamps, suitable jars for vases, household cement.

Procedure: Small metal candle holders are available at craft shops and can be attached to pieces of driftwood for attractive holders. To make lamps, attach the electric sockets to the wood; this may necessitate some drilling and possibly a rod to hold the socket. Be certain that the driftwood base is firm when making candle holders and lamps, so they will not be tippy. Some driftwood may have natural holes or crevasses where jars can be put; glue the jar to the driftwood, if possible. Collect a bouquet of flowers, arrange them in the jar, add water, and enjoy your creation. A flower pot may be substituted for the jar. Put a plant in the pot and you will have a unique planter.

driftwood collages

Materials: Pieces of driftwood, household cement, beachcombing "treasures" (shells, feathers, dried seaweed, bleached bones, pebbles, dried grasses, sand).

Procedure: Follow your own imagination and creative instincts. Glue the treasures onto the driftwood to make decorative seaside collages.

seaside animals & activities

Marine animal life is fascinating and richly varied. Most shore animals await your discovery, especially at low tide. Progging, which is poking, prodding, and peeking about for creatures in the intertidal area, can be mucky on rocky shores or in salt marshes. Be prepared to plunge right in, so to speak; wear old clothes, especially old sneakers (in my family they are known as clamming sneakers).

Take along plastic bags and plenty of waterproof containers, and be prepared for a safari with discoveries that almost always bring something new, even to inveterate proggers. Children, of course, are natural proggers, being generally undaunted by a little mud, and possessing boundless curiosity.

The waterproof containers can be used as temporary aquariums. Put seawater in them and be careful that the water does not become too warm. At the shore such an aquarium can be placed in shallow seawater or in wet sand; indoors, put the aquarium in the refrigerator. Place small animals in the aquarium, being careful not to overcrowd them. Then, close observation of the animals will allow intimate views of their structure, behavior, and adaptations, and is an entrance into the private worlds of these beings, overlooked by those who hurry on by. After completing observations in the temporary aquarium, always return the animals to their own habitats as soon as possible. However insignificant they may appear to us, they deserve our respect and care. (It is possible to set up permanent saltwater aquariums, but considerable care in establishment and maintenance is needed. A book with information on permanent aquariums is included in this chapter's bibliography.)

Tide pools are much like large aquariums, waiting for you to look into them. A tide pool is an area where water has been caught in a rocky depression as the tide goes out. Many plants and animals normally inhabit tide pools, such as small seaweeds, sponges, sea anemones, snails, minnows, barnacles, and small crustaceans. Other animals, such as large crustaceans and fish, are sometimes inadvertently trapped as the water recedes. Although tide pools provide a safe haven for these creatures, they can

Children are generally undaunted by a little mud!

also be dangerous. The intense summer sun can overheat tide pools. Also, the sun can evaporate the water, causing what is left to be highly saline. Rain can dilute the water, causing low salinity. Any of these variations can harm or kill the inhabitants of the pool. The activities with water salinity and temperature in Chapter 9 can be adapted for doing with tide pools.

Look under seaweeds at low tide. Get right down and lift up the weed; smell the wet seaweedy smell, listen for tiny creatures scuttling about, and watch. The seaweed is a protective host for many animals. Some may be the same as those found in tide pools, but there also may be larger crabs, a greater variety of snails, and starfish. If there is any kelp at the edge of the low water, pull up a

Get right down and lift up the seaweed.

piece. Very often the holdfast of the kelp will prove to be a home and a safe haven for several animals. Look for brittle stars, the delicate starfish relatives, sea slugs, and whatever other creatures may be hiding there. Lower down in the water at low tide, you can find sea urchins and sand dollars.

Beaches that are usually crowded with summer visitors are often

cleaned up, so animal life there is scarcer than it might otherwise be. But pick up a piece of dry seaweed on a beach; you will find it hopping with sand fleas. Salt marshes abound with animal life, especially snails, including the large whelks, numerous other mollusks, and crabs. There is no shore area that is devoid of life, although pollution can drastically reduce populations and eliminate some species entirely.

sponges

Sponges are plentiful, both in varieties and numbers, in tropical waters, but only a few species are found in colder areas. Since sponges do not move, it is easy to overlook them; some look like an encrusting mass over a rock. The Crumb of Bread sponge, for instance, looks like a rough green mat, but a close observation reveals holes resembling volcano craters. If picked up and rubbed between the fingers, this particular sponge will crumble like bread, as its name indicates. Cells from the small pieces that fall into the water may regroup to form a new sponge. (Be warned—most sponges have a bad smell.)

how do sponges eat?

Materials: A living sponge, temporary aquarium with seawater, food coloring, medicine dropper.

Procedure: Put the sponge into the aquarium. Take a small amount of food coloring into the medicine dropper and carefully deposit drops of coloring at several points close to the outside surface of the sponge. Watch to see what happens.

Almost immediately, streams of colored water will emerge from tiny pores in other areas of the

sponge, seemingly by magic. This indicates how actively the sponge filters water through its pores in order to feed on microscopic organisms in the water. Some sponges filter a ton of water to gain an ounce of body weight.

jellyfish & sea anemones

Jellyfish and sea anemones are close relatives; they belong to the coelenterate phylum, as do corals. Jellyfish are often found stranded on beaches, looking like globular discs of jelly. In the water they appear umbrellalike as they drift with currents, undulating slightly as they go. Like all coelenterates, they possess stinging tentacles, so be careful of them. Red jellyfish and a close cousin, the Portuguese man-of-war, are particularly toxic to people.

Jellyfish are relatively large and easily seen. The smaller sea anemones, however, are not easy to spot, unless you take the trouble to look for them. Look for something on a rock below the water's surface that has the appearance of a flower with a delicate ring of petals atop a short stalk. If you think you have found one, you can test it by touching it gently with a stick. If the petals withdraw in a magical vanishing act and the flower is transformed into looking like a small tin can, it is a sea anemone; but do not worry, the "flower" will bloom again. Doesn't its name describe it well?

feed a sea anemone

Materials: Sea anemone, temporary aquarium with seawater, small creature for the sea anemone to eat (sea worm, small crustacean), tweezers.

Procedure: Put the sea anemone into the aquarium. (Handle this

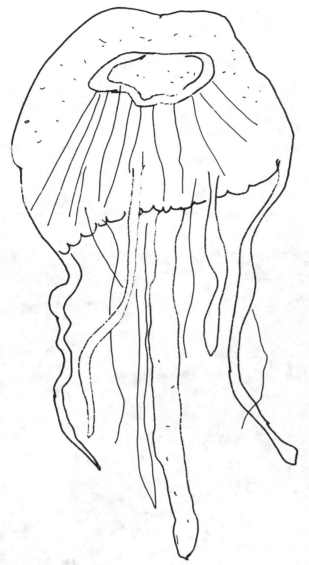

Jellyfish by a fifth-grader.

is colored with iridescent blues and greens and can grow to 1 foot (.3 m) or more in length, which can make it somewhat disconcerting—dispelling its beauty, if one comes upon it all of a sudden. It is a cousin to the earthworm, and, like its cousin, is often used for bait in fishing. However, the clam worm has hefty "jaws" and can bite; handle it cautiously. With caution, put a clam worm in an aquarium and watch how it swims with graceful undulations, sparkling in iridescence. This is why the clam worm has the scientific name of nereis, after the Nereids of Greek mythology, who were sea nymphs.

straining for worms

Materials: Strainer, temporary aquarium with seawater, seashore field guide (optional).

Procedure: Put mud or fine sand from an intertidal zone into the strainer. Pull the strainer back and forth in the water, straining out the mud or sand. Any worms that are present, and perhaps other small beings, will be caught in the strainer. Put them into the aquarium to observe them. Try identifying them with the field guide.

animal with care, or, if possible, do this activity with the sea anemone in place where it was found.) Wait for it to open up, showing off its flowery appearance. Hold the small creature near the anemone's tentacles with the tweezers, and watch.

The innocent-looking petals are in reality tentacles, armed with small stinging cells to aid the animal in catching its food. You may see the anemone paralyze the small creature with its stinging cells and move its prey to its mouth in the center of the ring of tentacles in order to consume it.

sea worms

The sand, silt, mud, and ooze on the bottoms of shallow shore areas have high populations of numerous species of worms, particularly flatworms, roundworms, and segmented worms. Look underneath a rock and you may find some, and possibly other kinds of animals. Watch them and try to identify them. When you are through, replace the rock carefully so as not to further disturb the underneath-dwellers. An especially beautiful sea worm is the clam worm, often found in mud flats. It

mollusks

The beautiful shells we admire at the shore are all remnants of mollusks, the soft-bodied animals that live protected by one or two shells. One of the most common mollusks seen on shores is the snail, a type of mollusk that includes moon snails, periwinkles, whelks, and conchs. Moon snails are round, squat, and often a few inches in width. You may be familiar with their egg mass that is sometimes seen on shores; it looks like a round collar of sand or the end of a "plumber's helper." Moon snails

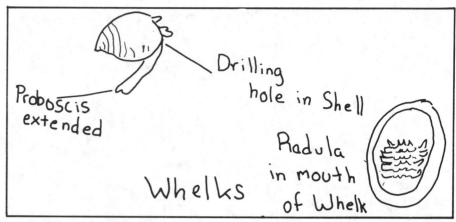

By a fifth-grader.

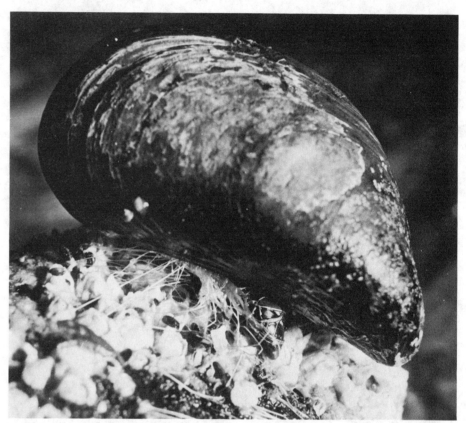

Notice the byssal threads that this mussel is using to attach itself to the rock.

are carnivorous and have a specialized rasping mouth part that enables them to drill holes in other mollusks to enjoy a shellfish meal. Whelks and conchs feed in the same manner. Periwinkles, which look like small moon snails, are vegetarians. They travel over shore areas at the traditional snail's pace, munching plant material as they

go, leaving a small cleared trail behind that marks their progress.

Bivalves—mollusks with two shells—are common. Mussels, which are blue-black bivalves, are generally found in large colonies. They may live in quiet water, but they are also able to live on exposed rocky areas where waves

and currents are strong. Mussels anchor themselves firmly in place by secreting strong adhesive strands, called byssal threads; try picking up some mussels and you will understand. On the other hand, scallops are unattached and can move rapidly. They open their shells, then snap them shut with such a force that the animal is

Hold a whelk shell up to your ear, and you may hear the sound of the ocean.

colors. Some sea slugs have stinging cells and an unpleasant odor, which protect them from predators, as if to make up for their lost shells. If you find some sea slugs, handle them cautiously and put them into an aquarium so that you can admire their beauty.

There are many crafts that can be done with mollusk shells; some are described later in this chapter. There also are activities that involve the animals themselves; a few of these follow. But first a warning: many communities have strict regulations about gathering shellfish. Check local ordinances before removing any shellfish from the shore, even temporarily.

molluskan mathematics

Materials: Paper, pencils.

Procedure: Study the population of a species of mollusk, such as snails or mussels. First, determine the boundaries of the area. Then count the number of the mollusks in a small sample area. Estimate how many times the small area fits into the total area. Multiply that number by the number of the mollusks in the small area. The sum will be an estimate of the total number of the mollusks in the area.

This kind of population study works with many other kinds of animals. It might be interesting to estimate the number of sand fleas in the dried seaweed on a beach, or the number of barnacles on the rocks of a particular area. Such population studies offer many opportunities for working with numbers.

what is a filter feeder?

Materials: Mussels, temporary aquarium with seawater, food coloring, medicine dropper.

Procedure: Put the mussels into the

moved by a kind of jet propulsion. A razor clam can move with surprising rapidity through sand or mud by means of a "foot" that it extrudes, but other clams, along with oysters and other bivalves are relatively sedentary.

Squid and octopi are mollusks that do not have shells. They are seldom seen near the shore, unlike another shell-less mollusk, the sea slug, which is easily found. Sea slugs are sea snails that have lost their shells during an early stage of development. They resemble slugs, their land-dwelling cousins, but they generally are far more beautiful, often covered with fleshy projections of fantastic shapes and aquarium, and watch to see if they anchor themselves onto the bottom or sides with their byssal threads. Carefully put drops of food coloring near them, and observe what happens.

Can you see the colored water being taken into the mussel and then being extruded? Mussels, along with all other bivalves, are filtered feeders. They take in seawater and filter out microscopic organisms for food, extruding the leftover water.

scallop jet propulsion

Materials: Scallop, temporary aquarium with seawater.

Procedure: Put the scallop into the aquarium. Wait until it opens up and shows its twinkling blue eyes in the mantle at the edges of the shells. Then put a stick or some other object in front of the scallop. The scallop's blue eyes will perceive the stick, and the animal will snap its shells shut, moving back with jet-propelled force.

It is likely that the scallop will demonstrate its jet propulsion talent as you try to catch it. Good luck!

sing an octopus song

This activity has nothing to do with a living octopus and is included for a change of pace. To the tune of "Skip to My Lou," sing the following words.

Eight long arms, two big eyes,
Salty tears when he cries,
Lives way down on the bottom of the sea.
Who can guess what he can be?

Watch him wiggle, see him slide;
You can't catch him if you tried;
Toss him a fish so he won't fuss;
He's a baby octopus!

Author unknown

crustaceans & two relatives

There are many varieties of crustaceans in the ocean; some we know well, such as crabs, shrimp, and lobsters. Do you know how to catch a crab? You must be quick and grab it carefully by the shell, holding onto its sides where it is the widest, behind the two large, pinching claws. Held in this way, it cannot easily pinch you. Respect the crab's capacity for self-defense and be sure that everyone with you does also. Crab's eyes are on stalks, which is handy for them because they can turn them in any direction, like periscopes. Some crabs can only crawl along the bottom, but a few can swim as well. Swimming crabs have hindmost pairs of legs that are shaped like paddles. Hermit crabs have no shells of their own. They use deserted snail shells and, like turtles, they carry their shelters with them.

Other familiar crustaceans are barnacles. The common acorn barnacles look like tiny white-plated mountain peaks, and they tend to live in large colonies, firmly anchored to a rock, a wharf piling, an old shell, or a boat bottom. As is true with most marine invertebrates, barnacles pass through larval stages when young. Baby barnacles look nothing like their parents. Furthermore, they float freely, adding to the number of the plankton population, until it becomes time to settle down. These young barnacles seem to be attracted to areas already colonized by others of their species. Although I have never seen it happen, it must be a literal head-on plunge, for the young barnacle cements the top of its head to the surface where it will spend the rest of its life. Then it secretes the calcereous plates that make its fine protective home, and it has settled down for good.

It is fascinating to watch barnacles feed because they swish food into their mouths with their feet! Barnacles are filter feeders. They open up their small top white plates and use their feathery feet to move water into their bodies, where microorganisms are filtered out for the animal to use as food.

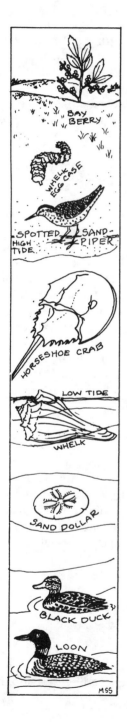

BAY BERRY

WHELK EGG CASE

SPOTTED SANDPIPER
HIGH TIDE

HORSESHOE CRAB

LOW TIDE

WHELK

SAND DOLLAR

BLACK DUCK

LOON

MSS

Put a rock with some barnacles in an aquarium, or watch some in the water by the shore, and you can see them feeding. You will notice, however, that those that are above the water level remain tightly closed. Above or below the water, barnacles can cause bad cuts to bare feet or to anyone who falls on them. Be careful. Barnacles also can cause economic problems because they grow readily on ship bottoms and are costly to remove.

Many crustaceans are tiny. You can often recognize them by the way they swim, using lots of legs in a frenetic manner. Look for small crustaceans in tide pools and underneath seaweed. Gribbles are shaped like sow bugs, which are small terrestrial crustaceans; others are shaped like tiny shrimps. Catch some and observe them for a while in an aquarium.

Have you ever seen horseshoe crabs? These are venerable seashore creatures, relatives of crustaceans. They are often called living fossils because they have persisted virtually unchanged through geologic ages. Their nearest relatives today are spiders and scorpions. Do not be put off by the somewhat threatening appearance of horseshoe crabs, for they are quite benign. They can eat very young shellfish, but are unaggressive toward larger animals. Their sharp, pointed tails are not intended to serve as weapons (although they can cause harm if stepped on), but are rather a means of righting themselves, if they become turned upside down.

Sometimes on the surface of tide pools you may see a cluster of tiny, dark creatures. These are a variety of springtails, which are primitive insects. They are blue-black in color and wingless. They have a thick coating of hair (in proportion to their minute size) that carries air and is said to enable them to breathe underwater for several days, if necessary. Often they congregate in large groups on the surface of the water, and they are especially worthy of note because there are very few insects that live in salt water.

invite a crab to dinner

Materials: Crab, temporary aquarium with seawater, food for the crab (pieces of fish or shellfish).

Procedure: Catch the crab carefully, avoiding its pinching claws. Place it in the aquarium. Put a piece of food nearby and observe how it feeds.

Watch, as close to the crab as possible, and see how the crab uses its various mouthparts in eating. Try looking through a magnifying glass.

spiny-skinned animals

The spiny-skinned animals, the echinoderms, live only in salt water. Starfish, sea urchins, and sand dollars are members of this phylum. Almost everyone can recognize a starfish, but few may know of its remarkable method of procuring food. The starfish wraps its body and legs around its prey, a

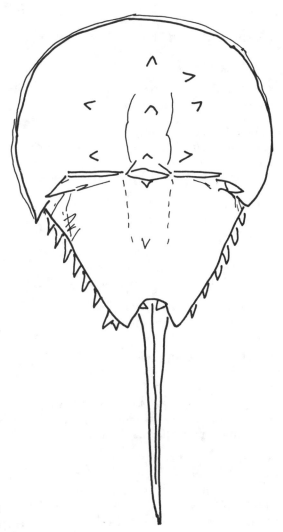

A ten-year old's drawing of a horse shoe crab.

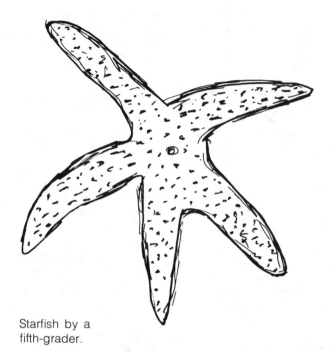

Starfish by a
fifth-grader.

clam, for instance. It then pulls hard on each of the clam's shells, very gradually forcing them to open. All it needs is an opening about the width of a knife blade; then it everts its stomach and slips it through the small opening between the shells into the clam, secretes an enzyme, and enjoys a juicy clam meal. How is the starfish able to pull so hard on the clam's shells? Starfish have tube feet that work on a water vascular system, which allows them to move about and to exert force on clams, mussels, or oysters to such a degree that the mollusk inevitably tires.

Sea urchins look like pincushions with many pins sticking out. Do not step barefooted on one of these animals! The spines are sharp, and, furthermore, some kinds of sea urchins in tropical areas have poisonous spines. The fuzzy spines and circular shape of sand dollars, sometimes called sea biscuits, are reminders that they are related to sea urchins, but they are much flatter in shape. Sea urchin shells and sand dollars are often found washed up on beaches, generally having lost most of the spines.

spy on a starfish walking & eating

Materials: Starfish, temporary aquarium with seawater, small piece of shellfish, or small clam or mussel.

Procedure: Put the starfish into the aquarium and watch how it moves, using its tube feet. Put the small piece of shellfish or the small clam or mussel near it. Observe what the starfish does with the food.

The starfish may move the small piece of shellfish toward its centrally located mouth on its lower side by using its tube feet. The small clam or mussel may be gripped and forced open just enough for the starfish to evert its stomach into the soft molluscan body and enjoy the meal out there.

The starfish's tube feet are remarkable. Hold a starfish up to your hair and then move it away slowly. You will notice how the tube feet will have caught onto several hairs that will be pulled as you move the starfish. Do not keep a starfish out of water for long because its water vascular system cannot survive prolonged exposure to the air.

fish

Ocean fish are generally too deep to be visible from the surface, although minnows and other small fish are often seen in tide pools or as they swim in a school in a shallow area.

fishing

Materials: Appropriate fishing equipment, from drop lines on up, and bait.

Procedure: Use equipment with proper bait and wish for fisherman's luck.

Whether a fish is caught or not, the time spent fishing is an opportunity for quiet appreciation of the ocean: the color of the water as it changes with the color of the sky, the smells of salt air, the lights and shadows on the waves, the sounds of a gull crying, or the waves lapping against the shore. (For activities with fish, see Chapter 6.)

sea turtles

Sea turtles, although seldom visible in the water, may be seen on southern beaches at certain times when the females come up on the sand to lay their eggs, leaving them buried in the sand. It is a lucky happenstance to be on a beach when the eggs are hatching and to watch the hatchlings emerge. Immediately they clumsily start to make their way down the beach, where they are easy prey for ever-alert shore birds, to the more protective environment of the water.

sea birds

There are many birds that prey on the small seaside animals. Gulls consume almost any small creature that they can catch. Even those that are protected by shells do not escape, for gulls carry these creatures up into the air and drop them in order to break the shell

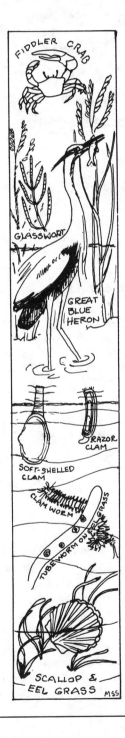

FIDDLER CRAB

GLASSWORT

GREAT BLUE HERON

RAZOR CLAM

SOFT-SHELLED CLAM

CLAM WORM

TUBEWORM ON EEL GRASS

SCALLOP & EEL GRASS MSS

and eat the occupant. If the shell lands on soft ground and does not break, the gull repeats the process. Have you seen shells high up on rocks above the high-tide line? They are signs of the meals of gulls. Gulls also eat dead animals, which makes them helpful in reducing pollution in harbors. As scavengers they thrive in the company of humans and their inevitable garbage dumps. It seems incongruous to find such a symbol of the ocean shore at the local dump, but gulls are not particular about the scenery, as long as the refuse offers good gull pickings.

Terns, another common shorebird, look somewhat like gulls, but they are smaller and have noticeably forked tails. They also eat small shore creatures and a great number of fish. Sandpipers are common on beaches, where they run down after the backwash of a wave in search of small animals that may have become dislodged by the water.

Many other shorebirds are fish-eaters. Herons, egrets, and ibises fish along the shore. Long legs and long bills are helpful adaptations for these feathered fishermen. Other birds catch fish by diving from the surface of the water.

Ducks, loons, and cormorants catch fish in this manner, aided in swimming underwater by their webbed feet. Have you ever noticed cormorants standing with their wings outspread? They look a bit silly, but it is necessary for them to stand that way to dry their feathers, since their plumage is not as water-repellent as that of other diving birds. A number of birds catch their fish by diving into the sea from the air. Ospreys, kingfishers, gannets, and brown pelicans fish from the air.

watching shore & ocean birds

Materials: Binoculars, field guides, paper, pencils.

Procedure: Watch shore and ocean birds, learn to identify them, sketch them, and study their behavior.

Many of the hints on bird watching and the activities in Chapter 7 on birds will be useful here. The wide range of visibility at the shore offers good vantage points for bird watching.

feeding gulls

Materials: Old bread, crackers, fish scraps, or selected garbage.

A thirteen-year-old's thoughts about gulls.

> I see a seagull flying across the water and I wonder how it would be to be a seagull. I could go almost any where, I could fly gracefully a cross the bay and with a few flaps I would gently fly away.
>
> If I was a seagull all seagulls would be my freinds. If some one threw out some garbage another seagull would tellme of it. I would never be lonely. Just how nice it would be to be a seagull sitting on the shore, at low tide, to fly across the land and water

Procedure: From boat or shore, toss food pieces to attract one gull. One is all that is needed. As soon as it shows up, all its friends and relations will rapidly arrive to join in the feasting.

Gulls are scavengers and are scarcely picky about their food. The flock will stay as long as the food supply lasts, and even afterward they will hang around hoping for more. Gulls are beautiful flyers. Feeding gulls allows you to appreciate close up their soaring style of flight, and it also lets you in on a great deal of gull conversation.

Sea otters are appealing.

sea mammals

Sea mammals can be seen at the surface of the water when they come up for air. Whales come to the surface, spouting as they rise, a sight that explains the old whaling expression, "Thar she blows!" Porpoises and dolphins gracefully arch their bodies through the water's surface. To see seals and sea lions, look for their dark heads showing above the surface of the water. If they are close enough, you may see their large, soulful eyes and even spot their whiskers.

These animals also sun themselves on rocks exposed as the tide goes out. The sea otters of the Pacific shore are seen most frequently as they rest in kelp beds, which serve as fine mattresses for these animals.

watching for sea mammals

Materials: Binoculars, field guides, pencils, paper.

Procedure: Be on the alert for sea mammals. If you are lucky and spot some, watch them through binoculars, sketch them, and record notes about them.

Look for sea mammals in their likely habitats. Often, seals have favorite rocks to sit on while the tide is out. Sea otters are found in kelp beds. Porpoises may be seen close to shore, but dolphins and whales are usually seen from boats off-shore.

other activities relating to sea animals

footprints in the sand

Procedure: Observe footprints on the beach and try to discern the stories they may tell.

From birds and mice to dogs and humans, visitors to the beach may leave tracks behind. Sand, like snow, can be a good writing board for track stories, and most of the snow-track activities in Chapter 12 can also be done at a beach. For directions for making plaster of Paris casts of tracks, look in the Index under tracks.

beachcombing

Procedure: Walk along the shore,

gathering interesting objects and "treasures."

What constitutes a treasure depends on your own choice. A few of the interesting objects, however, might be: skate and whelk egg cases, molted shells of crabs and horseshoe crabs, feathers and shells of many sorts and sizes. Driftwood and curious dried seaweeds are fun to find, but for the most part beachcombing involves materials associated with sea animals. Beach glass, oil cans, and plastic bottles are associated with the most ubiquitous animal of all, ourselves. Try to collect human litter as you go along.

Skate egg cases are like tough black purses with prongs at each corner; the embryonic fish has developed and left the case. However, baby whelks can be found in a whelk egg case, which looks like a long series of tan disc-shaped capsules on a central cord. Open a capsule and look for minute replicas of the adult whelk. On the shore, if you find a large whelk shell, hold it to your ear. Do you hear the sound of the sea? Make a collection of discarded crab or horseshoe crab shells, or of feathers or beach glass.

And by all means, collect shells. Shells have a fascination and beauty of design that have intrigued people throughout the ages. Some even have been used as currency. Wampum of the Indians was made from the white and purple of quahog shells. Many activities with shells follow.

comparing shells

Materials: Assorted shells, rulers, paper, pencils.

Procedure: Compare sizes and shapes. Measure length, breadth, and height. Describe shapes: circular, spiral, enlongated, and so on. Compare colors. Find other comparisons. Make sketches.

These comparisons should illustrate the tremendous variety of shells and lead to a basis for identifying different shells. Young children may enjoy sorting a collection of shells; without knowing any names, it is likely that they will put all snail shells in one group, bivalves, such as clams and mussels in another, and so forth.

Compare also the shell structure. Break a few shells apart and compare the layers. The shiny inside layer is mother-of-pearl, which at one time was used for buttons.

displaying shells

Materials: Some of the following may be useful: cardboard boxes, egg cartons, styrofoam containers, shelves, velvet, construction paper, cotton batting, fluffed-up tissue, sand, clear plastic film, salad oil, pencils, paper.

Procedure: Place shells in one of the above containers on velvet, colored paper, cotton, tissue, or maybe just sand. Cardboard dividers may be added and clear plastic film can be used over the top. Rubbing the shells with a little salad oil will give them added luster. A serious collector will label the shells, including name, where the shell was found, and the date.

You may find your own devices for shell displaying. For a major project, make a shell display table. Make a coffee-type table, but substitute for the top a tray with a glass covering. Arrange shells in the tray (sand is an effective background), cover with glass, and enjoy a table with memories of seaside visits.

crafts with shells & other beachcombing items

Materials: Shells, drill, string, glue, tin cans, other containers, plaster of Paris, putty, plywood, cardboard, driftwood, and other beachcombing items.

Procedure: Make shell necklaces, using drill (carefully) and string or dental floss. Knots in between the shells will help to keep them in position. Make shell wind chimes using drill and string; hang the shells from driftwood. Make mobiles with shells and other beachcombing items and driftwood. Make mosaics or collages by gluing shells onto plywood or cardboard and hang them on a wall. Make a "snowman" using sea urchin shells, or create other creatures using shells and glue. Make a beachcomber's bookend. Find a rock of suitable size and shape to be used for a bookend and test it with some books to see if it will hold them up. Cover its surface with putty (except the side that will be next to the books and the bottom, which you may wish to cover with felt when the process is finished). Arrange shells and other items decoratively on the putty and perhaps sprinkle sand between the items for a pleasing texture. Wait for a week or two until the putty dries, and the bookend will be ready for use. The same process may be used with a tin can to make a pencil holder or with other items that you may wish to try.

food from the sea

The pleasures of catching your own fish or digging your own clams seem to add to the enjoyment of the eating. Always check regulations about harvesting seafood. Permits or licenses often are required, the numbers allowed to be taken may be limited, and sometimes there are specified seasons for the taking of certain animals. Never eat shellfish from polluted areas, or from where there may be a danger of red tide. How about a pudding made with seaweed? Look in the Index under Irish moss pudding for this seaside specialty.

Seaweeds, shellfish, crustaceans (lobsters, crabs, shrimp), fish, turtles, seabirds and their eggs, seals and whales have been traditional foods for many cultures. Study these cultural uses. For example, some Indian tribes annually migrated in summer to shore areas to use the bountiful supplies of seafood available there, leaving large shell heaps that can be found today and tell of the Indians' activity. The supplies have greatly diminished, so that today conservation measures are necessary to protect sea animals. Study these measures, including international law on fishing rights. How do these help whales, currently an endangered species? Also study the impact of oil wells and spills on fish and other marine life.

sea music

Materials: Record or tape player, recordings or tapes of "La Mer" by Claude Debussy or "The Sea

Symphony" by Ralph Vaughan Williams, music and lyrics of sea chanties.

Procedure: Play and enjoy listening to the music about the sea. Have fun singing some of the old sea chanties.

There are also many poems about the sea. Read some to the children or have them create their own. Here is a haiku poem by a nine-year-old.

In the deep blue sea
  Seaweed bends in delight to
    The rhythm of the waves.

modern society's effect on the sea

Procedure: Study the wide-ranging

effects of humans on ocean ecology, and the significance that these effects could have on our lives.

Salt marsh destruction (see p. 107 for a salt marsh debate), pollution, overfishing, extermination of whales, and oil spills are only a few of the many ways by which we destructively alter ocean ecology. Seventy-five percent of the globe is covered by oceans. All life originated in the sea, and we are still dependent on the healthy functioning of ocean ecology. What can we do to preserve it?

bibliography

adults

ABBOTT, R. TUCKER, *Sea Shells of North America.* New York: Golden Press, 1968.

AMOS, WILLIAM A., *The Life of the Seashore.* New York: McGraw-Hill, 1966.

BERRILL, N.J., and JACQUELYN BERRILL, *1001 Questions Answered about the Seashore.* New York: Dover, 1976.

CARSON, RACHEL L., *The Edge of the Sea.* Boston: Houghton Mifflin, 1955.

GOSNER, KENNETH L., *A Field Guide to the Atlantic Seashore.* Peterson Field Guide Series. Boston: Houghton Mifflin, 1979.

HILLSON, C. J., *Seaweeds.* University Park: Pennsylvania State University Press, 1977.

MAGLAND, HANS J., *The Complete Home Aquarium.* New York: Grosset, 1976.

ROBERTS, MERVIN R., *The Tidemarsh Guide.* New York: Dutton, 1979.

URSIN, MICHAEL J., *Life in and around the Salt Marshes.* New York: Crowell, 1972.

children & adults

ADRIAN, MARY, *A Day and a Night in a Tide Pool.* New York: Hastings House, 1972.

BROWN, JOSEPH E., *Wonders of a Kelp Forest.* New York: Dodd, Mead, 1974.

GOLDIN, AUGUSTA, *The Sunlit Sea.* New York: Crowell, 1968.

KOHN, BERNICE, *The Beachcomber's Book.* New York: Viking, 1970.

LAYCOCK, GEORGE, and ELLEN LAYCOCK, *The Flying Sea Otters.* New York: Grosset, 1972.

LIST, ILKA KATHERINE, *Questions and Answers about Sea Shore Life.* New York: Four Winds, 1970.

MAY, JULIAN, *Plankton.* New York: Holiday House, 1972.

POZELL, ELSA Z., *The Beginning Knowledge Book of Sea Shells.* New York: Rutledge, 1969.

SCHREIBER, ELIZABETH ANNE, and RALPH W. SCHREIBER, *The Wonders of Seagulls.* New York: Dodd, Mead, 1975.

SHEPHERD, ELIZABETH, *Tracks between the Tides.* New York: Lothrop, 1972.

SHULZ, CHARLES M., *Snoopy's Facts and Fun Book about Sea Shores.* New York: Random House, 1980.

WATERS, JOHN F., *Some Mammals Live in the Sea.* New York: Dodd, Mead, 1972.

ZIM, HERBERT S., and LESTER INGLE, *Seashores.* New York: Simon & Schuster, 1955.

11

ponds, streams, swamps & other watery places

Freshwater areas are exciting to explore. Ponds, puddles, rivers, and streams are generally teeming with wide ranges of plant and animal life awaiting discovery; and swamps, marshes, and bogs may have even more to offer. I admit to a prejudice for such wet and squishy places, and I have never been disappointed leading a field trip of children or adults to these habitats. Curiosity and just a little sense of adventure will almost always bring new findings.

A helpful introduction to studies of freshwater life concerns the properties of freshwater, as well as its susceptibility to changes caused by people.

properties of water

Life as we know it cannot exist without water. About 70 percent of the earth's surface is covered with water, and all living things are made up largely of water— from 70 to 90 percent. Water is in the air, the soil, and even in rocks, as well as in oceans, ponds, and rivers. Our lives depend on the continuing water cycle, which goes on all around us all the time. Heat from the sun evaporates water on the earth and transforms it into clouds. Cooling conditions cause precipitation in the form of rain or snow. The rain water, or the snow after melting, percolates into the soil or runs off into lakes, rivers, and the seas, becoming available for use by living beings.

Water is a medium that can support life for many reasons. Pure water is nontoxic and is neither acid nor alkaline. It contains dissolved oxygen, a vital requirement for aquatic animals that do not breathe air. Water's density (its mass in comparison with its volume) is approximately the same as that of protoplasm (protoplasm is largely composed of water). Because protoplasm is the basic living matter of organisms, it allows them to be buoyant in water. Water's transparency allows animals with eyes to see under water and also permits sunlight to reach shallowly submerged plants, so that photosynthesis can take place.

When water freezes, unlike other substances, it expands and becomes lighter. Ice forms at the very top of the water surface, so ponds freeze from the top down. However, ponds seldom freeze solidly, so animals can continue to live in the water beneath the ice. Find a section of clear ice on a pond in winter; watch the water down below the ice and you may see water creatures moving about. Once we were surprised to see a lifeless-looking frog directly under the ice. Then, without warning, the frog gave a kick and disappeared from our windowlike view through the ice.

The surface tension of water is important to aquatic life. Molecules at the surface of any liquid are strongly attracted to each other, giving the exterior of the liquid a certain strength known as surface tension or film. This is why drops of liquid keep their shape while falling. The surface tension of water is particularly strong. It enables some creatures to walk on the water, but makes it difficult for small creatures to break through the surface of the water. Surface tension also allows water creatures to carry bubbles of air under the water for an oxygen supply.

activities with water

The following activities demonstrate various factors of water as a habitat. They are relatively simple and require no special equipment.

Freshwater areas are exciting to explore.

Field test kits and laboratory equipment can be used for more sophisticated studies of such factors as dissolved oxygen, pH (hydrogen-ion concentration), transparency, and the presence of certain pollutants.

water in the air

Materials: Glass, ice water, warm place (where there is some humidity).

Procedure: Fill the glass with ice water in a warm place. Watch how water from the air becomes evident as it condenses into a fog on the outside of the glass.

Perhaps you have never thought of it, but those wet glasses or bottles of ice-cold drinks in summer are continual demonstrations that there is water in the air. (The air inside many buildings in winter may be too dry for this experiment to work.)

water in soil

Materials: Freshly dug soil, cup, scales, oven (optional).

Procedure: Weigh the cup of soil. Dry it out in a slow oven or other warm place. When dry, weigh it again. Note the loss of weight, which indicates the amount of water evaporated from the soil.

Different types of soil may vary in water content. Sandy soils, for instance, are relatively dry. This same procedure will illustrate how water is contained in bread, other foods, or other natural items. Weigh a slice of bread, piece of apple, or other item; dehydrate by air or oven drying. Weigh again, and note how much water has been lost. Make percentage problems, such as what percent of the bread was water?

water cycle

Materials: Plastic bag, water, rubber band, sunny window or warm place.

Procedure: Put about two teaspoons (10 ml) of water in the plastic bag, blow air into it, and seal the opening with the rubber band. Place the bag in a sunny window or warm place and watch what happens as evaporation takes place.

This is a miniature water cycle. The water at the bottom of the bag represents a pond. The fog that accumulates on the inside surfaces of the bag shows how clouds are formed. Drops falling from the top down imitate the formation of rain. If the bag remains fairly warm, more of the water will stay in the air as vapor; this explains why humidity is often high on hot summer days. If the bag cools, there will be more condensation; this is why dew is found on the ground after cold summer nights.

testing water for acidity or alkalinity

Materials: Water from various sources (pond, river, puddle, rain, local water supply), litmus paper or pH kit from a swimming pool supply company, paper, pencils.

Procedure: Test the various waters with the litmus paper or the kit. Record whether the waters are neutral, alkaline, or acid. Look in the Index under litmus paper to find information about how to use it.

The results may vary. Some areas, such as bogs, are naturally acidic, while waters from limestone areas or sites near fields where lime has recently been applied to the soil are likely to be alkaline. Strongly acidic waters may be caused by acid rain, a threat to many water resources. Pollutants in the atmosphere cause acid rain, which may fall a great distance away from the polluting source. Especially in the northeastern region of the United States, acid rain has destroyed life in many lakes and ponds. Study acid rain as an environmental threat; what could be the far-reaching consequences of acid rain in the future, and what, if anything, can be done about it?

water pollution

Materials: A local body of polluted water, and/or reference materials about the local pollution, as well as about water pollution in general.

Procedure: Study the pollution story in a body of water. Use the reference materials to find out the cause of the pollution and its effects on the plant and animal life in the water.

Lake Erie is a classic example of water pollution. Phosphates and other pollutants released into the lake by industries and sewage disposal plants upset the natural balance of life in the lake. At first, green plants flourished on the fertilizer of phosphates, crowding out much of the other lake life. Then, the oxygen supply in the lake was depleted by the increased number of bacteria breaking down the great numbers of dead organisms. Ultimately, the lack of oxygen eliminated almost all life in the water. Within a few years, Lake Erie, which has been an important source of commercial fish, had "died." It required many years of cooperative and costly pollution-abatement efforts by the United States and Canada to help resuscitate the lake, which has recovered sufficiently so that commercial fishing is again possible. Information about the relationship between aquatic life and pollution is given later in this chapter.

transparency of water

Materials: Various freshwater areas (river, pond, bog), bottles, white paper, pencils.

Procedure: Fill each bottle with water from a different area. Hold each bottle against the white paper and describe its color. Record the observations.

Paint, crayons, or commercial paint color charts of appropriate hues may be used to indicate the various colors. Water transparency is important to the growth of water plants. The clearer the water, the more sunlight can penetrate, and the greater the amount of photosynthesis that can take place, allowing for more prolific plant growth. Can you make any correlations between the color of the water and the plant growth in the habitat?

ice is lighter than water

Materials: Ice cubes, water, cup.

Procedure: Fill the cup partly with water and put in the ice cubes.

The cubes will float, demonstrating that they are lighter than water. Use food coloring to make colored ice cubes; the cubes themselves will float, but colored meltwater from the cubes will tend to diffuse downward.

surface tension of water

Materials: Paper clip or needle, pan of water.

Procedure: Carefully place the paper clip or needle *on* the water in the pan. It can float. Look carefully and see the indentation in the surface film where the clip or needle is floating.

Greasing the paper clip or needle may make it easier to float it; also, be certain the paper clip is flat (not twisted). Water striders, who, as their name suggests, stride on the surface of the water, have slightly greasy feet, which help them to stay on top of the surface film. There are other ways to show surface tension. Fill a cup with water. Carefully slip pennies into the cup, one by one. The surface tension will allow the water to rise slightly above the edge of the cup. How many pennies can be added before the surface tension breaks? Push a small piece of velvet under the water. Surface tension will prevent the water from penetrating between the fibers of the velvet, and the layer of air will give the velvet a silvery appearance. Some aquatic animals have hairy coverings that retain air, useful to the animals for breathing. As with the velvet, the air gives these creatures a silvery appearance.

Float a paper clip and add a few drops of liquid soap or detergent to the water—the paper clip sinks immediately!

surface tension of water drops

Materials: Wax paper, pencil, birthday candle with the wick cut off, water.

Procedure: Put drops of water on a piece of wax paper. Observe them. With the pencil, move a drop around; join several drops together. Poke a drop with the pointed tip of the birthday candle.

Did the birthday candle make a hole in the drop, as did the pencil? Or did the drop seem to have a skin, the surface tension, which the candle could not easily break through? The wax should have greater difficulty breaking the surface tension for the same reason that water striders have slightly oily feet.

Water drops are shaped like small lenses; therefore, they can magnify. Hold the wax paper with the drops of water on it over a printed page, and look through the drops at the letters on the page. Try looking through drops of morning dew at the end of pine needles. Make a magnifier by drilling a hole about 1/16 inch (2 mm) in diameter in a piece of metal. Put a drop of water in the hole. Held in the right position, the drop will magnify objects seen through it.

water temperatures

Materials: Thermometers, pencils, paper.

Procedure: Take and record temperatures at different locations in one or more freshwater areas. Repeat periodically and compare the results.

Where is it the hottest? The coldest? What temperature is the water when it freezes, or melts, and is it warmer beneath ice? Since cold water contains more dissolved oxygen than warm, temperature is important to life in the water; warm water can support less life than cold. Thus, water temperature can be an important factor in pollution.

freshwater life

Freshwater areas abound with life. Large areas can support muskrats, beavers, otters, and many species of waterfowl, turtles, water snakes, frogs, salamanders, fish, and, in southeastern states, alligators. These large areas, as well as small freshwater areas, also support a teeming variety of invertebrate life. Even a roadside ditch may be filled with activity. Leave a container of water outdoors long enough, and it too will acquire inhabitants. Mosquitoes, whose larvae are aquatic, are notoriously adept at finding such places for laying their eggs.

As with salt water, the smallest organisms in freshwater are the members of the plankton community, drifting microscopic plants and animals that constitute the basic food supply of their environment. The smallest creatures that can be seen with the naked eye appear like tiny grains of moving pepper. Other water invertebrates are larger, some up to several inches, or centimeters, long. The makeup of invertebrate populations varies according to habitat, season, water conditions, and other factors.

Generally, the most common of these small animals are the insect larvae and nymphs, such as caddis fly larvae and mosquito larvae, and dragonfly, damselfly, and mayfly nymphs. Caddis fly larvae are of special interest since most of them build protective shelters, usually of plant material. A hook at the tip of the abdomen holds the larva in its house. At the front the insect can reach out its head and legs to creep about and find food, drawing its shelter with it. Dragonfly

POND LIFE

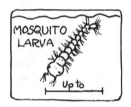
MOSQUITO LARVA
Up to

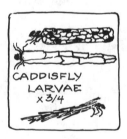
CADDISFLY LARVAE x 3/4

JET-PROPELLED
DRAGONFLY NYMPH up to 1¾"

nymphs are the dragons of the watery world. They are voracious predators, being equipped with a specialized mouthpart, known as a mask, which is capable of shooting out a fair length to catch hapless prey. Dragonfly nymphs also have a unique adaptation for rapid movement. Normally, they crawl about slowly using their six legs, but, when speed is necessary, they resort to a type of jet propulsion by suddenly expelling water from the anal cavity at the back of the abdomen. The mayfly has a particularly interesting life cycle. After hatching from their spring-laid eggs, these nymphs live in the pond until the following spring, when they emerge from the water to become adults. Adult mayflies are beautiful, fragile-appearing insects with long delicate tail filaments. As the name of their order, *Ephemoptera*, suggests, they have an ephemeral existence, living only from a few hours to two days at the most. During their brief adulthood, they do not eat—in fact, their mouthparts are useless for taking in food, but they do mate and the females lay their eggs in the water, thus ensuring that these beautiful insects will appear again the following spring.

Many adult insects are also commonly found in ponds. Numerous beetles have adapted to water living. They carry their air supply with them, and sometimes this air is clearly visible as a bubble at the end of the abdomen. Look for these bubbles with children, and they can see how beetles "invented" air tanks long before scuba divers came to use them. Whirligig beetles are often seen on the surface of a pond, circling about just as their name implies. Their third pair of legs are broad and paddle-shaped, which aids them in whirling through the water. They have remarkable eyes in that each one is in two parts: an upper part for looking up into the air, and a lower part for looking down into the water. Another adult insect, aptly named the water boatman, also has legs adapted for swimming; they look like a pair of oars. Water striders, which take advantage of the surface tension, have long legs that distribute their body weight, as well as a slightly greasy covering, both of which assist them in staying on top of the water surface.

Whirligig beetles, water boatmen, and water striders all have particularly descriptive names. Children observing these insects often invent equally descriptive names, sometimes even hitting on the "right" one. Many times on ponding expeditions, I avoid identification as such. The names or descriptions given by the children are the results of their own thoughtful observations. Such observations lead to their own understanding of these creatures, a more important goal than that of knowing the proper name. Of course, there comes a point when the children become interested in knowing the correct names. That is the time to bring out the field guide, for in knowing the true name of something we tend to feel closer to it.

Crustaceans, like insects, are abundant in freshwater. Many are tiny, but all may be characterized by their jerky motions and the frenetic activity of their legs. Scuds are characteristic and large enough to be observed easily. The water sow bug is another readily seen crustacean, and it greatly resembles its land cousin, the sow bug that is found under logs and rocks. Crayfish, which look like miniature lobsters, are freshwater dwellers that are not easily caught in dip nets, since by day they are liable to hide under rocks, coming out to feed during the night.

Other creatures that may commonly turn up in a dip net are pond snails, various worms (many insect larvae have a superficial resemblance to worms; look for indications of insect body parts or legs as with bloodworms, which are a type of midge larva), and even hydras. Hydras are fascinating little creatures. Small, delicate looking, and nearly transparent, they may be found anchored to pieces of vegetation, pebbles, or anything they can hang on to. These simple creatures can reproduce by budding (growing a new hydra out of the body wall) and sometimes move by turning slow somersaults. Like their ocean relatives, the sea anemones, hydras have stinging cells in their tentacles, which assist them in catching their prey.

Many plants are adapted for living in freshwater. Many have flexible central stems that can bend with currents or waves. Some have leaf and stem tissues that absorb minerals directly from the water, reducing the need for roots. Some have roots only to serve as anchors. Many underwater leaves are divided or ribbonlike, as are many seaweeds, in order to lessen their resistance to moving water. Some have additional floating leaves above, which are quite different from the filamentous ones below.

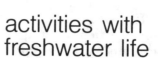

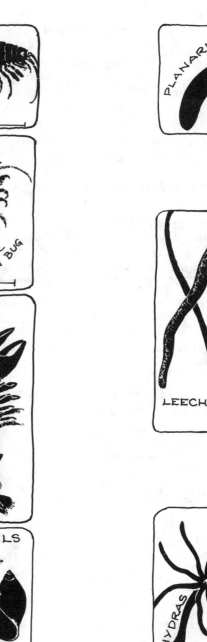

Water plants are useful to aquatic animals. They add oxygen to the water and provide shelter for innumerable small creatures. A number of water insects, fish, and amphibians lay their eggs on leaves or stems of water plants. Also, these plants serve as food for herbivorous water animals.

activities with freshwater life

Ponding (catching and observing small aquatic creatures) is a major exception to the general rule that the less equipment needed on a field trip, the better. Ponding re-

Water plants are useful to aquatic animals in many different ways.

quires a number of items, from jars and white plastic spoons to hand lenses and eyedroppers. The most important pieces of equipment are the dip nets. A dip net is easy to construct. Tape an ordinary kitchen strainer (a diameter of 6 inches, or 15 c, is a good size) onto a 3-foot (.9 m) dowel or an old broom stick or whatever other handy pole you may have around. Pressure on the strainer can cause it to break off from the handle;

caution dip net users to handle them carefully.

The small ponding items like the eyedroppers and hand lenses are easy to lose. A small piece of red mystic tape put around the glass or plastic portion of an eyedropper makes it much more visible when dropped on the ground. Colored strings or yarn attached to the hand lenses help in finding them and also allows them to be

worn around the neck. If you are using identification sheets of any kind, put them between two pieces of clear self-adhesive plastic to protect them from water and mud. Also put the plastic around paper-backed field guides to protect them.

Old clothes suitable for working at the water's edge are advisable for ponding. Unless it is cold, boots are not necessary, especially because they can serve as an invitation to go into the water. It is better to wear old sneakers and keep feet out of the water, which helps to keep the water unmuddied.

On ponding expeditions with children, you may have to overcome the "frog syndrome." This is a normal reaction of normal children—they want to catch frogs. You, however, want them to concentrate on finding the small pond creatures. One way to dispel the frog syndrome is to ask who knows how to hold a frog. Usually one or two children will know that frogs can best be held by holding them at the waist and securing their back legs. Do the children know that they should wet their hands before holding a frog and moisten the hands several times if holding it for any length of time? Explain that frogs need wet skin and become uncomfortable if they get too dry. Next, suggest that the first one to catch a frog take it around and show it to the rest of the group—holding it properly, of course—and then let the frog go back into the pond. Once this is done, the frog syndrome diminishes.

The next task is to help the children "think small." Frogs, as well as fish and turtles, are relatively large. The creatures you can catch with the dip nets will be small. Explain to the children that some of the animals may look like moving specks of pepper. Once the group becomes involved, the small size of the animals is no drawback. In fact, it serves to intensify feelings of excitement as the children discover more and more tiny creatures they have never seen before.

ponding

Materials: Dip nets, white or light-colored pans, dishes or other low-sided containers for observing

pond creatures, small plastic containers for "backflushing," white plastic spoons, eyedroppers, small jars with tops, hand lenses (optional), and pond life identification books (optional).

Procedure: Divide the students into groups of two or three. Give each group one each of the items listed under materials. Assign each group an area of shore for collecting. Have the students of each group collect and observe aquatic creatures in the following manner:

1. Sweep the dip net through the water or along the bottom of the pond.
2. Bring the net out and hold it upside down over the observing pan.
3. Fill the smaller "backflushing" container with pond water and pour the water through the net in order to wash all the contents of the net into the observing pan.
4. Let the contents of the pan settle down so that the small aquatic creatures may be seen against the light-colored background.
5. Use the spoon or eyedropper for catching sample specimens and

"BACK FLUSHING"

Pour water through back of strainer to wash organisms into pan.

put them into the jar for bringing back for inside observation.
6. Return the remaining creatures and the water in the observing pan to the pond.
7. Repeat the process and see what new creatures may be found.

Often the discoveries in the observing pan are exciting. For instance, a cry of "I've caught a *monster*!" may indicate that a large dragonfly nymph has been found, and these are indeed impressive looking. Some of the creatures may be put into the jars for further observation back in the classroom. However, if samples are not to be taken back, it can be fun to make a communal zoo. Fill a pail or other large container with water and have the children add creatures. If you limit the zoo to only one of each kind of animal, the children will look closely at their own to differentiate between the various kinds. White styrofoam egg cartons offer another way of sorting and observing pond creatures. Give the children egg cartons and have them put different creatures into each section: damselfly nymphs into one, scuds into another, water beetles in another, and so forth. Before leaving the pond, be certain to return all the animals from the zoo or egg cartons to the water.

If possible, visit the same freshwater area in different seasons. Note any differences in the composition of the animal population.

Ponding can be conducted on simpler scales. Try just using hands; take sticks, pieces of plants, or small rocks from the water, and see what creatures may be found. Lift larger rocks in the water, and perhaps a crayfish will scuttle away. Scoop up water in a small white cup and look closely to find what may be in it. I generally have a white plastic spoon in my field trip bag. Although small, it serves

Looking for discoveries in the observing pan.

well as an emergency piece of ponding equipment.

plankton collecting

(See directions for making and using plankton nets on p. 109.) The smallest kinds of freshwater life are found in the plankton community, these are mainly unicellular animals and plants that are found drifting in the water. Like their saltwater counterparts, plankton organisms provide the basic food supply of their environment, especially the one-celled algae, which use energy from the sun to make food and are at the bottom of the food chain. Older children will enjoy using a microscope for a close-up view of these organisms.

using water glasses

(See the directions for this activity on p. 114.) A water glass allows for clear viewing in water. Swimming with a face mask, with or without a snorkel, is another way to watch aquatic life in its own environment.

freshwater aquariums

Materials: Glass tank, soil (or gravel), water plants, water animals, pond water or tap water that has been left in an open container for a day, and a small plate.

Procedure: Put about 2½ inches (6 c) of soil (or gravel) on the bottom of the glass tank and plant some aquatic vegetation in it. Lay the small plate on the bottom and carefully pour the pond or tap water onto the plate to minimize disturbance of the soil and plants. When the freshwater aquarium is full, put the small aquatic creatures into it.

Air, light, and a biologically balanced community are the main points to consider in managing an aquarium. A low tank with a wide surface area will allow for more aeration than a tall, narrow one. Green plants are excellent oxygen-producers in an aquarium. If further aeration is necessary, use an electrical aerator. (Since the aerator may stir up soil, the bottom material should be gravel

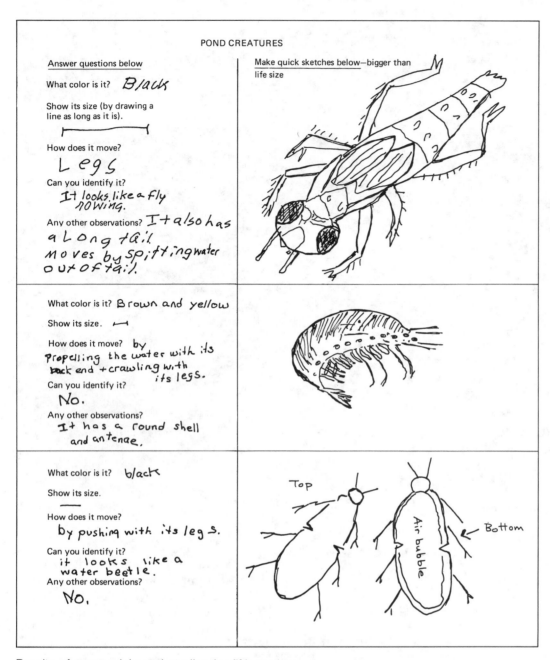

POND CREATURES

Answer questions below

What color is it? Black

Show its size (by drawing a line as long as it is).

├————————┤

How does it move?
Legs

Can you identify it?
It looks like a fly rowing.

Any other observations? It also has a Long tail. Moves by spitting water out of tail.

Make quick sketches below—bigger than life size

What color is it? Brown and yellow

Show its size. ┝┥

How does it move? by Propelling the water with its back end + crawling with its legs.

Can you identify it?
No.

Any other observations?
It has a round shell and antenae.

What color is it? black

Show its size.

How does it move?
by pushing with its legs.

Can you identify it?
it looks like a water beetle.

Any other observations?
No.

Top

Bottom

Air bubble

Results of some mini-pond studies by fifth-graders.

or pebbles.) Light is essential for the health of aquarium plants, but too much light is not beneficial for water creatures that are accustomed to living in murky depths. Also, too much sunlight may overheat the aquarium beyond the heat tolerance point of many of its inhabitants; be careful. To keep a biologically balanced aquarium, consider food chains and the needs of the individual animals. For instance, the highly predacious dragonfly nymphs eat almost any other small aquatic creature, even young tadpoles. If you do not want your tadpoles to be eaten, put them in another aquarium and provide other small organisms as meals for the dragonfly nymphs. For help in keeping an aquarium clean, keep some pond snails in it.

Aquarium keeping may be simplified, especially if the animals are to be kept only for a short time. Wide-mouthed jars serve very well as temporary homes for many beings. A bucket with pond water and a tangle of water plants is handy when you have only limited time at the pond. When time permits, put some of the water and plants into an observing pan; sort out the creatures that have been housed in the plant tangle and repeat the process until finished.

Look in the Index under tadpoles to find directions on how to keep them.

mini-ponds

Materials: Pond water and creatures, observing pans or any small light-colored container, and such optional items as hand lenses, pond life identification books, white plastic spoons, medicine droppers, pencils, paper, microscopes.

Procedure: Observe and study pond creatures in the observing pans.

Mini-ponds allow for close-up viewing of small aquatic animals. Hand lenses are useful, especially for watching tiny beings such as the smaller crustaceans. Spoons and medicine droppers help in moving animals from one container to another. A very miniature aquarium can be made with just one drop of water on a plate. A wee beastie can swim happily in such a "drop aquarium," whose small size limits the creature's traveling, making it easier to observe. Drawing or sketching animals, looking them up in identification guides, and studying their adaptations can all be done with close-up observations. The "oars" of the water boatman, the materials of the caddis fly nymph's shelter, or the tentacles of a hydra can readily be seen. Taking organisms from a mini-pond and observing them with microscopes is an activity older children will find interesting.

water slides

Materials: Two squares of thin glass, such as photographic slide cover glass, 2 x 2 inches (5 x 5 c), strips of 3/16-inch (4 mm) wide balsa wood that is 13 1/8 inches (33.3 c) long (or longer), waterproof glue.

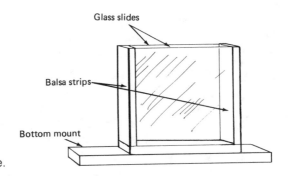

Water slide.

Procedure: Cut balsa strips into the following pieces: one piece 2 inches (5 c) long; two pieces, 1 13/16 inches (4.6 c) long; and one piece, 7½ inches (18.4 c) long. Coat strips on all surfaces with the glue for waterproofing and allow to dry. Glue strips to one piece of glass as shown in diagram. Allow to dry, then glue other glass square in place. Glue slide onto 7½-inch (18.4 c) strip and let it dry.

The slide is now ready for use as described in the following activity. It is a good idea to make several slides, especially if they are going to be used with groups.

water slide show

Materials: Slide projector (manually operated, not carousel), projection screen, water slides (see preceding activity), spoons, medicine droppers, pond water, and small aquatic animals.

Procedure: Fill a water slide about three-quarters full with pond water and carefully add creature to be viewed. Put slide into the projector and project image onto the screen.

It is fascinating to watch the small aquatic beings that have become so large on the screen. (The image is upside down, but this is not a detraction.) Details, otherwise unnoticed, become apparent, such as the fringe of hairs on the "oars" of the water boatman or the ten legs of the water sow bug. Also, the strength of surface tension can

be seen dramatically when an animal tries to break through it. Some creatures, especially the larger dragonfly nymphs, may not fit between the narrow confines of the two pieces of glass; make sure that animals to be put into the slide are small enough to be comfortable in it. A water slide show makes an exciting finale to a ponding expedition. Children are eager to put animals they have caught into the slides, as well as to watch the show on the screen, which is sometimes dramatic. Once on the screen, an enormous damselfly nymph grabbed and consumed a small crustacean before our very eyes. When the show is over, don't forget to return all creatures to the pond (except any to be maintained in aquariums).

duckweed experiments

Materials: Duckweed, paper cups or similar containers, water, fertilizer, pencils, paper.

Procedure: Fill half of the cups with plain water; fill the others with water with a small amount of fertilizer added. Put ten duckweed plants in each container. Put a pair of containers, one with plain water and one with fertilized water, in a sunny window. Place other pairs in different spots, such as warm, cold, shady, dark, and so on. Compare the growth of the plants periodically and record the results.

Duckweed is one of the smallest of the flowering plants. Its tiny leaves measure less than 1/8 inch (6 mm) in length, yet often so many of these small plants float together that they look like a large green mat covering an area of water on a pond or river. As their name implies, they are a favorite food of many ducks.

It might be interesting to conduct a similar series of experiments with freshwater algae and phosphate as a fertilizer, since phosphates from detergents can cause water pollution.

return to life, or "phoenix," experiments

Materials: Earth or mud from an area where standing or running water had been present in an earlier season, jar, water, hand lenses (optional), microscope (optional).

Procedure: Put the earth or mud in the jar and fill with water. Watch for any life to become evident after a period of time.

It is likely that sooner or later there will be small animals swimming around in the jar. Many habitats are frequently inundated by water in one season and dry in another. Some aquatic animals have adapted to such situations by having eggs that can withstand desiccation. When wet again, these eggs will hatch.

In winter, saw or chop a slab of ice from any convenient pond or river and let it melt in the classroom. Small creatures will become

He's caught one!

apparent, kicking about in the meltwater within a few hours.

fishing

Materials: Any appropriate fishing equipment, from a line on a pole to a rod and reel, and bait or flies.

Procedure: Select a place where there may be fish, use the equipment, and hope for fisherman's luck!

Regardless of the success, or lack of, fishing often is a time for tranquil appreciation of the watery habitat. For other activities relating to fish, see Chapter 6.

amphibians & reptiles

See Chapter 6 for information and activities relating to amphibians and reptiles. Amphibians are tied to water in that they must lay their eggs in water or extremely moist areas. Certain reptiles, such as alligators and some turtles, are aquatic.

Does this alligator realize its ecological importance?

In some areas in the southeastern states, alligators play important ecological roles by creating deep-water holes that they keep free of muck and vegetation. In dry seasons, when the surrounding wetland has no standing water, these alligator holes are refuges for the water-dependent animals of the area, such as fish, snails, and turtles. Some of these animals become meals for the birds and mammals that have followed them to the holes, as well as for the alligators. When the rains return, usually enough of the water-dependent creatures still remain to repopulate the wetland.

waterfowl & other birds

Materials: Binoculars, field guides, pencils, paper.

Procedure: Observe the birds of freshwater environments. Learn to identify them, sketch them, and study their adaptations and behavior.

From ducks and geese to bittern and red-winged blackbirds, a wide variety of birds inhabit, or frequent, freshwater areas. Many are seasonal; some may be year-round residents. Many of the hints on birdwatching and the activities outlined in Chapter 7 on birds will be useful here.

animal track casts

Materials: Half-gallon milk carton, scissors, plaster of Paris, water, mixing stick or spoon, petroleum jelly, pencil.

Procedure: Find a clear animal track and make a plaster cast of it by following the directions in the illustration on page 95. When it is finished, on the bottom write the date, location, and, if known, the kind of animal that made the track.

Muddy shores are excellent places

for spotting animal tracks and studying the stories they may tell. Common tracks near freshwater areas include duck, goose, deer, raccoon, otter, muskrat, and beaver. Plaster of Paris casts can easily be made in the mud.

muskrats & beaver

Materials: Reference materials on muskrats and beaver, and, if possible, a habitat where muskrats and beaver may be found.

Procedure: Study these two

mammals and their adaptations for aquatic life. If possible, observe the animals and signs of their activity.

Both muskrats and beaver have many adaptations for living in freshwater. As is true with many mammals, it is easier to see signs of their activity than to view the animals themselves. We have waited at the edge of a beaver pond at dusk, hoping at least to hear the slap of a beaver's tail, and have come away only with mosquito bites and feelings of

gratitude for the bats who appeared and we assumed were hunting the mosquitoes. Muskrat and beaver lodges are easy to spot, as are their footprints on muddy shores. Trees cut by beaver are testimony to the incredibly strong teeth of this rodent. Beaver dams create ponds, effecting great changes in the ecology of an environment. It may be slightly reassuring to realize that humans are not the only animals that can cause a major ecological change in an area.

diverse freshwater areas

Freshwater areas can be classified roughly into two main types: those with moving water and those with relatively still water. Moving water areas are rivers, streams, creeks, brooks, and springs. Rivers generally are larger than streams, creeks, and brooks, and springs are seeps from an underground water supply. Ponds have relatively still water, as do lakes, swamps, marshes, and bogs. Ponds are open bodies of water, smaller than lakes, often shallow enough so that rooted plants may grow in them. Wetlands may have some open water. Swamps are wetlands characterized by a dominant growth of trees and shrubs; marshes have herbaceous vegetation such as cattails or rushes. Bogs are wetlands, generally acidic, rich in plant residue, and characterized by such plants as sphagnum moss and other acid-tolerant vegetation. Local areas may have different interpretations for these wetland terms, but most of us immediately understand the allusions of such

expressions as feeling "swamped" or "bogged down."

From a hydrologist's viewpoint, freshwater areas are accidents. Water flows downhill, a simple but basic hydrological principle, which, surprisingly, many very young children comprehend. A pond occurs when the contours of the land act as a dam for a flow of water, trapping the water behind it. Sooner or later erosion wears through the dam, and the trapped water will flow more freely on its downhill trip to the ocean.

Meanwhile, the pond may have gone through a period of succession from a young, bare-bottomed pond, shy of minerals and skinny on life, to a mature pond with organic mud on the bottom and rich in nutrients. In the pond's old age, it gradually becomes filled in with vegetation, changing into a swamp, marsh, or bog. Ultimately, the dam breaks down and the area is completely drained. Since this process of pond succession may take anywhere from between one to many thousands of years, no one can see the complete process in a lifetime, but we can recognize the stages of succession by the type of environment. For instance, a crystal-clear pond is at a young

stage; one with cattails at the edges and slightly murky water is somewhat older.

At whatever stage, freshwater areas are of great value to humans. Boat traffic on the Mississippi River, the local lake that serves as a water supply, rainbow trout from a stream in the Rocky Mountains, or the old swimming hole are but a few examples. Swamps, marshes, and bogs, all wetlands formerly considered wastelands, are achieving new status. Many have been filled in by people to suit their needs for dry or developable land, but those that remain are slowly achieving recognition of their vital ecological roles. Such wetlands contribute to flood control, groundwater supplies, pollution filtration, and they support a significant variety of plants and animals.

activities with diverse freshwater areas

comparing freshwater areas

Materials: A variety of freshwater areas (rivers, ponds, swamps, and others), freshwater identification guides, clippers, pieces of white poster board (at least 8½ x 11 inches, or 21.6 x 28 c), self-adhesive plastic (cut to sizes to match the poster board pieces), pencils, paper, old newspapers.

Procedure: Visit a freshwater habitat. Estimate and record the area of standing water and/or the area of water-saturated soil. Note the prevalent plants of the area and clip samples of typical growth. Arrange each sample on a piece of poster board and cover it with clear self-adhesive plastic. On the back, record the date, name of habitat, name of plant if known (use field guide), estimated percentage of that plant type in relation to the total plant population of the habitat, and any other pertinent information. Put plant samples that are wet between layers of newspaper, and mount them on poster board after they are dry. Visit other freshwater habitats and repeat the study. Back inside, organize the materials from the different habitats into a display and compare the results.

It is likely that the results will demonstrate that in the different freshwater areas, different plant types are found to be predominant, although a few plant types may prove to be common in all the areas. Most plants have distinct preferences for particular environmental conditions. Rushes and sedges may be the predominant plants in a marsh, willows common along a river, and cattails crowding at the edge of a pond; duckweed, however, might be found in all three areas. This comparative study illustrates that plants, when found in significant numbers, are excellent indicators of the conditions in that habitat and can help in identifying types of freshwater areas.

This is a relatively sophisticated study, suited for older children,

and it can be enlarged. Test different waters for acidity or alkalinity. Compare the colors of the different waters. Take ponding equipment and survey the aquatic animals in each habitat. The compositions of the animal populations may vary, like the plants, indicating different aquatic conditions. Black fly larvae, for instance, indicate well-oxygenated water and are adapted for living in swiftly flowing rivers and streams. Whirligig beetles, however, do not need water with a high oxygen content; they live in still or gently moving waters.

The types of animals populating a freshwater habitat can indicate the presence, or absence, of pollution. Water sow bugs, dragonfly nymphs, and certain others are able to tolerate slightly polluted waters. Finding a few of these creatures along with a great number of pollution-tolerant animals, such as mosquito larvae, bloodworms, and rat-tailed maggots would indicate pollution. On the other hand, water can be judged unpolluted when a great number of pollution-intolerant creatures, such as water boatmen and mayfly larvae, are present, with few, if any, pollution-tolerant species.

These comparative studies may also demonstrate pond succession. Clear water with few plants indicates an early stage. Cattails, waterlilies, and other water-loving plants growing in organic mud indicate later stages, while the vegetation of a marsh and little open water clearly show the end stages of succession.

Studying and comparing ponds, rivers, swamps, and bogs will increase understanding and appreciation of these watery habitats. To find a pitcher plant in a bog, for instance, is to find a living demonstration of the theory that the high acidity of bogs,

caused by the great accumulations of peat from sphagnum moss, makes nutrients such as nitrogen difficult for some bog plants to obtain. A pitcher plant is carnivorous in part; its pitcher shape forms a trap for small animals, namely insects, from which the plant is able to obtain its needed nitrogen.

rate of brook, stream & river flow

See the activity on p. 106 that describes how to find the velocity of water in a creek.

follow a brook

Materials: Brook, vehicle, and/or maps.

Procedure: Trace the route of water in a brook from its source to its eventual destination, the ocean.

Do at least some of this activity by walking beside and observing the brook. Depending on the distances involved, use a vehicle to follow the progress of the brook to a river and on to the ocean. Stop at several sites to observe the waterway. Has it become larger? Does it flow faster? Use maps to follow any part of the route that cannot be done by foot or vehicle.

how does water erode?

Materials: Garden hose, water, a slightly inclined area with relatively bare earth.

Procedure: Turn on the hose and let the water flow through the area, like a miniature river. Have the children build dams, ponds, and canals with earth, and watch how the course of the water flow may change and how the water erodes the earth.

An excellent location for this activity is an area under pine trees, as the pine needles and soil underneath are adaptable materials for building dams and the like. This is an absorbing activity for young children, and while they are making or repairing pine needle and mud dams, they are learning about erosion as well.

A modification of this activity is possible indoors. Line a large, low wooden box with plastic sheeting; leave a hole at one end for a drain. Put sand or soil into the box. Raise the end of the box opposite the drain. Pour water into the high end of the box and see what happens. Experiment with digging out a path for the water to follow, making dams, and so on. Experiment also with raising and lowering the high end of the box. Put sod in the box. Does it make a difference?

pebbles & sand

Many freshwater areas, especially streams and rivers, have pebble-lined shores; for activities with pebbles see pp. 102–103. Other freshwater areas, particularly lakes, have sandy shores; for activities with sand, see pp. 103–106.

values of freshwater areas

Materials: Data from previous freshwater studies and/or appropriate reference materials.

Procedure: Study aspects of the significance of freshwater areas to the environment and to humans, both historically and today.

There is a vast array of subjects for studies. Freshwater areas have numerous ecological roles. They supply food; the Indians consumed freshwater fish, waterfowl, and plants, such as wild rice, and we do today. Lakes and rivers are used for boat transportation. Many rivers and streams supply waterpower. Freshwater areas are used for water supplies, and wetland areas

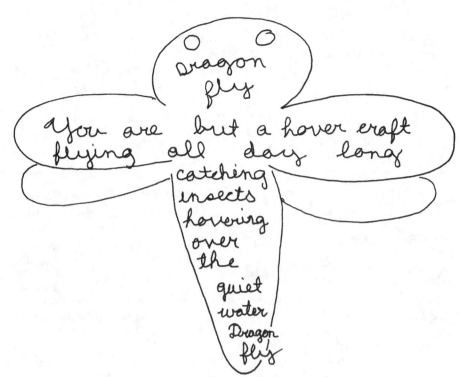

A young teen-ager's picture poem about a dragonfly by a pond.

can filter pollution. Many wetland areas contribute naturally to flood control. Rivers, ponds, and lakes are greatly used for recreation, such as boating, swimming, and fishing.

These subjects offer opportunities for follow-up studies in natural history and science as well as in other disciplines, such as language arts, mathematics, art, and social sciences, as indicated by the following examples. Make population surveys of waterfowl at a pond in different seasons. Study how the Indians of a locality utilized products from the freshwater areas. Try weaving with cattails as the Indians did. Using a local map, measure and estimate the percentage of the community's total area that is covered by freshwater or wetlands. Study the community's water supply. Find

out where the water comes from, how it is purified, and how much water the average family uses daily. Learn about the local regulations for protection of wetlands and whether further conservation measures are necessary. Study how electricity is generated by water power. Draw a picture of a swamp, illustrating both plant and animal inhabitants. Write descriptions or poems about a pond or a river.

Here is how Thoreau once described Walden Pond:

Walden is blue at one time and green at another, even from the same point of view. Lying between the earth and the heavens, it partakes of the color of both. Viewed from a hill-top it reflects the color of the sky, but near at hand it is of a yellowish tint next the shore where you can see the sand, then a light green, which gradually deepens to a uniform dark green in the body of the pond.

bibliography

adults

Amos, William H., *The Life of the Pond*. New York: McGraw-Hill, 1967.

Andrews, William A., *Freshwater Ecology*. Englewood Cliffs, N.J.: Prentice-Hall, Inc., 1972.

Coker, Robert E., *Streams, Lakes, Ponds*. New York: Harper, 1968.

Credland, Peter, *Rivers and Lakes*. New York: Grolier, 1975.

Janus, Horst, *Pond Life in the Aquarium*. Princeton, N.J.: Van Nostrand, 1966.

Klots, Elsie B., *The New Field Book of Freshwater Life*. New York: Putnam, 1966.

Needham, James G., and Paul R. Needham, *A Guide to the Study of Freshwater Biology*. San Francisco: Holden-Day, 1962.

Niering, William A., *The Life of the Marsh*. New York: McGraw-Hill, 1966.

Ursin, Michael J., *Life In and Around Freshwater Wetlands*. New York: Crowell, 1975.

children & adults

Busch, Phyllis S., *Puddles and Ponds*. Cleveland: World, 1969.

Earle, Olive L., *Pond and Marsh Plants*. New York: Morrow, 1972.

Hagaman, Adaline P., *What is Water*. Chicago: Benefic, 1960.

Hamberger, John, *Birth of a Pond*. New York: Coward-McCann, 1975.

Headstrom, Richard, *Adventures with Fresh Water Animals*. Philadelphia: Lippincott, 1964.

Laycock, George, *Exploring the Great Swamp*. New York: McKay, 1978.

Lubell, Winifred, and Cecil Lubell, *In a Running Brook*. New York: Rand McNally, 1968.

McClung, Robert M., *Aquatic Insects*. New York: Morrow, 1970.

Reid, George K., *Pond Life*. New York: Golden Press, 1967.

Reynolds, Christopher, *The Pond on My Window Sill*. New York: Pantheon, 1969.

Vessel, Matthew F., and Herbert H. Wong, *Watching Animals Find Food*. Reading, Mass.: Addison-Wesley, 1970.

12

winter, with nods to fall & spring

"If winter comes, can spring be far behind?" The ceaseless cycle of the seasons is always apparent outdoors because any one season contains clues about the ones to follow. During the fall, the natural world prepares to survive the rigors of winter, at the same time preparing for the renewal of growth in the spring. Fall, winter, and spring overlap each other, so that a study of winter includes the winter preparations of fall and the beginning of growth in the spring.

The length and severity of winter varies with latitude and other geographical factors. The season itself may appear fickle in some areas, bringing one year a blizzard in May and the following year torrents of rain in January. In the northern hemisphere, winter technically starts on the shortest day of the year, December 21, when the sun is at its southernmost point. Winter ends on March 21, the vernal equinox, when the sun is over the equator and days and nights everywhere are of equal length.

fall

Days and nights are again of equal length about September 23, the autumnal equinox and the official inception of fall. Thereafter, the hours of daylight become shorter and shorter, while the sun's rays become less direct. Temperatures drop, and cooler latitudes experience frosts.

Plants react to these shorter days of autumn. Annuals, which will die at the end of the growing season, have ensured their reproduction in the coming spring by producing prodigious numbers of seeds. Stems and leaves of biennials will die their first winter. Their roots remain alive, and the second-year plant will produce seeds as a means of ensuring continued reproduction. Many perennials may die to the ground in winter, but the roots live through winters for many years, sending up new growth each spring. Woody shrubs and trees survive winter in a state of dormancy.

Animals also react to the shortening daylight hours. Squirrels grow heavier coats, muskrats make winter homes, chipmunks gather seeds for winter food supplies and woodchucks have already stuffed themselves to acquire fat to sustain them during hibernation. Monarch butterflies and many species of birds migrate southwards. Frogs disappear from the edges of ponds to hibernate in the bottom mud; many adult insects die, leaving behind their eggs to hatch their progeny in the spring.

fall activities

days become shorter

Materials: Clock, compass, yardstick, thermometer.

Procedure: Record weekly or at other periodic intervals the times of sunrise and sunset; also note the compass points of the position of the sun at these times (if visible). On the same days at ten o'clock in the morning (or at any other set time), measure the length of the shadow of a yardstick held vertically, with one end on the ground. Record the length and also the temperature at that time.

These observations of the length of days and the position of the sun illustrate the sun's role in fall changes. After the autumnal equinox, the hours of daylight become shorter and the sunrises and sunsets are farther and farther to the south. Temperature readings decline, while the shadow from the yardstick becomes longer as the sun's rays become less direct. (Note that these activities are appropriate at any time of year to illustrate the sun's role in seasonal changes.)

frost

Materials: Thermometer with high and low indicators.

Procedure: Record the first, and subsequent, frosts in your locality. Observe and record which plants are first affected.

Geographical and other features may cause some areas within a given locality to experience frosts before others. If this is true in your area, can the reasons be determined?

fallen leaves

Materials: Construction paper in

Make discoveries outdoors in winter!

red, yellow, orange, purple, tan, brown, green, and any other fall leaf colors.

Procedure: Divide the children into groups, so that each group can have a different-colored piece of construction paper. Take a collecting walk and have each group find leaves on the ground to match the color of the group's paper. If there are quantities of certain kinds of leaves, set a rule that the groups collect only one leaf of each kind. Make a display of the leaves inside.

Take a collecting walk a week or two later and see how the colors have changed. (For other fall leaf activities, see Chapter 2.)

plant spring flowering bulbs in the fall

Materials: Spring flowering bulbs, such as snowdrops, daffodils, or tulips.

Procedure: Follow planting instructions for the bulbs and plant them at proper depths and distances apart for each species.

Here is the promise of spring in a fall activity, which will be well rewarded when the flowers appear.

how animals prepare for winter

Procedure: Observe and discuss a variety of animal winter preparatory activities.

Look for diverse activities such as squirrels burying acorns, birds migrating (for bird migration activities, see Chapter 7), as well as the family dog's growth of a heavy winter coat. Discuss how humans also prepare for winter by bringing in the harvest, insulating houses, getting out warm winter clothing, and putting on the car's snow tires. Read to the children Aesop's fable, "The Ant and the Grasshopper."

winter

Winter poses challenges to the natural world, especially in areas where temperatures frequently are below freezing. For plants, winter's main challenge is similar to that of a drought because water is unavailable for plant use when it is frozen in the ground as ice, or above the ground as snow. Plants, therefore, exist without a water supply and, to survive, must conserve what moisture they have. Deciduous trees and shrubs, having shed their leaves, have leaf scars sealed with a corky layer, and their next year's buds are covered with scales, both moisture-conserving adaptations. Evergreen shrubs and trees often have thin or small needlelike leaves, or leaves with waxy coverings, to conserve moisture.

Snow also is a challenge for plants. A heavy snow can break limbs off trees, but some trees are adapted so that snow tends to fall off them. The conical shape of many spruces is an example. Lack of snow cover can expose some plants to the dangers of freezing and thawing, but a continual snow cover insulates them against such temperature changes.

The cold of winter brings severe conditions for many animals. Those that are cold-blooded have approximately the same temperature as their surroundings and become increasingly sluggish with the lowering of temperatures. Most cannot move when the weather approaches freezing, and they enter a period of dormancy. A turtle, for instance, may pass the winter dormant in the mud at the bottom of a pond, or a spider may lie dormant in the protection of a curled-up leaf. Many insects survive in immature stages or as eggs. Warm-blooded animals that do not migrate or hibernate need to

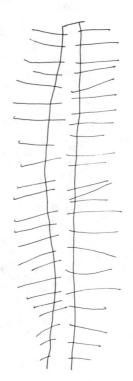

"A tree in winter that's lost all its leaves." Title and drawing by a five-year-old.

maintain their body temperatures. Many mammals grow thick winter coats, while birds can fluff up their feathers to provide added insulation. Many mammals and birds also seek shelter to conserve warmth.

The scarcity of cold-blooded animals and lack of green plant growth in winter disrupt the food webs of warmer seasons. Animals that in summer may eat grass and tender leaves, or frogs and insects either migrate, hibernate, or alter their feeding habits. Foxes, for instance, subsist entirely on the prey that they can catch; in summer foxes also eat fruits and vegetables. Some animals use food supplies gathered during summer and fall. Honeybees have stored honey for their winter food, while beavers eat from their underwater caches of logs. A few animals, such as woodchucks and ground squirrels, hibernate and sleep right through winter's food shortages and other vicissitudes.

Winter's snow is a mixed blessing for animals. For many it offers protection, shelter, and insulation. Several feet of snow can protect mice in their tunnels underneath from predators above, shelter them from winds, and insulate them from cold extremes of weather. The same snow depth may allow rabbits to nibble buds and ends of twigs, which otherwise would be high above their reach, but it makes it difficult for deer to paw to the grasses on the ground below. Deeper snow hinders deer as they run, making them more vulnerable to predators, although snow can hinder a predator's travel as well. Some animals adapt to walking on the surface of the snow. The snowshoe hare grows extra fur on its feet, and the grouse develops comblike fringes along the edges of its toes in the fall; thus, both have winter "snowshoes," an idea that children find intriguing.

The snowshoe hare is also known as the varying hare because its brown coat of summer turns to white, allowing it to continue protection by camouflage when snow is on the ground. Weasels also grow a winter coat of white, making them less visible to their prey. Many arctic animals, such as polar bears and snowy owls, are white permanently.

Why study nature in winter when many plants and animals are dormant, some animals have migrated south, and many of those that remain are concealed beneath the cover of snow? At a glance, an icy, snow-covered landscape may appear barren and lifeless. But such looks are deceiving. Snow can be a great indicator of wildlife activity. It serves as a writing board for all kinds of animal stories told by the tracks that are left on its surface. Also, signs of animal activity, such as chewed evergreen cones, show up well against the white back-

The snowshoe hare in its winter coat.

ground. The barrenness of dormant trees and shrubs reveals nests, woodpecker holes, galls, and openings for diverse animal homes previously concealed by leaves. Frozen swamps, ponds, and other wetlands allow for close-up inspections of beaver lodges, muskrat homes, and other natural features. Winter bird feeders near windows allow close-up viewing of birds in action. Winter offers unique opportunities for natural history experiences, and the activities of this chapter should serve as propaganda for winter nature study.

However, a word of warning is in order. Just as winter poses harsh conditions for wildlife, so it does for humans. Cold toes or shivering bodies are not conducive to the enjoyment of discoveries and learning. And certainly any risk of hypothermia (subnormal body temperature) should be avoided. When going out in the cold, insist that warm socks, boots, leg cover-ings, sweaters, jackets, hats, and mittens or gloves are worn by both the children and accompanying adults.

A lesser warning is that flexibility, one of the important maxims of outdoor teaching, becomes more important in winter. You may go to bed with a carefully planned program on the insulating properties of snow all set for the following morning, only to find upon awakening that a warm air mass, aided by an all-night rainstorm, has melted and washed away almost every trace of yesterday's snow cover. Yet, had temperatures been colder, the rainstorm could have been a blizzard, perhaps forcing cancellation of the program because of bad road conditions. In such cases, remember—flexibility!

activities with temperatures

winter temperature variations

Materials: Thermometers, clipboards, paper, pencils.

Procedure: Take temperatures in a variety of areas: sunny, shady, at the edge of a building, on an asphalt parking lot, at the base of a tree, in tree branches, in the pocket of an overcoat, on the surface of the snow, or buried down in the snow.

The temperatures will vary. See if the children can figure out why. One time some third-graders put a thermometer into a manure pile from which steam was rising. The result was a surprise to us all because, while the other temperatures taken had been around freezing, the manure pile was cooking along at 110°F (43° C)! This and the other temperatures were recorded on a large drawing of a thermometer on a piece of cardboard, which gave the children a clear, visual comparison of the different temperatures.

There are many possible variations with temperature-taking activities. Take and record daily or weekly temperatures. Make graphs of the results. Find the coldest and the warmest temperatures in a given month. Compute monthly temperatures to find the average. Compare the temperatures with those in the weather report in the local newspaper. Have temperature guessing contests; who can come the closest?

Substitute snowballs for thermometers. On a mild day place even-sized snowballs in a variety of locations. The comparative temperatures of the different locations will be evident by the order in which the snowballs melt. Even-sized ice cubes can be used instead.

make-it-yourself icicle

Materials: Open tin can, hammer, nail, string, water.

Procedure: Use the hammer and a nail to make a hole in the bottom of the tin can and holes at the top edge for hanging up the can with the string. Fill the can with water and hang it outdoors in freezing weather.

Your icicle should grow, but the temperature and the size of the hole will effect the rate of growth. Try coloring the water for variation. If it is cold enough, the water in the can may freeze, causing the can to bulge. The children may be curious about this; if so, have them take some plastic jars, fill them with water, put the tops on securely, and then leave the jars outdoors in freezing weather, overnight if possible. By morning the jars should be broken, and the children may have learned something about how water expands when it turns to ice.

activities with snow

Children have no trouble finding activities with snow by themselves. Snowmen, snowballs, tunnels, forts, and houses in the snow all teach their young makers about snow and its various properties. The following activities will also

Finding out the different depths of the snow.

teach about snow, but by more structured methods.

snow crystals are beautiful

Materials: Black construction paper (one piece for each child) chilled in a refrigerator freezer, hand lenses, clipboard, paper, pencils, snowstorm.

Procedure: Give each child all the materials above (except the snowstorm). Give the black papers last and go out immediately before the papers warm up. Have each child catch a few snowflakes on the paper, examine them with hand lenses, and, weather conditions permitting, draw and/or describe one or more crystals.

Often individual flakes may be seen on dark clothing during a snowstorm. Enjoy these ephemeral crystals when you can see them, for each one is a unique beauty. No two snowflakes are ever alike.

make a snow gauge

Materials: Wide-mouthed jar (or large can), ruler, masking tape, paper.

Procedure: Mark off in inches or centimeters on the masking tape from one to the number of inches or centimeters of the height of the jar. Put the tape vertically on the outside of the jar. Put the jar outdoors in an open area. After a snowfall, record the depth indicated by the gauge (make sure the snow in the jar is level before taking the reading). Record also the date and times of the start and the end of the snowstorm.

Make several gauges. Put them in different locations, and after snowstorms record and compare the results. For measuring deep snowfalls, use a measuring stick, as described in the following activity.

how deep is the snow?

Materials: Measuring stick, clipboard, paper, pencil.

Procedure: Measure snow depths and record the results in a variety of areas: open area, beside buildings, under trees, in the woods, or in snowdrifts. Compare the results. If snow gauges also have been used, include their readings.

snow temperatures

See the Winter Temperature Variations activity earlier in this chapter, and take temperatures on the snow and at various depths in the snow in different locations. Can the children realize that snow acts as an insulator? Ask them why snow is sometimes called a blanket. Have them burrow into the snow to understand its protection, and remind them that igloos are snow houses that insulate their occupants from the cold outside.

a snow melt guessing game

Materials: Clear plastic cups, waterproof marker.

Procedure: Mark lines on the plastic cups about an inch from the bottom. Ask each child to fill a cup with enough snow so that when the snow melts, there will be water in the cup right up to the marked line. Put the cups in a warm place indoors, wait, and then see how much water is left in each one when the snow has melted.

A simpler method is to have had the children guess how much snow is needed to make a cup of water when melted. Have them put snow in a pot and melt it on the stove. Try this with new snow and with old; there may be interesting differences.

Try snowball melting games. Outdoors ask the children to make snowballs that are equal in size. (This may prove to be an interesting educational experience in itself, as the children try to figure out how.) Inside, impale half the snowballs on pencils and hang them off the edge of a table by anchoring the other ends of the pencils with books. Have the children guess how long it will take for the first drop of water to fall off. Put the other snowballs in separate dishes and guess how long it will take before a whole snowball has melted.

what makes good insulation?

Materials: Small, equal-sized jars (or pill vials), rubber bands, various materials for insulation such as aluminum foil, cotton cloth, woolen fabric, cotton, newspaper, or cardboard.

Procedure: Have each child fill a small jar with as much snow as can be squeezed in, and, indoors, wrap their jars with one of the different insulating materials. Give two rubber bands to each child to hold the material in place. Put the jars in a warm place. After a period of time, unwrap the jars and see how much snow has melted in each one.

The one with the most water will have had the poorest insulation. Which one had the best insulation? You can also do this with ice cubes of even size.

do colors affect melting?

Materials: Equal-sized squares of construction paper in black, white, and other colors, black paint, paintbrush, two dowels.

Procedure: Put the different colored squares of construction paper on the top of the snow in a sunny location, and record the times taken for the different ones to sink into the snow. Paint one of the dowels black, and stick both dowels in the snow in a sunny location. Observe and record the melting rate by each dowel.

These experiments may help explain rates of snow-melt in backyards, driveways, and other areas. Compare the melting patterns by the dowels with those around nearby plants and tree trunks. Do further experiments using squares of aluminum foil or other materials the children choose.

how clean is snow?

Materials: Containers for snow and water, paper towels, magnifying glass.

Procedure: Melt snow and filter the water through a paper towel. How much dirt remains on the towel? Look at it with the magnifying glass.

Compare snow from various locations, as well as new and old snow. Where does the dirt come from?

snow sherbet

Warning! This activity requires clean, uncontaminated snow. Do not try this in urban areas or any other area where the snow may be dirty or contaminated, including areas subject to acid rain.

Materials: Cups, spoons, orange juice powder.

Procedure: Gather fresh, clean, new-fallen snow in the cups. Add orange juice powder, stir, and enjoy an orange sherbet wintertime treat.

Make snow ice cream by mixing snow, cream, sugar, and a few drops of vanilla.

snow shadow pictures

Materials: Stick.

Procedure: Have a child draw the shadow on the snow of another child with the stick.

play wolves-in-the-snow

Procedure: One person assumes the role of lead wolf. All the others are wolves that go in single file after the lead wolf, taking care to step exactly in the footsteps made by the lead wolf.

Can the children figure out how this way of traveling helps wolves to conserve energy? If a group has been restless or perhaps beginning to show signs of "getting out of hand," this is a good way to channel energies and preserve order.

play fox & geese

Procedure: In the snow, tramp out a big wheel with spokes through the middle. When playing, no one may go off these paths. One person is the fox and tries to catch all the others who are the geese.

This is good as a toe-warming activity.

make a snow scene

Materials: White chalk, colored paper.

Procedure: Have the children draw snow scenes with chalk on colored paper.

Hold up a piece of plain white paper while the children are making snow scenes and have them guess what it is. Answer: A picture of white geese eating saltines and flying in a blizzard over the North Pole.

snow sculptures

Materials: Snow that sticks together, items suitable for adding details to the sculptures.

Procedure: Make sculptures of animals or other objects and add whatever items are needed for details.

Of course, snowmen will win the popularity contest of favorite sculptures to make. Young children may need a little help in rolling the big balls and lifting them into place. If the weather is below freezing, try spraying the sculpture carefully with some water, which will freeze and harden it.

activities with plants

winter twig collection

Materials: Clippers or knife, identification guide, plastic spray.

Procedure: Collect twigs that have buds and leaf scars from different kinds of plants. Identify the twigs using the identification guide. Spray the twigs with several coats of plastic spray. When they are dry, mount them on the display board and label them.

Winter is a good time for learning identification of trees and shrubs by their twigs. Younger children enjoy twig matching games. Have several examples of different kinds of twigs. Give each child a twig and have the children find the others who have twigs that match their own. Many twigs are of different colors. Go out on a "rainbow hunt," looking for different colored twigs, such as yellow willow, green sassafras, purple-blue flowering dogwood, or red osier dogwood.

Winter is also a good season for evergreen identification because evergreens are particularly conspicuous when deciduous trees and shrubs have shed their leaves. Notice, when observing shapes outdoors, how many evergreens

WINTER TWIGS

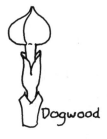

Dogwood

Horse Chestnut

Tree of Heaven

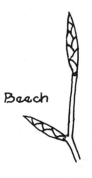

Beach

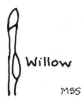

Willow

MSS

have a conical shape, an adaptation that helps snow to fall off. Take evergreen twigs indoors for close-up observation and identification.

rhododendron thermometers

Materials: Rhododendron leaves.

Procedure: On a day when the temperature is well below freezing, notice how the rhododendron leaves are curled up. Cut a sprig of the leaves, bring it indoors where it is warm, and watch.

As if by magic, the leaves will uncurl. Take them back outside. Leave them for a while and, presto, they will curl back up! Rhododendron leaves curl up as a moisture-conserving adaptation. When it is below freezing, the air also is dry and the leaves will curl. Compare the amount of leaf curl with the temperature and find how it correlates. (If you look during dry summer weather, you will notice how the leaves have again curled.)

forcing twigs

Materials: Clippers, jars of water.

Procedure: Toward winter's end, clip twigs of forsythia, pussy willow, red maple, or other shrubs and trees, and put the stems in water. Observe what happens (and enjoy it as a foretaste of spring).

Leaves and perhaps flowers will appear. Experiment with bringing twigs in at weekly intervals and compare the results. What are the differences and why?

tree silhouettes

Materials: Paper, pencils (or charcoal, pastels, drawing pens, or other mediums).

Procedure: Sketch tree silhouettes

to show the basic shape of the tree.

Winter is a good time for sketching tree silhouettes. The silhouettes vary greatly, and many trees can be identified by the shapes of their silhouettes. On a smaller scale, weed seed stalk silhouettes can also be observed and drawn.

activities with animals

bird feeders

Winter is a good time to feed birds, and there are many kinds of bird feeders that can be made by all ages. For bird feeder activities, see Chapter 7.

hibernation

Materials: Books with information on hibernating animals, fever thermometer, timepiece that indicates seconds.

Procedure: Study how a hibernator's metabolism slows down to conserve body energy. Have the children take their own temperatures, and count their heartbeats and number of breaths in a minute. Have them repeat these tests after resting and after exercising. Compare the results.

During four months of hibernation, an animal uses about the same amount of energy as it would in four days of activity. A hibernating woodchuck's heart rate

JUMPING MOUSE
HIBERNATING

slows from the normal of about eighty beats a minute to three or four per minute; its temperature drops to 38°F (3.3°C), and it breathes only once in every five minutes. The children's experiments with their own temperatures and rates of heartbeat and respiration will aid them in understanding how hibernators' slow metabolism helps them through the long hibernation period. If you live where winters are severe, find out which animals hibernate in your locality. (If you are in a hot climate, it might be interesting to find out if any animals in the area estivate, which is to become dormant during the heat of summer.)

hidden animal game

Materials: Construction paper, crayons, scissors.

Procedure: Have the students draw, color, and cut out an animal of their choosing (decide beforehand whether the animals should be real or imaginary).

Have each child "hide" his or her animal outside in a given area, leaving the animal in plain sight, but using camouflage for concealment. When all the animals are hidden, have the children hunt for them.

Which animals were the most obvious? Can the children think why? Were there any animals that no one found? Would the animals be easier to see if they could move? This activity can be done with bare ground or when there is snow. The snowshoe hare, ermine, snowy owl, and ptarmigan are animals that camouflage well in snow.

animal track stories

Materials: Animal track guide.

Procedure: Find animal tracks in

the snow. Identify them, using the track guide. Follow them to find what story they may tell.

Animal track stories in the snow generate excitement as the plot of the story is unraveled, clue by clue. Play "track detectives" and watch for the following clues: size and shape of the tracks, number of toes showing, claw marks (if any), length of stride and sidewise width, and the overall pattern. Are there tail or wing marks? Which direction was the animal going, and where do the tracks lead?

To preserve an animal track story, sketch the tracks and record all the observations about them. Remember that in populated areas many tracks may be those of dogs and cats. Make a pet track survey of the area.

Much can be learned about tracking by making tracks ourselves. Have the children walk, run, jump, and hop in the snow. How do these tracks vary? Do short and tall children leave the same track patterns? Have some

Measuring the stride of squirrel tracks in the snow.

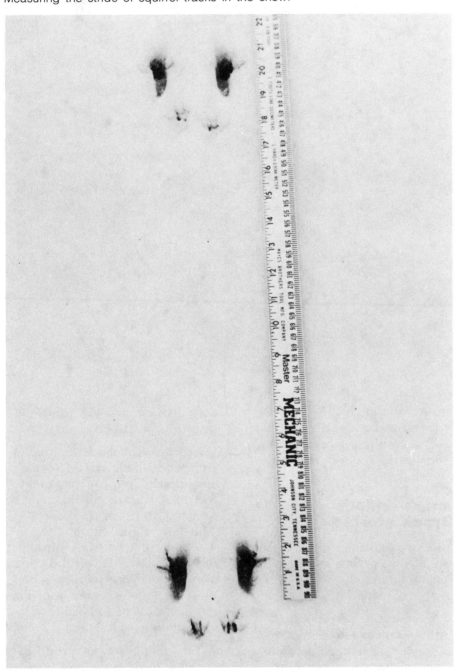

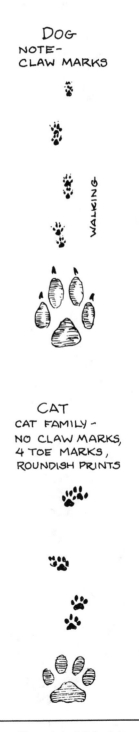

DOG
NOTE-
CLAW MARKS

WALKING

CAT
CAT FAMILY -
NO CLAW MARKS,
4 TOE MARKS,
ROUNDISH PRINTS

children make a track trail for others to follow; what track stories can they include in the trail? Long hind footprints in front are an identifying clue to rabbit and squirrel tracks. Try to make these kinds of galloping tracks in the snow; it's difficult!

Young children like to make "angels" in the snow. Lying on their backs in the snow with their

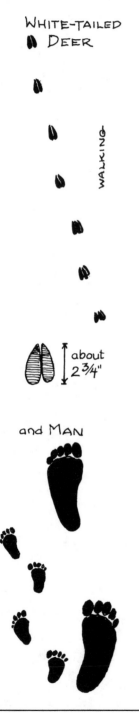

WHITE-TAILED DEER

WALKING

about 2¾"

and MAN

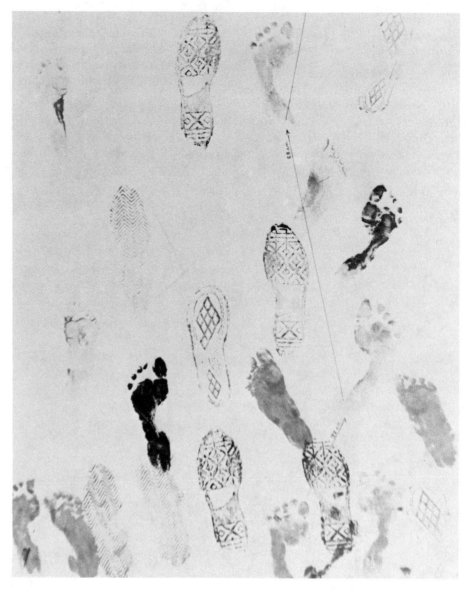

A footprint mural.

arms out straight, they move their arms back and forth. Then they carefully get up and the snow surface shows signs of angels.

make indoor track stories

Materials: Potatoes or pieces of styrofoam, paring knives, poster paint, aluminum pie plates, large pieces of paper.

Procedure: Carve tracks for printing on potato halves or styrofoam. Put small amounts of paint in the pie plates. Dip

carved tracks into the paint and print on the paper.

Use larger containers for the paint and a long roll of paper, and the children can put their feet in the paint and make their own footprints on the paper. This can be fun, but also messy. Try to have a pet walk through the paint and then on the paper. You can get nice footprints on the paper this way, but you may also get a lot of footprints elsewhere as well.

A very simple way of printing tracks is to draw a small track

"JUMPERS"
RABBIT
↑ SQUIRREL
↑

"GROUND JUMPERS"
USUALLY PUT
FRONT FEET
DOWN ONE AFTER
THE OTHER ~
JUMPING ANIMALS
WHICH LIVE IN
TREES USUALLY
USE FRONT FEET
TOGETHER ~

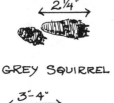

← 2¼" →

GREY SQUIRREL

← 3"-4" →

↑ HIND FOOT   ↑ FRONT

COTTONTAIL
RABBIT

(bird tracks are the easiest) on the top of an ordinary pencil eraser with a ball-point pen. Press the eraser down onto paper to make track patterns. When the tracks become faint, apply more ink to the eraser with the pen. Tracks can also be made with stencils; cut a track stencil and spray with spray paint to make tracks. A large piece of styrofoam can be used to show track stories; simply make indentations of tracks with a pencil in the styrofoam.

signs of animals hunt

Materials: Lists, pencils.

Procedure: Divide the children into groups and give each group a pencil and a list with the following animal signs to find on it: mammal home, sign of mammal feeding activity, mammal scat, bird home, sign of bird feeding activity, piece of bird or mammal covering, insect home, sign of insect feeding activity, insect eggs, insect cocoon, and a gall. Have each group record on the list where it found each item.

This is excellent for a group outdoor exploration because finding the items gives a definite focus to the expedition together. With so many eyes wide open for looking, many questions are bound to arise about other discoveries on the trip. This is a time to capitalize on the children's self-aroused curiosity. Help them to figure out answers themselves and also suggest looking things up in reference materials when back indoors.

This activity can also be done as a scavenger hunt. Set a specified time limit, and the group that finds the most items on the list wins. Afterwards discuss together the different items that were found. A group of children with a background in natural history might enjoy a hunt that required finding specific animal signs, such as woodpecker holes, a twig chewed by a deer (deer bite with their molars, leaving a jagged cut), or a twig chewed by a rabbit (rabbits cut with their sharp front teeth, leaving a 45-degree angle cut).

lively leaf litter

Materials: Shovel, magnifying glass.

Procedure: Dig down through snow in the woods and bring up some leaf litter. Observe the litter carefully indoors to see how many creatures have been wintering there.

As the litter warms up, a surprisingly large number of small creatures may become active, and you can see them. Watch for these small animals with a magnifying glass. If possible, replace the animals and their litter where you found them.

winter & people

Materials: Books with information on how different cultures have solved problems of winter survival.

Procedure: Using the books as references, study and make reports on how different societies adjusted to coping with the problems of winter.

Find out how snow, ice, and cold affected native Americans, the early settlements at Plymouth and Jamestown, and the covered wagon trains traveling westward. Think of ways that our urbanized modern society adapts to winter weather. Study the Laplanders, Eskimos, and other societies that live in extremely cold climates. It is said that the Eskimos have fifteen words in their language to describe snow. Ask the children if they can figure out why.

natural history in an art museum

Procedure: Visit an art museum and look for animals, plants, mountains, rivers, seashores, and other aspects of the natural world.

This is an enjoyable expedition, especially for a cold, unpleasant winter's day. The picture galleries will surely provide opportunities

Bird watching in the art museum.

for discoveries in natural history. However, also look at sculptures, tapestries, decorations on vases and other containers, jewelry, silver, and even furniture. How many clawed feet can the children find on the legs of tables and chairs? Ancient Egyptian art and hieroglyphics are full of delightful animal discoveries for children to make.

winter poems

Enjoy with the children Robert Frost's poem "Stopping by Woods on a Snowy Evening."

Whose woods these are I think I know.
His house is in the village though;
He will not see me stopping here
To watch his woods fill up with snow.

My little horse must think it queer
To stop without a farmhouse near
Between the woods and frozen lake
The darkest evening of the year.

He gives his harness bells a shake
To ask if there is some mistake.
The only other sound's the sweep
Of easy wind and downy flake.

The woods are lovely, dark and deep.
But I have promises to keep,
And miles to go before I sleep,
And miles to go before I sleep.

Then ask the children to write winter poems of their own.

One last look at winter: It can be a time of silence, a rare commodity in our industrial society. Gentle snowstorms soften human noises, often obliterating the sounds of cars on a highway or a distant jet plane. Go out early in the morning after a snowfall. In the woods, in a field, or in your neighborhood or backyard, there will be relative stillness, interrupted perhaps only by birds chattering or ice snapping a branch. Go out with children. Be silent and share together the calm that allows for peaceful feelings.

spring

Moving on toward spring, we know that "March winds and April showers always bring May flowers." Whether the timetable of this rhyme suits your region depends on where you are, latitudinally and geographically. The winds, showers, and flowers will appear as the daylight hours lengthen and warmer weather comes. As the snow melts, rivers and streams may flood. The brown winter-washed landscape belies the fact that greenery is on its way. The intricate preparations of fall to ensure the renewal of growth in the spring slowly unfold. Seeds left behind by annual plants in fall will begin to sprout; biennials soon send up their second year's growth; the roots of perennials once again nourish the development of the new season's plant. Snowdrops and crocuses appear, among the earliest of the fall-planted bulbs. Soon the buds of deciduous trees and shrubs open to display flowers and tender, new leaves. Mammals, including the family dog, start to shed their winter coats. Woodchucks and ground squirrels may again be seen after their long periods of hibernation. Frogs and turtles are back at their ponds. Insect eggs hatch, cocoons release moths and butterflies. Birds sing. Spring is here.

After winter's cold, spring outdoor explorations are especially inviting. Many fall outdoor activities can be resumed. The lengthening daylight hours, changing positions of the sun, and consequent rising temperatures can be studied, just as the opposite processes were studied in the fall (see earlier in this chapter). Who studied migration in the fall? In spring, you can study the northward migration of birds; record the dates when different species reappear. Following are suggestions for other early spring activities.

spring activities

signs-of-spring walk

Materials: Cards, pencils.

Procedure: Take a walk to look for signs of spring. Look for such signs as pussy willows, skunk cabbage flowers, fattening buds on trees and shrubs, newly arrived bird migrants, and their spring songs. List the spring signs on the cards.

Beward of mud and wet places in the spring. I speak from experience: on one signs-of-spring walk with my own children, a fateful decision on my part to take a shortcut home turned five enthusiastic walkers into four cold, wet youngsters and one mother in the same condition. The shortcut led us deeper and deeper into wet places, usually dry in summer. I ended up with ice water up to my waist, carrying my bedraggled youngest, while the other three were immersed according to their heights. Fortunately, home was not far. We quickly warmed up, and the walk swiftly became an adventure. Outdoor activities can include a touch of adventure now and then, which brings a special depth to the experience that is obtainable in no other way.

Repeat signs-of-spring walks. Keep a list as spring progresses. Record the first crocus, daffodil, frog calls, ferns unfolding, turtle sunbathing, or dandelion flower. This activity will help keep eyes open and observations going.

how fast does grass grow?

Materials: Yardstick, paper, pencils.

Procedure: Choose a clump of grass for measuring the rate of growth of grass blades. Measure the tallest blade every three days and record.

Is the same blade always the tallest? Continue watching the growth of the grass through the spring. When do the seed heads appear?

spring wild flowers

Materials: Wild flower identification book, clipboards, paper, colored pencils (or crayons).

Procedure: Study early spring wild flowers. Make colored sketches of each different species and record dates and habitat.

Many early spring wild flowers grow in the woods, taking advantage of sunny conditions before tree leaves appear and shade the forest floor. Make a display of the early spring wild flower picture collection.

insects' return

Materials: Insect identification guide (optional).

Procedure: Observe and record the renewal of insect activity.

Snowfleas, tiny primitive insects, are sometimes seen on the surface of snow, but otherwise, except for the legendary crickets on the hearth, winter is noticeably devoid of insect activity. When the temperature rises above 54°F (12.2° C), honeybees will venture from their hives. As warmer weather comes, other insects will appear, some hatching from eggs laid in late summer or fall, some emerging from cocoons, and others as adults that have passed the winter in dormancy. Watch for and note the dates of the first honeybee, butterfly, bumblebee, dragonfly, ant, blackfly, mosquito, and the first ladybug, who may bring good luck with the reciting of the old rhyme:

Ladybug, ladybug, fly away home,
Your house is on fire, your children are gone.
All but one, and her name is Ann.
She crept under the bread-pudding pan!

When spring comes, summer's on its way.

bibliography

adults

BROWN, LAUREN, *Weeds in Winter*. New York: Norton, 1976.

COUCHMAN, J. KENNETH, and others, *Snow and Ice*. New York: Holt, 1971.

HEADSTROM, RICHARD, *Whose Track Is It?* New York: Washburn, 1971.

MURIE, CLAUS J., *A Field Guide to Animal Tracks*. Boston: Houghton Mifflin, 1975.

QUINN, JOHN R., *The Winter Woods*. Old Greenwich, Conn.: Chatham Press, 1976.

RUSSELL, HELEN ROSS, *Winter Search Party*. New York : Nelson, 1971.

STOKES, DONALD W., *A Guide to Nature in Winter*. Boston: Little, Brown, 1976.

TRELEASE, WILLIAM, *Winter Botany*. New York: Dover, 1967.

children & adults

BERRILL, JACQUELYN, *Wonders of Animal Migration*. New York: Dodd, Mead, 1964.

BRANLEY, FRANKLYN M., *Big Tracks, Little Tracks*. New York: Crowell, 1960.

BUCK, MARGARET WARING, *Where They Go in Winter*. New York: Abingdon, 1968.

COLE, JOANNE, *Plants in Winter*. New York: Crowell, 1975.

COSGROVE, MARGARET, *Wintertime for Animals*. New York: Dodd, Mead, 1975.

DAVES, BETTE J., *Winter Buds*. New York: Lothrop, 1973.

GRAHAM, ADA, and FRANK GRAHAM, JR., *Let's Discover Winter Woods*. New York: Golden Press, 1974.

WEBSTER, DAVID, *Track Watching*. New York: Watts, 1972.

13

everything is hitched to everything else: ecology by day & night

"When we try to pick out anything by itself, we find it hitched to everything else in the universe," said John Muir, the renowned naturalist. The natural world is made up of innumerable, intricate interrelationships, like the widening and intermixing ripples caused by raindrops falling in a placid pond. Any small change in an interrelationship causes a series of repercussions in ever-widening areas. A volcano erupts, and volcanic ash is spread through the atmosphere thousands of miles away. A housing development is built in a wetland, which may change the watertable and increase flooding in some distant area. Also, the destruction of the wetland's natural plant and animal community will cause readjustments in neighboring ecosystems—readjustments that in turn will affect others in ever-widening areas.

Ecology means the relationship of organisms to each other and to their environment. The word *ecology* is derived from the Greek, *oikos*, meaning household, and in this instance, the household is the whole earth. Interrelationships are central to an understanding of ecology, and these interrelationships depend on the adaptations of plants and animals for their life needs and on the changes continually occurring in the natural world. A tree falls in the forest. What might happen to the shade-tolerant species that had been growing underneath it, or to the eggs in the bird's nest that fell with the tree? Older children can comprehend the concept of ecology, but it is generally difficult, if not impossible, for elementary school children to absorb the concept. (Complex ecological relationships are often not understandable until a child is in high school, and some are difficult even for adults to comprehend.) However, concrete examples, such as the changes that could result from that tree falling,

illustrate the concept. Such examples will build a basis for a child's future theoretical understanding of ecology and its significance to us all.

No ecosystem, no life anywhere on earth, could exist without the sun. The sun's energy is vital to the process of photosynthesis, which produces the basic food of all life. The sun also warms the earth, making it habitable, while it warms the air of the atmosphere. The effect of the sun's warmth on air is one factor that causes varying weather conditions. These different weather conditions, and the resulting differences in climate, have direct influences on plant and animal life. Palm trees cannot live in the arctic and polar bears cannot survive the heat of the tropics.

Air, water, and the materials of the earth are necessary for life as we know it. The oxygen and carbon dioxide in air are used by plants and animals. Life began in water, and without water, plants and animals cannot live. Most plants need soil for growing, and the type of plant that may grow in a given area depends on the makeup of the soil as determined in part by the minerals contained in the underlying bedrock. Since animals depend on plants for food, the components of soil indirectly influence the animal life of an area. The rich, deep soils of the prairie support an abundance of grasses, which support many grazing animals and their predators— quite a different ecosystem from a dry, sandy desert area where vegetation is sparse and animal populations relatively low.

Variations of sunlight, weather, climate, soil, and water, therefore, determine the types of plants and animals that can live in a habitat. These plants and animals develop interrelationships between themselves as well as with the habitat,

Like the ripples caused by raindrops in a pond.

constituting a dynamically balanced community subject to continual natural changes. For instance, a habitat with ample food plants for a large population of rabbits will in all likelihood also support such predators as foxes, coyotes, hawks, or owls, all of which enjoy meals of rabbits. Eliminate one species of the predators and the populations of the other animals will change. That might mean that there would be more rabbits, but, unless there are enough food plants to support the extra rabbits, some will die of starvation. More likely, the population of the other predators will increase and offset the rabbit surplus. In either case, a natural dynamic balance will be restored.

Enter the human animal into this habitat and it is probable that the natural balance will be drastically altered. A housing development, a school, and perhaps a shopping center would cause most of the predators to seek hunting territories elsewhere. The rabbits might remain, although their numbers would be greatly diminished by lack of food and protective cover, and by dogs and automobiles. Human changes would reverberate through the whole habitat, disrupting normal population fluctuation; new ranges of fluctuation would arise, perhaps only to be altered again by the effects of air and water pollution.

ecology activities

Since everything is hitched to everything else, all the activities in this book could be called "ecology activities." The activities in this chapter, however, are limited to those dealing with the components of habitats (sunlight, weather, climate, soil, and water) and with interrelationships of living things to each other and their habitat by day and by night.

activities with sunlight

The simplest approach to learning about sunlight is to feel it. In winter or summer, ask a group of children to close their eyes and face the sun to feel its warmth on their faces; this is effective, especially when contrasted with feeling the temperature in shady areas. Measuring the varying lengths of days in any season shows another aspect of the influence of sunlight; look in the Index for the activity entitled Shortening Daylight Hours. The sun's role in photosynthesis is vital; look in the Index for the Plants Need Sun activity. The direct use of solar energy by humans is important also; consult the Index under solar energy for related activities.

measuring the amount of sunlight in an area

Materials: Light meter, pencil, paper.

Procedure: Use the light meter to measure the light in different habitats, and keep a record of the data.

Repeat the measuring at different times of day and in different weather conditions, such as sunny, hazy, cloudy, or foggy. Observe the plants growing in the different habitats; are they the same or different?

activities with weather & climate

Weather affects habitats day by day and season by season; over a period of years, the normal average of the weather conditions determines the climate. Most of the activities in this book can be done in a warm season or climate; however, for activities in a cold season or climate, see Chapter 12 on winter.

Weather is an ever-present factor in outdoor teaching. When possible, use weather conditions positively. This is by far easier said than done; if the conditions are too harsh for the comfort of the group, remember that flexibility is a maxim of outdoor teaching, and seek shelter. However, a warm, summer rain can be turned to advantage. Feel the drops, watch what happens when they strike the ground; are puddles forming? How about tiny erosion gullies? What happens to the rain that falls on roofs or on streets or other paved areas? How are other animals coping with the rain? Enjoy the experience; it will be educational in a variety of ways.

how strong is the wind?

Materials: Pieces of thread and several different weights of string, pencils, paper.

Procedure: Hold a piece of thread at arms's length and pretend that it is an arm of a clock. If it hangs vertically at six o'clock, there is no wind. If it moves to seven, a light breeze may be blowing. If it stays at nine, use one of the heavier pieces of string. Keep a record of the results.

Compare the results with the Beaufort scale as shown in the illustration, and have the children learn to recognize calm, light air, slight breeze, and the others. When there is light air, can the children tell which way the wind is blowing? Have them wet a finger and hold it up; the side that feels cool is where the wind is coming from. The direction tells the name of the wind; for instance, if it is blowing from the north, it is a north wind. When the wind is stronger, have the children feel it blow against their faces. Close eyes and listen. Can they hear it? Smell it? Don't forget to fly kites on a windy day!

how much did it rain?

Materials: Wide-mouthed jar, ruler, waterproof tape, waterproof pen.

Procedure: Mark off 6 inches (15 c) on the tape with the pen. Attach the tape vertically on the jar, with zero at the bottom. Put the jar out in an open area. After a rainstorm, check the level of water in the jar to find out how much rain fell, and empty out the jar so that it will be ready for the next rainfall. Keep a record of the results.

cloud calendar

Materials: Paper, pencils.

Procedure: Make a drawing each day of how the clouds look that day; describe them also. Put the date on the drawing and description, and note whether it was sunny, partly sunny, overcast, or rainy.

Don't forget to look for animals, fantastic beasts, and other objects that may be seen in cloud shapes.

Smoke rises straight up. / Less than 1 mile per hour. / CALM ⓪	Large branches in motion; umbrellas hard to hold; telephone wires whistle. / 25–31 miles per hour. / STRONG BREEZE ⑥
Smoke drifts; weather vanes still. / 1–3 miles per hour. / LIGHT AIR ①	Whole trees in motion; walking against wind difficult. / 32–38 miles per hour. / MODERATE GALE ⑦
Leaves rustle and weather vanes move. / 4–7 miles per hour. / SLIGHT BREEZE ②	Twigs break off the trees. / 39–46 miles per hour. / FRESH GALE ⑧
Leaves and small twigs in constant motion; light flag extended. / 8–12 miles per hour. / GENTLE BREEZE ③	Slight building damage. / 47–54 miles per hour. / STRONG GALE ⑨
Dust, dry leaves, loose papers raised; small branches move. / 13–18 miles per hour. / MODERATE BREEZE ④	Seldom happens inland; trees uprooted; much damage. / 55–63 miles per hour. / WHOLE GALE ⑩
Small trees in leaf start to sway; crested wavelets form on inland waters. / 19–24 miles per hour. / FRESH BREEZE ⑤	Very rare; much general damage. / 64–72 miles per hour. / STORM ⑪
MASSACHUSETTS AUDUBON SOCIETY / LINCOLN, MASSACHUSETTS 01773	Anything over 73 miles per hour is a HURRICANE ⑫

Try to catch one in a drawing before it fades into something else.

make a simple barometer

Materials: Water, food coloring, bottle, cork to fit bottle with one hole in it (to fit glass tube), two 2-inch (5 c)-long glass tubes, 3-inch (7.5 c)-long piece of rubber tubing (to fit glass tube), candle, matches, string, adhesive or masking tape.

Procedure: Fill the bottle with water and add food coloring to color the water. Fasten the glass tubes together with the rubber tubing and insert one glass tube through the cork. Put the cork securely into the top of the bottle; seal it closed with wax melted from the candle. Invert the bottle and suck water into the tube; tie the tube to the bottle's neck so that it forms a U. Hang the bottle upside down, using the string and the tape to hold the string in place. (Plastic tubing may be used instead of the glass and rubber tubing, but it is difficult to seal completely with wax.)

When the air pressure is high, the pressure will push on the water in the tube, causing the level of the water in the tube to be lower; when the air pressure is low, the level in the tube will be higher.

daily weather reports

Materials: Thermometer, weather vane or compass, thread, string, rain gauge, simple barometer.

Procedure: Have the children make daily weather reports using materials and techniques of the previous weather activities. Include temperature, wind direction (use the weather vane or feel the wind direction and use the compass to tell the direction), wind speed, amount of precipitation, cloud description, and air pressure.

weather lore

Procedure: How many bits of weather lore do the students know? Make a collection of them written on the blackboard. Which ones seem to "work"?

Weather lore varies in different localities. A few examples for starters follow.

Red sky at night, sailors' delight;
Red sky in morning, sailors' take warning.

When the dew is on the grass,
Rain will never come to pass.
When grass is dry at morning light,
Look for rain before the night.

When smoke descends,
Good weather ends.

In New England, strangers are often told, "If you don't like the weather, wait a minute."

Use a hand lens to look closely at rocks.

activities with rocks & soil

Rocks are at the bottom of it all because the entire surface of the earth is underlain by bedrock. Sometimes we see this bedrock exposed, especially in mountainous places, or we see it rising along the sides of a superhighway that has been blasted through the rocky hill. More often, however, the bedrock is covered with various layers of soil and vegetation. The minerals in the bedrock contribute directly to the mineral content of the soil. Soil contains finely ground rock, which generally comes from the bedrock of the area; soil also contains water, air, and organic matter from decayed plants and animals.

Children are natural rock collectors, and often are interested to learn about the three different kinds of rock: igneous, sedimentary, and metamorphic. Igneous rocks were molten liquids that have cooled to become solid, just as water, when cooled enough, turns to ice. Sedimentary rock is the result of rock erosion into leftovers of silt or sand, forming layers of sediments, which, under pressure, are squashed together to become rock hard. Generally, the layers can be seen in sedimentary rocks. Metamorphic rocks are either igneous or sedimentary rocks that with heat or pressure have undergone chemical changes. Insects and frogs undergo metamorphoses, or changes in form and structure; rocks do also, but over a considerably longer time span. The earth, after all, has been around for nearly four billion years. If you pretend that four billion is one year, the amount of time that humans have been on earth is the equivalent of the last twelve seconds of that year.

Rocks are easily found. Look at city buildings. Most are made of natural or manufactured rocks. Look at rocks along the sides of highways; often you can see layered sedimentary rocks. Look for rocks with fossils in them; they tell stories of ancient times. Sometimes in cities you can find modern "fossils"; look on concrete sidewalks for footprints, usually dog, cat, or human, made while the cement was wet. Look for rocks that have a white stripe around them; they are "lucky" stones and are supposed to bring good fortune.

Make rock rubbings by placing a piece of paper over the surface of a rock and rubbing the broad side of a crayon over it. Paint an enlarged view of the design or texture of a rock surface. Look for animal shapes in rocks. Also, see Chapter 9 for how to make rock mosaics and do other crafts with rocks. For a little rock fun, take two pieces of quartz into a dark place and hit them together. Sparks will fly!

sorting rocks

Materials: Assortment of rocks.

Procedure: Have the children sort the rocks into categories.

There are many possible categories: color, weight, shape, texture, hardness. Young children, for instance, can sort rocks to

match the colors of crayons. A project for older children is to sort rocks using the geologist's scale of hardness, from 1 to 10.

A rock of a soft mineral, such as talc, that can be scratched with a fingernail is 1 or 2 on the scale. If the mineral can be scratched with a copper penny, but not with a fingernail, it is 3 on the scale. If it can be scratched with a knife, but not with a penny, it is 4 or 5. If it can scratch glass, it is 6 or higher, and if it can scratch quartz, it is 7 or higher. The hardest mineral, diamond, is 10 on the scale, which means that diamonds can scratch all other minerals.

make a "sedimentary rock"

Materials: Half-gallon milk carton, plaster of Paris, water, mixing container, large spoon, sand, earth, gravel, colored chalk.

Procedure: Unfold the entire top of the milk carton. Mix plaster of Paris and water together and have the children add sand, stirring it well. Pour or spoon this mixture into the bottom of the milk carton. Allow it to harden, then repeat the process with earth instead of sand. Keep adding layers in this manner; use the gravel, the colored chalk, and whatever other ingredients the children may want to try. If any of the layers do not seem to dry properly, sprinkle a little plaster of Paris powder on top, and the layer should dry. When it is all dry, carefully peel off the milk carton and behold the children-made "sedimentary rock."

test soil for acidity & alkalinity

Materials: Pink and blue litmus paper, lemon juice, baking soda, water, small containers, soils, pencils, paper.

Procedure: First, experiment with the litmus paper. Put a pink and a blue piece of litmus paper into a container of lemon juice (or other acid, such as vinegar); the pink piece will not change color, but the blue piece will turn pink. Put a pink piece and a blue piece into a container of baking soda mixed with water. The results will be the opposite; the alkalinity of the baking soda will turn the pink litmus paper blue. Test soil by allowing it to wet the litmus paper; if the soil is dry, mix in a small amount of neutral water. As with the lemon juice and the baking soda, if the soil is acid, the blue paper will turn pink; if the soil is alkaline, the pink paper will turn blue. If the soil is neutral, the papers will not change color. Record the results and repeat the test with other soils.

If the soils tested show differences of acidity and alkalinity, notice the kinds of plants growing in the different soils. Evergreens, for instance, are acid-tolerant and the soil beneath them generally is acidic. For a more accurate rating of the soils, obtain a soil-testing kit from a garden supply store. Many of these kits are simple enough to be used by children.

test soil for compactness

Materials: Metal rod or thin, sturdy stick, paper, pencils.

Procedure: Push the rod or stick into soil. Rate the soil's compactness as follows: very easy, like pushing into soft ice cream; easy, like pushing into a snowball; hard, like pushing into modeling clay; very hard, so hard that the rod almost cannot be pushed in. Record the results and repeat with other soils.

The degree of soil compactness determines the kinds of plants that can grow in a habitat. Plantain, for instance, is a weed that can grow in very compact soil. This plant was carried with the colonists to America and became known by the Indians as the plant that follows in the white man's footsteps, since not only did it come with the white settlers, but it quite literally grew in areas where there had been many footsteps.

test soil for moisture

Materials: Trowel, paper, pencils.

Procedure: Dig a small amount of soil; feel it and squeeze it. Rate its moisture content as follows: dry, falls apart and sifts through fingers; slightly moist, looks moist, but does not stick together; moist, sticks in a clump; very moist, feels wet; wet, water drips out. Repeat the test with other soils, keeping records of the results.

Most plants have distinct preferences for wet, dry, or in-between habitats. Notice the different plants that grow in the soils of varying degrees of wetness. (For determining soil moisture by weighing it and drying it, look in the Index under soil moisture.)

sift soil

Materials: Hardware cloth of different degrees of mesh.

Procedure: Sift some soil through coarse hardware cloth; what is left? Sift the soil through a finer mesh, and repeat through a very fine mesh. Examine the items left behind.

Sometimes the discoveries are exciting. Sifting soil once with some preschoolers produced a slug, which began to move in an assured fashion with its tentacles out across a small hand. Perhaps the small watchers had never before seen a slug; finally one commented, "Why, it looks like a snail!" This was an acute

Sedimentary rocks of the Grand Canyon.

observation, because slugs are members of the snail family that do not have shells.

soil soup

Materials: Three or four equal-sized jars with tops, water, three or four different soils, pencils, paper.

Procedure: Fill the jars about two-thirds full with water. Add into each an equal amount of different soil; put on the tops and shake each jar hard. Set the jars down side by side. Watch how the different soils settle and record the differences.

Different soils are composed of different-sized particles. The largest particles, such as small pebbles and sand, will settle first; the smallest particles, such as those in silt, will settle last. Repeat the experiment using aquarium gravel, sand, and chalk dust in separate jars, and in one jar combine all three.

activities with habitats

An intensive study of the components and interrelationships of a particular habitat, combined with comparative studies of neighboring habitats, leads to an understanding of the ecology of the area and ecological principles in general.

habitat explorations

Materials: Recording sheets, clipboards, thermometers, trowels, thread, metal rods, plastic bags, pencils, piece of string about one yard (or one meter) long, masking tape, felt-tipped pens, roll of large paper suitable for making large charts.

Procedure: Prepare your own recording sheets. The following three pages provide examples of the types of information to include in your habitat study. Locate an area that includes several different habitats, such as open field, edge of woods, deciduous woods, small stream, evergreen woods. Divide the children into pairs. Assign each pair a habitat, or, depending on the number of pairs, assign some pairs areas midway between two different habitats. Mark each pair's study area with a circle two yards (or two meters) in diameter, using the string as a compass. (Indicate the boundaries with twigs, pebbles, or by scratching the ground surface with a stick.) Give each pair the first eight materials listed above and have them conduct the experiment and observations of their study area as indicated on the recording sheets. When finished, have each pair bring with them their sheets, collections of signs of animals, plant samples, and soil sample.

Move indoors and give each pair a large piece of paper for making a chart. Have the masking tape, pens, and scissors ready. Have each pair write their type of habitat at the top of the chart and record all the data gathered, as well as tape to the chart the plastic bags with the soil and plant samples and the signs of animals.

Generally, children in the sixth through ninth grades can do the experiments and the collecting in their study areas independently, although the leader should be free to visit the groups to help and encourage. The chart-making usually becomes an engrossing and creative activity. This habitat study requires little or no prior knowledge of natural history on the part of children or leader. It is truly a learn-it-yourself activity.

Without any need to use the term *ecology*, ecological principles become clearer when the data and materials of the charts are compared. Questions arise about why different plants were found in the different habitats, and why signs of certain animals were found in some habitats, but not others. What interrelationships might exist between the plants and animals? How do they correlate with the effects of soil moisture and compactness, temperature, and wind on the habitat?

I know of a teacher who did this habitat study with a class in the fall, and then used the material on the charts with the class for the rest of the school year. There are many follow-up possibilities. For instance, identify the plants and animals of the habitats. Find out the food needs of the animals; which ones depend on the plants, which are predators, and which are the prey? Relating the animals in this way demonstrates a food chain of the area. Make graphs of the comparative data found in the habitats. Use the factual data for bases for problems in arithmetic. Research how the Indians might have used the habitat. What evidences of modern people were found in the habitats? Draw items found there. Make dioramas of the habitats.

This habitat study can be varied easily. Younger children who cannot do the work independently enjoy doing it as a group. A whole group studies a habitat together with a leader and afterward makes the chart together. Other groups do other habitats, so that there are different charts for comparisons. The studies can be made more sophisticated: use light meters to determine amounts of sunlight; set out rain gauges to measure rainfall over a period of time; use litmus paper to determine the soil's acidity or alkalinity. Return to the habitats during different seasons and repeat the studies.

habitat study

temperature

Put the thermometer in each position listed below for about a minute. Read each temperature and record it below.

_____ At shoulder height (hold thermometer carefully; keep your fingers off the bulb)
_____ At the surface of the ground
_____ Below the ground (use a trowel to dig a small hole about the depth of the trowel blade; put the thermometer into it)

soil moisture

Use the trowel to dig up a small amount of soil. Feel it in your hands and record below how it feels.

_____ Dry (falls apart and sifts through your fingers)
_____ Slightly moist (looks moist but does not stick together when squeezed)
_____ Moist (clumps together when squeezed)
_____ Very moist (feels wet when squeezed)
_____ Wet (water drips out when soil is squeezed)

soil sample

Dig a small sample of soil and put it into a plastic bag.

soil compactness

Take the metal rod and push it into the soil in several different places. How easy or difficult is it to push the metal rod into the soil? Check the best description below.

_____ Very easy (like pushing into soft ice cream)
_____ Easy (like pushing into a snowball)
_____ Hard (like pushing into modeling clay)
_____ Very hard (so hard that you almost cannot push the rod in)

wind speed

Hold a piece of thread at arm's length and pretend that it is the arm of a clock. If it hangs vertically, it is at six o'clock and there is no wind. Record below whether the thread stayed at six o'clock, or moved to seven, or eight, or nine o'clock.

_____ Holding thread over your head
_____ Holding thread at your waist
_____ Holding thread down near the ground

animal life

1. Collect signs of animals or animal activity (for example, feathers, nibbled-on acorns) and put each one into a plastic bag. Don't forget to include any signs of human activity, too.

2. Describe below any signs of animal activity that cannot be collected (for example, footprints, burrows).

_____

_____

_____

_____

_____

_____

_____

3. Identify, describe, or sketch below any live creatures found on or in your plot.

_____

_____

_____

_____

_____

_____

live creatures

(continued on next page)

plant life

Bring sample leaves back with you for use on the chart, if you wish.

How many trees are in the area? _____
Identify them if you can. Describe them and draw a leaf from each one.

_____
_____
_____
_____
_____
_____

How many bushes are in the area? _____
Identify them, if you can. Describe them and draw a leaf from each one.

_____
_____
_____
_____
_____
_____

How many different varieties of other plants are in the area? _____
Identify, if you can, the five most common ones. Also, describe them and draw a leaf of each one.

_____
_____
_____
_____
_____
_____

They have been working on a habitat study.

fringes of a shopping center parking lot where a sparrow's nest may be seen through the bushes.

outdoors in the night

"Time to go to bed!" Children expect to hear this in the evening, not the morning. Many animals, however, do "go to bed" in the morning, after having been active all night. The protective cover of darkness offers concealment for many animals, although many nocturnal predators have adaptations that help them to hunt in the dark and counter the effects of night concealment. Owls, for instance, have large eyes that are adapted for night vision. Also their hearing is acute; barn owls can catch a mouse in total darkness, when they cannot see at all, by hearing exactly where the mouse is. Furthermore, owls have soft feathers on their wings and even down to their feet, which enable them to fly almost silently, giving a mouse little warning of impending danger and, more importantly, not getting in the way of their listening as the owls fly.

Our night vision in no way approaches that of owls, although after twenty minutes or so, human eyes do adjust so that we can see far better than when we are first out in the dark. Night is a good time for us to concentrate on using our other senses. In the dark we often have to rely on our sense of touch as we may have to grope our way along a path. Ask the children how things feel to them. Does the bark of the tree feel the same as in the day? Maybe it is cooler or damper. Try smelling what you are feeling; you may be surprised to find some distinct differences, unnoticed before.

Try to listen carefully in the dark.

make an ant's nature trail

Materials: Cards, scissors, pencils, craft sticks, masking tape, pieces of string two yards (or two meters) long.

Procedure: Divide the children into pairs and give each pair the materials listed above. Have each pair make a nature trail as seen from an ant's point of view. Put down the string to delineate the trail. Interesting points along the trail, such as the tallest blade of grass, a nibbled-on acorn, or boulders (which might look like pebbles to humans) are described with signs made on small cards, attached to the craft sticks with the tape, and stuck into place.

This activity sharpens observation for details. Upon completion the children should visit the other ant nature trails. Noticing differences between the mini-habitats of the ant's trails lays a basis for an understanding of simple ecology concepts.

Remember that ecology studies are not limited to country or suburban areas that have green spaces. Every place outdoors constitutes some kind of a habitat, be it the edge of a city sidewalk where hardy weeds are competing for space through the cracks, or the

Owls are adapted for night-time hunting.

You might hear a mouse scurrying by or the flutterings of bats overhead. Remember that bats use echo location, which not only enables them to locate and catch insects in the air, but also informs them exactly where you are, and by no means will they fly up against you. Try some listening activities outlined in other chapters. Listen for frogs and toads in the spring (p. 70); listen for crickets telling the temperature (p. 63). Listen to the loud sounds of the insect orchestra on a late summer evening and try to locate an individual musician. If you are by the sea shore, listen for the scuttlings of crabs, which can be very active at night.

Touch things, smell them, listen, and also look in the darkness. Night gives a new perspective. Enjoy the silhouettes of trees and buildings or even of parked cars. Ask the children how differently things may look to them. Don't forget to look up. Perhaps some children may know the constellations of the Big Dipper or Orion, the Mighty Hunter. Look at other groups of stars. What shapes can be seen? Animals? Trees? Tell stories that are suggested by pictures seen in groups of stars.

Also, try looking for earthworms (p. 59), as well as mammals (p. 93). Night can be an exciting time to share the outdoors with children.

bibliography

adults

ALLEN, DURWARD L., *The Life of Prairies and Plains*. New York: McGraw-Hill, 1967.

BROWN, VINSON, *Knowing the Outdoors in the Dark*. Harrisburg, Pa.: Stackpole, 1972.

BUCHSBAUM, RALPH, and MILDRED BUCHSBAUM, *Basic Ecology*. Pittsburgh: Boxwood Press, 1957.

REID, KEITH, *Nature's Network*. Garden City, N.Y.: Natural History Press, 1970.

RUSSELL, HELEN ROSS, *City Critters*. American Nature Study Society. Cortland, N.Y.: Wilkins, 1975.

SLOANE, ERIC, *Eric Sloane's Weather Book*. New York: Hawthorn, 1977.

children & adults

BENDICK, JEANNE, *Adaptation*. New York: Watts, 1971.

BRITISH MUSEUM OF NATURAL HISTORY, *Nature at Work*. New York: Cambridge University Press, 1978.

DARLING, LOIS, and LOUIS A. DARLING, *Place in the Sun*. New York: Morrow, 1968.

KEEN, MARTIN L., *Be a Rock Hound*. New York: Messner, 1979.

KIRK, RUTH, *Desert Life*. Garden City, N.Y.: Natural History Press, 1970.

PETTIT, TED S., *Wildlife at Night*. New York: Putnam, 1976.

POLGREEN, JOHN, and CATHLEEN POLGREEN, *Backyard Safari*. New York: Doubleday, 1971.

PRINGLE, LAURENCE, *Ecology*. New York: Macmillan, 1971.

PRINGLE, LAURENCE, and JAN ADKINS, *Chains, Webs & Pyramids*. New York: Crowell, 1975.

RUSSELL, HELEN ROSS, *Soil*. Boston: Little, Brown, 1972.

SIMON, SEYMOUR, *Science in a Vacant Lot*. New York: Viking, 1970.

STONE, A. HARRIS, and HERBERT SPIEGEL, *The Winds of Weather*. Englewood Cliffs, N.J.: Prentice-Hall, Inc., 1979.

WYLER, ROSE, *The First Book of Weather*. New York: Watts, 1966.

14
keeping in step with nature

Industrial society has "thrown monkey wrenches" into many ecological systems, resulting in water pollution, smog, habitat destruction, flooding, threats of radioactivity, extinction of numerous species of plants and animals, and a host of other environmental disturbances. Any one of us may feel helpless in the face of such problems; what can we personally do? Obviously, society has to act collectively to live more in harmony with the environment, and each of us can take small steps in that direction.

Living in harmony with the natural world involves understanding and appreciation of nature, which is largely what the activities of this book are about. However, it also requires an adjustment of priorities, so that we can adapt ourselves, and our society, to live within the natural limits of the environment. This chapter offers some suggestions for keeping in step with nature in this way, and you may find some that will suit your tastes, your family's way of life, or your students' needs. The children will learn from the examples we set in everyday living, and this is important education because our present environmental problems will one day belong to them.

outdoor recreation

An easy way for all ages to keep in touch with the natural world is to be involved in outdoor recreational activities, especially noncompetitive recreation. Take a walk, alone or with others, and explore the outdoors as you will. It is nice to leave the car, bus, or train behind for self-sufficient travel, and besides, feet can go many places that cars and other motorized vehicles cannot.

Hiking, cross-country skiing, and outdoor skating, like walking, all allow time for looking about or stopping to listen, touch, or smell. Jogging, although it brings quiet time to appreciate being outdoors, generally does not allow for stops for closer looks. Backpacking requires planning and a fair amount of equipment, but it offers opportunities for firsthand experiences with many different habitats. Family or group camping brings participants together, allowing for shared outdoor experiences with the inevitable surprises that nature provides. (I still laugh when I remember the night an armadillo ran into our tent!) Water activities, like canoeing, rowing, sailing, swimming, and fishing also bring us into contact with the natural world. Fishing brings to mind hunting, often a controversial issue, although some of the most sensitive naturalists I know are hunters. The Indians lived in great harmony with the natural world, and they were hunters. A relaxed bicycle ride allows time for enjoying the roadside scenery, and I was intrigued recently to read of an adult education class, "Bird Watching for Bicyclists." (For safety's sake, do not forget to wear bicycle helmets.)

Simply being outdoors brings contact with nature. Bask in the sun, sit on a rock and chat with a friend, sit under a tree and read, or go up in the tree and read. In the spring of sixth grade, I used to do history homework in an apple tree, and since then, robin songs have always reminded me of ancient Rome! For outside reading comfort, however, nothing can beat a hammock between two shady trees. No hammock? Try a walk along a paved sidewalk and contemplate the force that just one weed must possess to struggle through a hairline crack for its existence. Children who play outdoors cannot avoid close contact with nature, even in city parks or vacant lots. A child's curiosity, sharp eyes, and appreciation of natural things keeps his or her mind wide open for nature's messages. Have you ever received a bouquet of dandelions from a small hand? If so, you understand.

Keeping in step with nature.

Outdoor recreation brings contact with the natural world.

outdoor cooking

Cooking over an open fire has been a traditional outdoor activity with children. Perhaps it takes us all back to our origins, our long-ago ancestors cooking over fires in caves. Open fires, however, are dangerous because they can all too easily cause forest fires. Also, especially in areas of high use, the wood supply is limited and the smoke may be polluting. Often outdoor burning is prohibited or inappropriate. In such cases use a camping stove or cook-out grill. Some of the following open-fire cooking projects can be adapted to these mediums.

For many years a successful ending for a winter nature program for four- and five-year-olds has been a winter picnic. A blazing fire and hot cocoa have kept us all warm as we cooked bread twists on long sticks. Bread twists can be made with any muffin dough that is sticky enough to wrap around the end of a stick. Use your own favorite recipe, a commercial mix, or the commercial refrigerated ready-to-bake muffins. Wait until the fire has settled down, and cook the dough on the end of the stick over low flames and coals until golden brown. Then remove the bread twist from the stick (watch out that it is not too hot) and let the young cook fill the hollow center of the bread twist with peanut butter and raisins, jam, or a small sausage or weiner, both of which also can be cooked on sticks over the fire. By this time, even if some of the dough is not entirely cooked through, the finished product almost always tastes delicious. (To conduct heat more evenly through the dough, try putting aluminum foil over the end of the stick first.)

Cook popcorn over an open fire using an old-fashioned popper with a wire basket and a long handle. Use a hand-held folding grill on supports, and anything that can be put between the two sides can be cooked over the fire: hot dogs, hamburgers, other meats, and bread for toast. Put a cooking grill over the flames, and with pots and frying pans anything can be cooked that does not require an oven. Also, try roasting unhusked corn (turn the ears frequently) and potatoes wrapped in aluminum foil. Once I tried to cook a cake in a pot over the fire. My advice is, don't try it. The results were so unsatisfactory that a dog who came by the following morning was not even tempted by the remains of the doughy mass, which had been tossed into the coals. A reflector oven may do a better job. For children a happy ending to open-fire cooking often comes with toasting marshmallows. If you have graham crackers and plain chocolate bars available, you have the ingredients for "s'mores." Put pieces of chocolate on a graham cracker, then a toasted marshmallow, and put another cracker on top. Delicious, filling, and very, very sweet!

When the cooking is over, never forget to extinguish the fire completely. This is the kind of action that should become second nature to young open-fire cooks. Besides, the steam and hissing noises that come from putting water on the coals are exciting to create. When the fire is completely cooled, it still has a use. Look in the remains for charcoal. Do you have some paper? You and the children can draw charcoal pictures of the scene or of something special discovered while the cooking was going on.

growing & preserving vegetables

A child who has planted carrot seeds, has watered them, kept up with the weeding, thinned the seedlings, and finally has the reward of the first fresh carrot may find that no carrot before has ever tasted as sweetly flavored or has such a perfect degree of crunchiness. With any age there is great satisfaction in growing one's own food; it gives a feeling of self-sufficiency and return to basics. Families or groups can garden together, or children can plan and maintain their own gardens.

Plants need sun, air, soil, and water to grow. It is nice to have a large enough, sunny area of one's own for a garden. However, lacking such, there are other possibilities. Many urban and suburban areas have space reserved for community gardens, which have benefits far beyond the particular plots of ground. Working beside other gardeners, either beginning or experienced, allows the exchange of all kinds of information, from seed types to pruning tomatoes, and inevitably everyone learns. If there are no community gardens near your area, can you start one? Is there a neighbor who will let you use some land for a garden? Do you have some shrubbery or flower beds about your dwelling with room for tucking in a few vegetables in the front or anywhere the sun may penetrate? Even when the amount of produce is small, the benefits to heart and soul will be way out of proportion to the actual quantity of the harvest. Apartment dwellers may have balconies or the use of rooftops for tubs or window boxes with vegetable plants. A few sample plants can be grown indoors. Parsley, for instance, grows quite well inside, and it is handy to have right there in the kitchen when a sprig is wanted. If growing is not feasible, find out if there are farms in the local area that permit people to come and pick their own produce. This is rewarding: a means of obtaining truly fresh food as well as having had the experience of harvesting it.

Vegetable growing is both easy and difficult. Many factors are involved, ranging from the type of soil and the expertise of the gardener to the amounts of rain, sun, and cool and hot weather in the season, and sometimes, luck. If you and the children you are working with are beginning gardeners, take care to ensure success, otherwise it is easy to become discouraged with growing. Follow instructions in a reliable book (some are listed in this chapter's bibliography) or consult with experienced gardeners or with local sources of information, such as 4-H groups or your county agent. Together with the children, find out how to prepare the soil, if fertilizer is needed, and what seeds or young plants may be the easiest growers for beginners. Remember that the start of the garden is only the beginning and that the children must be committed to a long-term project. Watering, controlling weeds, cultivating, or mulching are among the chores that come before picking the vegetables. After the picking, be prepared for truly enjoyable meals.

Will there be any extra produce? Share some with friends or neighbors who do not have access to garden-fresh vegetables. Some

Working together to preserve apples.

children are adept at selling. Let them market some of the vegetables, and the gardening experience will expand to include business experience as well.

Another means of coping with extra produce is to preserve it. Freezing or canning is not difficult once you become familiar with the processes, and most general cookbooks give clear directions for both. Even very young children

can help with preparing the vegetables. Are you freezing lima beans? Which child can shell the most? Sometimes a contest or a game thrown into the work makes it seem to go much faster. Making jams, jellies, marmalade, pickles, relishes, and other conserves also preserves food, and the products add delicious touches to meals throughout the winter.

In the old days a great deal of

vegetable and fruit storage was done in "cold cellars." Apples, pears, celery, varieties of cabbage, onions, leeks, potatoes, and many other root crops, such as carrots and beets, keep well for varying lengths of time in a cold place, where the temperature is in the midthirties F (around 3°C). After about ten days of curing in a warm place, pumpkins and squash can be kept at a little below 50°F (about 20°C), or even at a cool room temperature. Some vegetables will last right through until early spring.

If you and the children feel experimental, it is fun to dry foods. Dried apples are super-delicious; they have a special sweetness and are always welcome snacks during summer hiking trips. To dry apples you can use a commercial dehydrator, but a homemade rack serves well. Make a simple rectangular frame (the size is your choice) by nailing four pieces of wood together. Then put a piece of thin material over the frame (an old sheet or nylon glass curtain will do), and thumbtack the material tautly to the frame. Peel and slice the apples as you would for pies, spread them out over the frame, and put them outside in a sunny spot or in a warm corner inside. Drying will take at least several days. Depending on the thickness of the material, you may need to turn the apple slices over a few times. When they are dry, store them in tightly sealed containers. To use, simply eat. Or, if they are not devoured before, rehydrate them by soaking them in water for about an hour and use them for cooking in your favorite apple recipe. Apples can also be dried by coring them, slicing them into rounds, threading a string through the center holes, and hanging them up. A batch strung up over the kitchen table comes in handy for dessert snacks. Just reach up and take one or two for sweet munching. Experiment with drying other fruits and vegetables, but do not try raw potatoes; they turn into an unappetizing black color.

wild foods

Another step toward self-sufficiency is in the use of wild foods. However, this is a subject that calls first for a number of warnings; not so strong to scare you away completely, but strong enough to ensure caution. Many plants are toxic, some downright fatal; be absolutely certain of the identification of any plant you eat; it is so easy to make mistakes. If it is your first experience with a certain plant, eat only a small portion, and wait a reasonable length of time to be sure that it does not disagree with you. People react differently to different plants; some people, for instance, are allergic to strawberries. Never use plants for food that may have been subjected to insecticides or other toxic substances. For this reason, do not pick plants growing along well-traveled roads because of exposure to pollution by automobiles, and be careful of plants growing in urban soils that may be contaminated with arsenic from lead paint. Some wild foods are plentiful, but others are not, and some are rare enough to be on endangered species lists. Practice conservation ethics and pick judiciously, even from the plentiful species.

A postscript of a warning has to do with wild foods and children. Never forage for wild foods with a group of children that you do not know well. Words of caution that you may give may not be heard as you intended them, or perhaps not heard at all if the child's attention is elsewhere. However, if you feel that the children you are working with are mature enough to be able to understand precautions and act cautiously, it can be rewarding to find new tastes and literal nourishment from nature.

Collecting wild foods gives a good excuse for an outdoor expedition with a family or with a group, and it sharpens observation abilities, as the children must learn to distinguish the edible plants from others. Use a reliable wild foods book (several are listed in this chapter's bibliography) for assistance. Although there is generally a plentitude of wild foods available, start small. Learn and try one edible plant at a time. You are in for some treats, and free ones at that.

In early spring there is no better wild food to start with than the dandelion, one of our best-known weeds. Dandelion greens must be picked while still young and tender; once the plant has gone to bud and flower, the greens become bitter. Be certain that you and your copickers recognize the dandelion's deeply notched leaves growing in rosettes. Pick an ample supply because these greens, like spinach, shrink when cooked. Back in the kitchen have the children help in extracting blades of grass while rinsing the leaves; it can be a tedious job to do alone. The cooking, however, is simple. Pour boiling water over the greens and cook until "fork tender," about five minutes. Drain them, add a little butter, season with salt and pep-

Be cautious with wild edibles. Try just one at a time, and only a little bit at first. Be ABSOLUTELY CERTAIN about proper identification.

per, and enjoy. They are not only delicious, but also filled with healthy vitamins and minerals. Sometimes a child finds them a little bitter. If so, try dandelion fritters a little later in the season. I have never known anyone, young or old, to turn them down. Have the children pick the golden yellow dandelion flowers with as little stem on them as possible. Have ready a beaten egg with a little milk added, a bowl of cracker crumbs, and a frying pan with some melted butter in it. Dip the blossoms first into the egg mixture, and then into the cracker crumbs. Sauté them briefly, about a minute or two, until they are golden brown and a little crispy. You will be surprised at how fast these will vanish.

During the summer many wild berries come into season. Many times these berries are easily recognizable; sometimes, however, they can be confused with other berries that may not be healthful,

or may be worse. Be certain of identification and then be prepared to enjoy wild strawberries, blueberries, huckleberries, raspberries, or blackberries on outings with children. These fruits never taste better than when eaten as they are picked from the plant. With a little restraint, however, you can enjoy blueberry muffins or pancakes or other favorite recipes calling for wild berries.

If you go to the seashore during the summer, look for the seaweed known as Irish moss. If you find it, you can make a pudding that will go nicely with your berries. Irish moss grows on rocks exposed at low tide. The plants are short, dark, and freely forked, and they are generally crowded together, so that at a distance they may look like a moss. Use a guide book or ask a person knowledgeable about the shore to make sure you have the accurate identification. Irish moss was used by the Indians and by people living by the sea as a

thickening agent in cooking; the recipe given here is adapted from a cookbook of my grandmother's.

First soak a half-cup of dried Irish moss in water for fifteen minutes (or use one cup of fresh moss). Add the moss to three cups of milk in the top of a double boiler and cook over boiling water for twenty-five minutes. Strain and discard the moss. Add a third of a cup of sugar, an eighth of a teaspoon of salt, and a teaspoon of vanilla. Stir the mixture and pour it into individual molds. Chill and serve plain or topped with berries, crushed and sweetened, that you and the children have picked. My family likes chocolate seaweed pudding, which is easily made. Melt a square and a half of unsweetened chocolate, add a half-cup sugar and a third of a cup of boiling water, and stir until smooth. Add this to the above recipe just after straining and omit the third of a cup of sugar. Seaweed pudding is delicious!

Many children enjoy wild teas. Spearmint is a good one for a starter. Perhaps you have some spearmint in your garden or know of a patch nearby. The smell should aid in identification. Have the children gather some spearmint stalks and remove the leaves. Allow for about a dozen leaves per cup. Pour boiling water over the leaves, let steep for five minutes, and serve. Sweetened with a little sugar or honey, almost everyone likes this fragrant tea. You can extend the enjoyment of spearmint tea throughout the winter by drying some of the mint leaves. Pick a quantity of the mint stalks and hang them upside down in a warm place. When they are dry, remove the leaves and put them in a tightly sealed container. Use them as you would the fresh leaves.

Wild foods not only bring nature into our everyday lives, but also can lead to interesting studies about our relationships with certain plants. Spearmint, for instance, was a well-known garden herb in medieval Europe and was brought to America by the colonists. Blueberries are native to America. Reportedly the French explorer Samuel de Champlain found Indians gathering blueberries for winter use near Lake Huron in 1615. Presumably the Indians preserved the berries by drying them in the sun. Have the children dry blueberries the way the Indians did. When blueberry season has gone by, you can soak the berries in water and make Indian-style blueberry muffins.

raising animals

Most children like animals, and most children can take the responsibility for taking care of animals. Pets and children seem to go together. Dogs, cats, rabbits, hamsters, gerbils, guinea pigs, white mice, and parakeets are common pets that children enjoy and can

Carefully readying their sheep for the 4-H fair.

take care of. A child learns responsibility and care for other beings by having charge of a pet, as well as learning about the animal itself. If space or other factors limit a family's ability to have these kinds of pets, try goldfish or tropical fish. Children can learn a lot from fish as well. Pets that can be kept in a classroom are also educational, especially for children who may not be able to have animals at home.

When space permits, many non-farm families and some kinds of school and other children's groups embark on projects of raising small farm animals, such as sheep, goats, chickens, ducks, or geese. Children, depending on their ages, can take some or complete care of any of these animals. Pigs, a family cow, rabbits, and honey bees are also possibilities. Home-grown wool, fresh goat's or cow's milk, fresh eggs, local honey, and meats such as lamb, chicken, duck, goose, pork, and rabbit all increase feelings of self-sufficiency and teach that modern society does not have to depend on stores for everything.

However, before undertaking to keep any of these animals, find out the animal's requirements and ensure that those requirements can be met. Also, check local regulations about keeping animals. Some animals (pigs, for example) may be prohibited, and others may necessitate permits. If neighbors live close by, it sometimes is advisable to check with them also. Most important of all, if this is to be a children's project, include the children in the planning, or, if possible, have them do the planning themselves, with a little adult

guidance. Also, be certain that the children are ready to carry out the necessary responsibilities, as taking on the care of other beings should be considered a serious commitment. Furthermore, be forewarned that raising animals for meat may pose difficulties; think about it before you start. In modern society most of us are insulated from the killing of animals, and we don't even consider the fact that when we buy meat in the supermarket, someone has had to kill an animal for us. If you or the children feel

uncomfortable about the idea of eating animals that you have raised, the feeling is a natural consequence of our way of life and you need not feel guilty if you cannot get over it. Keep bees for their honey or raise chickens for their eggs, instead.

Chickens can be delightful, and truly fresh eggs are delicious. Chickens need a house or inside area large enough so that the flock will not feel crowded. They also need ample food and water, nest-

The chickens wish they could help with book writing.

ing boxes for laying eggs, roosts for sleeping on at night, and, if at all possible, an outside yard. Chickens love to go outdoors, and when their door to the chicken yard is opened in the morning, they will crowd and rush to go out, much like children running out the school door at the start of recess time. Some hens develop distinct personalities, especially among the bantams, or small chickens, who can be quite witty as well. Our bantams, who run freely about the place, love to hide their eggs, and we find the eggs in the most surprising places, from bicycle baskets to a box of roofing nails in the workshop. The hen responsible for the latter became fondly known as "Mrs. Nails."

There are many good books to help the beginning chicken raiser, just as there are for most small animals. There may be local sources of information available, knowledgeable persons or families to answer questions, and for youngsters, the 4-H programs in animal husbandry are excellent.

If raising animals is not possible, try to find a farm to visit. Many urban children, for instance, have never seen a cow up close, and they are surprised to see the udder where the milk actually comes from before it gets into the familiar supermarket cartons. If the farm permits children to have a try at milking a cow or gathering chicken eggs, they can begin to feel some of the basics in food production. As a followup to a farm visit, make butter with the children. Pour a pint of room-temperature heavy cream into a jar; have the children sit in a circle and pass the jar around for everyone to shake. After a fair amount of shaking, when the cream looks liked whipped cream, give every child a dollop of the cream in a paper cup, and let them stir the cream in the cups with craft sticks. When little lumps appear, the cream is turning into butter, a seemingly miraculous transformation that each child can see happening right there in the cup. The liquid that is left is butter milk and tastes good. Have crackers available to put the butter on, and the children are in for a real treat—butter that did not come from a store, but that they made themselves.

conservation awareness

Major environmental problems cannot be solved by individuals alone, but it is vital that individuals be aware of the issues and have an understanding of them because an informed citizenry usually makes the right choices. Start laying the bases of understanding with children now.

The issue of endangered species is one that appeals to children. Most youngsters have an innate care for animals and are able to project their care to species of animals that live in distant areas and that they have never seen. Have the children study endangered species, from wolves, whales, and eagles to endangered reptiles, amphibians, fish, or even invertebrates. Extend the study to include endangered plants. It is almost inevitable that at some point the children will ask "why," and the door has been opened for consideration of a major environmental issue that has no easy answer. Habitat destruction? Insecticides? Water pollution? Elimination of another species that may be a vital link in the food chain? Acid rain? All of these answers can interrelate and can prompt further questions.

Habitat destruction, for instance, often directly affects ourselves. Paving over a salt marsh to make a parking lot not only destroys the habitat of the many salt marsh plants and animals, but also may result in reduced fish catches for fishermen out to the sea from the area, and erosion and flooding of nearby properties.

Once a child's curiosity has been aroused about environmental problems, how can it be cultivated? Keep an environmental bulletin board in the classroom and encourage students to bring in clippings from newspapers, pamphlets, and magazines that deal with specific or general conservation issues. You can also include write-ups from the students about environmental subjects seen on television. Some students may become interested in participating in a conservation association to find out more, as well as to be able to bring in more materials.

Once the children have had some experience in becoming informed about environmental issues, help them to share their information with others, so that, like energy traveling through a food chain, conservation awareness will spread from one individual or group to another. Have the students make posters about specific issues and put them up in the school, the local library, or other public buildings. Have them write and give a play about a particular problem. Stage a debate (look up Salt Marsh

Debate in the Index). Hold a contest for energy conservation suggestions. This will start participants thinking about the need for energy conservation, as well as producing some ideas to try out.

Have the students study a local land-use issue and send a report to the local newspaper. Have them study broader issues and use the information in letters to appropriate state or federal agencies or legislators. Try always to assist the children to consider immediate and ultimate human needs, as well as those of the environment.

pollution

Everything has to go somewhere. This ecological maxim is abundantly demonstrated by pollution. Smoke combines with moisture in the air and becomes smog. Laundry phosphates seep into rivers, causing the water to become polluted. Nonreturnable beverage cans litter roadsides. Needlessly loud machines create noise pollution.

activities with pollution

How many kinds and examples of pollution in your area can the children list? Try to find out the causes of some of the examples given. Check for information available in local newspapers or from local conservation groups. Can you and the children formulate constructive solutions to any of the problems?

Noise pollution can be subtle and invidious. Find out with the children if our ears become accustomed to a certain amount of noise pollution. Have the children sit in different areas of the school yard, just to listen. They may be surprised to hear things they had not noticed hearing before. If possible, repeat the activity near an area of heavy traffic or any other particularly noisy spot nearby.

pick up litter

Materials: Bags or other suitable containers for litter.

Procedure: Clean up all litter in a particular area.

This is a tried and true activity with groups of children. For a variation have each child count the number of trash items that he or she picks up during a specific three-day period. What would happen if it became second nature for everybody to pick up litter in this way? Do the children notice that different areas acquire different kinds of litter? What does this tell about the areas? Some litter, such as a plastic six-pack beverage holder, is dangerous to wildlife; perhaps some of the children have seen a picture of an animal with its head caught in one of the plastic loops. For fun after a group collecting project, use pieces of the litter to make trashmobiles and junk sculptures.

what litter is biodegradable?

Materials: Eight half-gallon milk cartons, scissors, masking tape, soil, and eight of each of the following: wooden match, apple core, beverage container top, short piece of string, plastic container cover or bag, candy wrapper, metal foil from a gum wrapper, green leaf.

Procedure: Make eight containers by cutting the tops off of the milk cartons. Put in soil and bury one of each of the previously listed items in every container. Keep the milk containers in a warm place and keep the soil damp. Once weekly for eight weeks dump out the contents of one of the containers; note and record the appearance of each buried item.

After the eight containers have been emptied, notice which items had begun to decay; these are the biodegradable ones. Have half the class write stories about what might happen to one of the biodegradable items if it was dropped on the ground under some trees. Have the other half write stories about what might happen to one of the nonbiodegradable pieces dropped in the same place.

Plastic is especially long-lasting. Also, it is a petroleum derivative, which means that it is costly in terms of energy consumption. Ask the children if they think it would be helpful to the environment if we used less plastic. Have them make a home survey of all the items made of plastic. How many of these items would serve as well if made of other materials?

make your own smog

Materials: Half-gallon bottle, water, matches.

Procedure: Put about half a cup of water into the bottle and shake it around. Light a match, let it burn a little, blow it out, and drop it immediately into the bottle. As quickly as possible put your mouth over the opening and blow hard. When you stop blowing, look quickly to see the smog form in the bottle.

test for air pollution

Materials: Index cards, pencils, vaseline, masking tape.

Procedure: Rub a thin coat of vaseline over the centers of the cards. Tape each card onto a flat surface in a different location. Write the name of the location on the top of the card and leave all the cards in position for a day. Then collect and compare what has collected on the cards.

Use a magnifying glass for a close-up look at the pollution or dust particles. Once we found that a card in the kitchen collected more particles than the one put beside the road, which certainly was a surprise.

water pollution

Monitoring pollution in freshwater areas is an important step in determining controls. Several water pollution activities are included in Chapter 11 on ponds. Does your local or state health department analyze water for bacteria count? If so, have students bring in samples from different freshwaters and you can send the samples in for analysis. D.O. (dissolved oxygen) testing is useful in identifying possible pollution. Simple D.O. kits are available from laboratory supply houses, as are other materials that older students can use for doing chemical analyses of different waters.

energy conservation

The old New England adage, "Eat it up, wear it out, make it do, or do without," is coming back into style in light of the increasing needs to practice energy consumption. Turning down thermostats, insulating buildings, carpooling, using public transportation, using less water, saving electricity, using alternative energy sources, and recycling are familiar calls. In what practical ways can we help children assimilate these directives? The following activities may be useful as is, or they may lead to further ideas of your own.

energy activities

solar baked apple slices

Materials: Four styrofoam cups, black paper, scissors, masking tape, apple, knife, thin plastic wrap, rubber bands, white paper, aluminum foil, newspaper.

Procedure: Line two cups with black paper, using the tape to hold it in place. Cut two equal-sized slices of apple and put one slice in each cup. Cover both cups with the plastic film, holding it in place with the rubber bands. Use the paper and tape to make a cone. Fit an apple cup into the small end of the cone and hold the cone in place by fitting it into another cup. Repeat the process with the second apple cup, but first cover the inside of the paper with aluminum foil. Put both apple cups outside in the sun or in a sunny window; place each on crumpled newspaper facing the sun.

Watch to see which apple slice cooks faster. The cooking time will depend on the strength of the sun in your locality at the time of day and on the day of the year that you are doing the experiment. The first apple slice to be done should be the one in the aluminum foil cone. Eat the slice. It should taste hot and good! Try the other slice and find out if it is as well cooked.

A simple way to demonstrate use of the sun's energy is to melt ice cubes. Put an ice cube on a plate in the sun and another on a plate in the shade. Not only will the one in the sun melt faster in the sun's heat, but the water left will evaporate faster also.

do colors absorb solar heat differently?

Materials: Three styrofoam cups, black paper, scissors, masking tape, aluminum foil, water, three thermometers, paper, pencils.

Procedure: Cover one cup with black paper using the tape to hold it in place. Cover another cup with aluminum foil. Fill all three cups with the same amount of cold water. Put them in the sun or in a sunny window and place a thermometer in each. Check and record the temperatures periodically.

The black cup should give the highest temperature. Have the children repeat the experiment, using other materials to cover the cups. Sand or soil may be used in the cups instead of water.

2 STYROFOAM CUPS LINED WITH BLACK PAPER.

AN APPLE SLICE IN EACH—

COVER WITH PLASTIC FILM HELD WITH RUBBER BAND.

MAKE TWO PAPER CONES— LINE I WITH ALUMINUM FOIL— LEAVE I WHITE.

PAPER CONE

APPLE CUP

CUP HOLDING THINGS TOGETHER

AIM COOKERS AT SUN— HOLD IN PLACE WITH CRUMPLED NEWSPAPERS.

ALUMINUM FOIL

which material stores solar heat the longest?

Materials: Cardboard box, five styrofoam cups, five thermometers, water, salt, crumpled paper, soil, and sand.

Procedure: Fill each cup with one of the different materials, putting in a thermometer at the same time. Put the cups in the box, close the box, and put it in the sun. When it has had time to become warm, remove the cups to a shady place and check the thermometers periodically.

The temperatures will show the children which material stores solar heat the best. If the children have done the previous activity about color and heat absorption, ask them if they think it would be a good idea to paint the box black before putting it in the sun.

nonrenewable resources reports

Materials: Reference materials with information about coal, oil, and natural gas.

Procedure: Have each student write a report on one aspect of coal, oil, and natural gas as energy materials.

Here are some suggestions for topics: how oil is formed, how coal is mined, how natural gas is transported, how using one of these resources is helpful or

harmful to the environment, what are the different products made from crude oil?

stop drafts with a dragon

Materials: Muslin, denim, or heavy cotton, and sewing materials, dry sand or sawdust, felt, and other materials for decoration.

Procedure: On the wrong side of the material sew a long tube as shown in the diagram, leaving a 3-inch (7.6 c) opening in one end. Turn it right side out and fill it with sand or sawdust. Sew up the opening. Cut teeth, legs, and spines from the felt and sew them on (or sew the spines on while sewing the tube). Use buttons or more felt for the eyes. Place the dragon at the bottom of a drafty door or window to keep the cold air out.

Drafts can also be stopped by other long, thin creatures, such as snakes or dachshunds. Have children make heat conservation surveys at home by recording temperatures in the center of rooms, by windows, by doors, by the heat source, and in other areas where the temperatures vary. Then determine the best places to put creature draft stoppers. Can the children think of ways to keep other cooler areas warm? Where would insulation be helpful? (Look in the Index under insulation for an activity with it.) Have each child

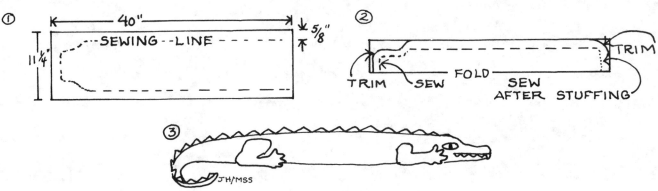

① ← 40" → ↓ 5/8"
11 1/4" ---SEWING--LINE - - - - -

② TRIM — SEW — FOLD — SEW AFTER STUFFING — TRIM

③ J·H/MSS

draw a picture showing heat being wasted.

math that is all wet

Materials: Reference materials with information about your local water supply.

Procedure: Have the children learn about the water supply, including the number of gallons used daily, the maximum amount of gallons available daily, and the number of living units served. Then solve math problems, such as the following: the average consumption per living unit per day; the number of added units the supply could serve; the amount of water saved if every unit flushed a toilet one less time per day; and if two percent of the units have faucets that drip a tablespoon of water an hour, the amount of water saved if all the faucets were fixed.

fun with recycling

Materials: Styrofoam trays (such as the ones supermarkets use to package meats), printing ink, pencil, brayer (roller), paper.

Procedure: Draw a picture on the bottom of the styrofoam tray with the pencil, pressing hard enough so that the lines are indented. Roll the ink over the drawing in the styrofoam with the brayer. Press the styrofoam, ink side down, onto a piece of paper, and see how the picture turns out.

There are numerous ways that children can enjoy reusing materials; see Robin Simon's book entitled *Recyclopedia*, listed in this chapter's bibliography. Have a milk carton recycling show. Ask each child to make something different using milk cartons, and then explain and demonstrate the new use to the rest of the class. How about planters, blocks for little children, or toy houses; there are many possibilities.

Roll out the barrels! Another way of using them before they are filled with this year's potato harvest.

bibliography

adults

BEHRMAN, DANIEL, *Solar Energy.* Boston: Little, Brown, 1976.

CENTER FOR SCIENCE IN THE PUBLIC INTEREST, *99 Ways to a Simple Lifestyle.* New York: Doubleday, 1977.

COE, MARY LEE, *Growing with Community Gardening.* Taftsville, Vt.: Countryman Press, 1978.

DOAN, MARLYN, *Starting Small in the Wilderness.* San Francisco: Sierra Club, 1979.

FERNALD, MERRITT LYNDON, and ALFRED CHARLES KINSEY, revised by Reed C. Rollins, *Edible Wild Plants.* New York: Harper, 1958.

GIBBONS, EUELL, *Stalking the Wild Asparagus.* New York: McKay, 1962.

HERTSBERG, RUTH, BEATRICE VAUGHAN, and JANET GREENE, *Putting Food By.* Brattleboro, Vt.: Stephen Greene, 1975.

JOFFE, JOYCE, *Conservation.* Garden City, N.Y.: Natural History Press, 1970.

LEOPOLD, ALDO, *A Sand County Almanac.* New York: Oxford University Press, 1949.

LORENZ, KONRAD Z., *King Solomon's Ring.* New York: Crowell, 1952.

MACLATCHIE, SHARON, *Gardening with Kids.* Emmaus, Pa.: Rodale Press, 1977.

MITCHELL, EDWIN VALENTINE, ed., *The Pleasures of Walking.* New York: Vanguard, 1979.

SCHATZ, ALBERT, and VIVIAN SCHATZ, *Teaching Science with Garbage.* Emmaus, Pa.: Rodale Press, 1971.

THOREAU, HENRY DAVID, *Walden.* New York: Crowell, 1961.

WEISBURG, CLAUDIA, *Raising Your Own Livestock.* Englewood Cliffs, N.J.: Prentice-Hall, 1980.

children & adults

ADAMS, FLORENCE, *Catch a Sunbeam.* New York: Harcourt, 1978.

BURGESS, THORNTON, W., *The Burgess Book of Nature Lore.* Boston: Little, Brown, 1965.

ENVIRONMENTAL ACTION COALITION, *It's Your Environment.* New York: Scribner, 1976.

GAMBINO, ROBERT, *Easy to Grow Vegetables.* New York: Harvey House, 1975.

HARRISON, C. WILLIAM, *The First Book of Hiking.* New York: Watts, 1965.

KOHN, BERNICE, *The Organic Living Book.* New York: Viking, 1972.

LIMBURG, PETER R., *Chickens, Chickens, Chickens.* Nashville, Tenn.: Nelson, 1975.

MILES, BETTY, *Save the Environment: An Ecology Handbook for Kids.* New York: Knopf, 1974.

MITCHELL, JOHN, and MASSACHUSETTS AUDUBON SOCIETY, *The Curious Naturalist.* Englewood Cliffs, N.J.: Prentice-Hall, Inc., 1980.

SIMONS, ROBIN, *Recyclopedia.* Boston: Houghton Mifflin, 1976.

STEVENS, CARLA, *Your First Pet.* New York: Macmillan, 1974.

appendix

Children enjoy making natural history crafts for gifts. The following list indicates many such crafts that are included in the book.

gift craft items	activities
Place mats, bookmarks, postcards, window decorations, wall hangings—all decorated with leaves, flowers, seed heads, or other plant materials	Preserving Leaves with Wax Paper, page 18 Preserving Leaves with Clear Self–Adhesive Plastic, page 18 Leaf Prints Using Paint, page 18 Leaf Spatter Prints, page 19 Decorative Plant Cards, page 36 Seaweed Prints, pages 111–113
Dried flowers & other dried arrangements	Drying Flowers & Seed Heads for Arrangements, page 37 Dried Arrangements in Plaster of Paris, page 37 Sand Casting, page 105
Mosaics	Seed Mosaics, page 48 Pebble Mosaics, page 103 Crafts with Shells & Other Beachcombing Items, page 125
Collages	Driftwood Collages, page 114 Crafts with Shells & Other Beachcombing Items, page 125
Mobiles	Maple Seed Dragonfly, page 50 Driftwood Mobiles, page 114 Crafts with Shells & Other Beachcombing Items, page 125 Bird Mobiles & Other Art Projects, page 87
Necklaces & pendants	Seed Necklaces, page 48 Crafts with Shells & Other Beachcombing Items, page 125 Preserving Leaves with Clear Self–Adhesive Plastic, page 18
Wind chimes	Crafts with Shells & Other Beachcombing Items, page 125
Pencil holders & other containers	Preserving Leaves with Clear Self–Adhesive Plastic, page 18 Crafts with Shells & Other Beachcombing Items, page 125 Decorative Plant Cards, page 36
Lamps & candle holders	Driftwood Candle Holders, Lamps, & Vases, page 114

gift craft items	activities
Bookends	Crafts with Shells & Other Beachcombing Items, page 125
Dolls	Applehead Doll, page 48 Corn Husk Doll, page 50
Animals made with natural materials	Cone Birds, page 49 Walnut Shell Turtle, page 51 Maple Seed Dragonfly, page 50 Acorn Snake, page 48 Stone Animals, page 103 Sand Clay, page 105 Crafts with Shells & Other Beachcombing Items, page 125
Wave bottles	Wave Bottle, page 102
Terrariums	Terrariums, page 35
Bird feeders	Easy Bird Feeders for Young Children, page 81 Simple Feeders You Can Make, page 81
Bird houses	Build a Bluebird House, pages 81–82

index

notes